D0203735

Mixed Bloods and Other Crosses

Mixed Bloods and Other Crosses

Rethinking American Literature from the Revolution to the Culture Wars

BETSY ERKKILA

PENN

University of Pennsylvania Press

Philadelphia

Copyright © 2005 University of Pennsylvania Press
All rights reserved
Printed in the United States of America on acid-free paper

10   9   8   7   6   5   4   3   2   1

Published by
University of Pennsylvania Press
Philadelphia, Pennsylvania 19104-4011

Library of Congress Cataloging-in-Publication Data

Erkkila, Betsy, 1944–
   Mixed bloods and other crosses : rethinking American literature from the Revolution
to the culture wars / Betsy Erkkila.
      p.   cm.
   Includes bibliographical references and index.
   ISBN 0-8122-3844-3 (acid-free paper)
   1. American literature—History and criticism.   2. Literature and society—United
States.   3. Racially mixed people in literature.   4. Social conflict in literature.   5.
Minorities in literature.   6. Ethnicity in literature.   7. Violence in literature.   8. Racism
in literature.   I. Title.

PS169.S57E75   2004
810.9'3552—dc22   2004055459

*This book is dedicated to my students,
my heartbeat. . . .*

Contents

Preface

The United States has been and continues to be constituted out of the international flow of capital, people, writing, culture, and goods across the borders. What Frederick Jackson Turner called "the Frontier" was not a vacant or virgin wilderness upon which the United States imprinted itself: the land was inhabited by thousands of indigenous Natives and hundreds of different cultures with multiple languages, customs, rituals, myths, and traditions. During the eighteenth century, the North American continent was also the site of an imperial war among the British, French, and Spanish empires for colonial possession and rule in the Americas. In the years leading up to and following the revolt of the American colonies against the British Empire in 1776, the American struggle to define itself and its destiny in the New World was marked not only by scenes of blood violence and contest over the land; it was also marked by scenes of cultural confrontation, exchange, and mixture across boundaries that were never finally settled or secure.[1]

Mixed Bloods and Other Crosses focuses on this historical and psychological drama and trauma of blood and boundaries at the center of American New World culture and politics. Beginning with a chapter on the symbolics of blood in American literature and history, the book moves from a consideration of contests about blood and boundaries—territorial, sexual, racial, class, national, cultural, and aesthetic—in the Revolutionary period and the nineteenth century to a discussion of the ways anxieties about blood, mixture, and crossing inform recent debates about the boundaries of culture, the canon, and the disciplines and the relation between aesthetics and politics, identity and difference, nationalism and cosmopolitanism, the local and the global. Rethinking American literature as a dynamic and fluid field of cultural and political struggle, I examine scenes of mixture and crossing, miscegenation and incest, doubling and hybridity, inversion and reversal that subvert, alter, or undo the boundary-building imperatives of American history.

Mixed Bloods draws on the work of theorists of linguistic, racial, cultural, and border hybridity, particularly the writings of Mikhail Bakhtin, Homi Bhabha, Edward Said, James Clifford, and Gloria Anzaldúa.[2] As a term that emerged simultaneously with the classificatory imagination of the Enlightenment, *hybridity* was originally used to describe crosses of different species of plants and animals in botany and zoology. While the Oxford English Dictionary (OED) records a few examples of this word in the seventeenth century, as Robert Young has observed, "'Hybrid' is the nineteenth century's word," a word that came into its fullest human usage with the ascendancy of capital, nation, and empire in the West and Western prohibitions against sexual, racial, and cultural mixture with the dark others of the imperial imaginary.[3]

And yet, as I argue in *Mixed Bloods*, in the Americas mixture of all kinds occurred from the moment of historical contact. The first recorded use of the term *mulata* in English—"a maid-childe, that is borne of a Negra, and a fayre man" (OED)—occurred in 1622, only a few years after the first Africans debarked in Virginia in 1619. Almost two centuries later, Thomas Jefferson responded to the question of what constituted a *mulatto* under Virginia law by using the terms *pure blood, Negro blood, mixture,* and *cross* to calculate mathematically how many "crossings" of "white pure blood" and "mixed blood" it would take to "clear" Negro blood from white blood: the "third cross clears the blood," and the offspring "is no longer a mulatto," he determined.[4]

Although I will use the primarily nineteenth-century term *hybridity* in particular historical and theoretical contexts, it is not the overarching figure of this study. I have chosen to focus instead on the dialectics of *blood* and *boundaries, mixture* and *crossing* because this dialectics comes closer to describing the linguistic and metaphoric frames, lived histories, and fluid and contested political and cultural field at the center of this study. While the term *hybrid* has been used historically to describe the offspring of racial and sexual mixture and by recent theorists to describe the doubleness of language, the potentially subversive and resistant relationship of colonized to colonizer, and the mixed identities of those who inhabit the borderlands, it does not convey the blood violence that accompanied America's boundary-building imperatives in the New World; nor does it adequately signify the anxieties about class mixture, black and female sexuality, sexual inversion, same-sex merging, and even capitalist exploitation that were expressed through the metaphorics of blood in the Americas.

Thus, for example, in the following passage from Edward Long's *Candid Reflections . . . On What Is Commonly Called the Negroe-Cause, By a Planter* (1772), anxieties about class mixture, black and female sexual appetite, bestiality, and sodomy are all signified through the figure of Anglo-Saxon *blood* and the specter of its corruption through the circuits of exchange and generation—of capital and slaves, migrants and goods—that linked Africa, Europe, and the Americas in the eighteenth century: "The lower class of women in *England,* are remarkably fond of the blacks, for reasons too brutal to mention; they would connect themselves with horses and asses if the laws permitted them. By these ladies they generally have a numerous brood. Thus, in the course of a few generations more, the English blood will become so contaminated with the mixture . . . as even to reach the middle, and then the higher orders of the people."[5]

In 1775 John Adams made use of a similar metaphor of English blood purity to mark his identification with a particular class, race, sex, region, and nation, and his fear of corruption by other non-English inhabitants of the New World. Confessing his "overweening Prejudice in favour of New England" in a letter to Abigail Adams, he writes: "The People are *purer English Blood*, less *mixed* with Scotch, Irish, Dutch, French, Danish, Sweedish &c. than any *other*; and descended from Englishmen too who left Europe, in *purer Times* than the present and less tainted with *Corruption* than those they left behind them."[6] Adams expresses the widespread and persistent American belief in the superiority of Anglo-Saxon blood, a superiority that would lead to fear of mixture not only with blacks, Indians, Mexicans, and Asians but with other European nations, including Scotland and Ireland.

As I argue in Chapter 1 and other chapters in this study, it is in and through the metaphorics of blood and its various New World permutations as space, race, sex, class, region, nation, and globe that Americans have struggled and continue to struggle over the meanings of democracy, citizenship, culture, and national belonging, and the idea of America itself as it was constituted and contested in its relations with others and the world. In fact, as this study will suggest, the persistence of phobias and fantasies of blood mixture and contamination in the national imaginary may account for the fact that despite the country's constitutional commitment to an ideology of justice, freedom, and rights, the American republic continues as a house divided in which some are more equal, more human, and more entitled than others to the founding ideals of life, liberty, and the pursuit of happiness.[7]

While *Mixed Bloods and Other Crosses* is centrally concerned with the "crosses" of sex, race, class, and blood in American literature and culture, it also focuses on other crosses: the ways acts of *crossing out* or repression in the official writings of the culture—the deletion of the antislavery passage from the original version of the Declaration of Independence or Jefferson's decision to cross out his admission that the "purchases" of Indian lands "were sometimes made with the price in the one hand and the sword in the other" in *Notes on the State of Virginia*[8]—come back to haunt American history and the national fantasy; the ways history and "blood" impinge on the putatively "pure" realms of culture, literature, and aesthetics in the writings of Jefferson and Phillis Wheatley, Poe and Dickinson, Melville and C.L.R. James; the ways the mixture and hybridity of language become a force for resistance and New World transformation in the writings of Wheatley and Abigail Adams, Whitman and C.L.R. James; and the ways modern subjectivity and the Freudian unconscious bear the historical markings of the dark, savage, sexual, and alien others that were expelled by the disciplinary logic of the Western Enlightenment and its legacy of blood in the Americas. As Gloria Anzaldúa writes in an address to whites in *Borderlands/La Frontera*: "Admit that Mexico is your double, that she exists in the shadow of this country, that we are irrevocably tied to her. Gringo, accept the doppelganger in your psyche."[9] My title, *Mixed Bloods and Other Crosses*, is meant to suggest this historical dialectics of blood and boundaries, mixture and crossing, at the center of American New World culture and the ways this dialectics has come to function as one of the sacred fetishes and central "crosses" that the culture bears.

Cross *n.* **1.** The instrument of crucifixion; the particular wooden structure on which Jesus Christ suffered death; a market-place, market; the Christian religion, especially when opposed to other religions. **2.** A trial or affliction. **3.** A trouble, annoyance; misfortune, adversity; sometimes anything that thwarts or crosses. **4.** The point where two lines or paths cross each other; a crossing, cross-way. **5.** An intermixture of breeds or races in the production of an animal; an instance of cross-fertilization in plants; an animal or plant, or a breed or race, due to crossing. **6.** An instance of the mixture of the characteristics of two different individuals; something intermediate in character between two things. **7.** A contest or match lost by collusory arrangement between the principals; a swindle; to be a thief, live by stealing.

Cross *v.* **1.** To crucify. **2.** To lay (a thing) across or athwart another; to set (things) across each other; to place crosswise. **3.** To lie or pass across; to intersect. **4.** To pass over a line, boundary, river, channel, etc.; to pass from one side to the other of any space. **5.** To delete or eliminate by or as if by drawing a line through. **6.** To meet or face in one's way; esp. to meet adversely; to encounter. **7.** To thwart, oppose, go counter to; to bar, debar, preclude from; to contradict, contravene; to cheat or double-cross. **8.** To breed together, being of distinct races or breeds, to interbreed.

—Oxford English Dictionary

Chapter 1

Blood, Sex, and Other American Crosses

What then is the American, this new man? He is neither an European nor the descendant of an European: hence that strange mixture of blood, which you will find in no other country.

—*J. Hector St. John de Crèvecoeur,* Letters from an American Farmer

And "blood," too, that word of all words—so rife at all times with mystery, suffering, and terror—how trebly full of import did it now appear.

—*Edgar Allan Poe,* Narrative of Arthur Gordon Pym

What a libel upon the heavenly Father, who "made of one blood all nations of men!" And then who are *Africans? Who can measure the amount of Anglo-Saxon blood coursing in the veins of American slaves?*

—*Harriet Jacobs,* Incidents in the Life of a Slave Girl

Blood. The image saturates the literature of the American founding and the years of ongoing political and cultural struggle over the Revolutionary ideals of freedom, equality, justice, rights, and citizenship. In the period leading up to the American Revolution, the prospect of a break with mother England was feared by many as a collapse of America into what James Otis called "a meer shambles of blood and confusion."[1] Urging reconciliation and prudence in the defense of American liberty in *Letters from a Farmer in Pennsylvania* (1767–1768), John Dickinson imagined separation from England in the blood-drenched image of amputation from the body of the mother: "Torn from the body to which we are united by religion, liberty, laws, affections, relations, language, and commerce, we must bleed at every vein."[2] Whereas in *Common Sense* Tom Paine sought to demystify monarchy and hereditary succession as devilish superstitions that had "laid . . . the world in blood and ashes," the loyalist Jonathan Boucher defended the divine right of patriarchal kingship against the "reserved right of resistance" by evoking similar images of "perpetual dissensions and contests," a return to the "state of nature," and the world as "an *aceldama*, or field of blood."[3]

Even after the war, Benjamin Franklin looked upon the Revolution as a mistake, a "bloody Contest" that could have been prevented had the colonies approved the Albany Plan of Union he proposed in 1754.[4] To Jefferson, writing in *Notes on the State of Virginia* (1787), the Revolution was an "open wound" that needed to be stanched by a return to republican reason, law, and order. And yet, as I shall argue in Chapter 2 and other chapters in this book, the bloody wound of the American Revolution would remain open: the ideological contradictions that were left unresolved during the period of the founding would continue to bleed, not only through Jefferson's life and work but through American literature and history.[5]

Rituals of American Blood

The real or imagined threat of blood violence and anxious appeals to blood kinship underwrite the language of the founding documents. In the original version of the Declaration of Independence, the constitutional rights of the colonies and their claims to self-sovereignty, liberty, representation, consent, and the right of resistance are grounded in blood—both the "blood" they have expended in their emigration and settlement of America and the "common blood" they share with their "British brethren." The failure of the king, the Parliament, and the British people to recognize these rights leads to charges of familial violence, murderousness, and abuse.

The Declaration presents a gothic and near-hysterical image of the American colonies under siege, "exposed to all the dangers of invasion from without and convulsions within." In a lengthy list of grievances, the king is charged with endeavoring "to bring on the inhabitants of our frontiers, the merciless Indian savages," inciting "treasonable insurrections of our fellow citizens," obtruding the slave trade's "assemblage of horrors" on the American people, exciting slaves "to rise in arms among us," and sending "over not only soldiers of our common blood, but Scotch and foreign mercenaries to invade and destroy us." Like the king, the British people are accused of disavowing "the ties of our common kindred" and being "deaf to the voice of justice and of consanguinity." "These facts," the colonists conclude, "have given the last stab to agonizing affection, and manly spirit bids us to renounce forever these unfeeling brethren."[6] The original version of the Declaration of Independence is, in effect, written in blood. It is through the evocation of an aggrieved image of a bleeding America and an appeal to blood rights, "common kindred," "consanguinity," and "common blood" that the American colonies legitimate their declaration of freedom, independence, and revolt against the British state.

Only a month earlier, Chief Cornstalk (Shawnee) had invoked a similar image of blood to affirm the commonality—the common ground and destiny shared by Native Americans and white people in the New World: "Our white Brethren who have grown out this same Ground with ourselves—for this Big Island being our Common Mother, we & they are like one Flesh and Blood."[7] The difference between Cornstalk's more inclusive use of the term *blood* and its organic connection to the earth as "Common Mother" and its more exclusive and racially inflected use in the Declaration of Independence—with merciless Indian savages, enslaved Africans, mercenary foreigners, and even Scotsmen being marked as outside the "common blood" of the Anglo-American colonists—suggests the paradoxical and violent dialectics of blood and boundaries in the New World. On the one hand, blood is associated with fluidity, kinship, commonality, and flow; on the other hand, blood marks a boundary, a line of distinction between bodies, regions, races, classes, cultures, peoples, and nations.

Although blood does not figure explicitly in the Constitution, the trace of an Old World order in which subjects are organically connected to the monarch through blood endures in the constitutional use of the term "Corruption of Blood" in article 3 to describe the "Forfeiture" of civil rights or life that a person will suffer if convicted of the crime of "Treason." As envisioned by the founders, the legal relation of the individual to the state is a relation of blood that will be severed in perpetuity for the crime of treason: juridically the United States is, in effect, a blood union in which the boundary between the inside and the outside of the body politic is marked by *pure* or *corrupt* blood.

The fear of national dismemberment, of an American republic bleeding at every vein, propels the Constitution's abstract appeals to "Justice," "domestic Tranquility," "the Blessings of Liberty," and the creation of a "more Perfect Union." This specter of blood violence is associated not only with Indians on the borders but with the dangers of foreign invasion, wars between the states, "domestic Violence," and "Insurrections" within the body of the republic itself. The appeal to "We the People" and "the Union" in the preamble to the Constitution is at best the abstract, legitimating fiction of an elite class of white men who wanted a more "energetic" form of national government. As the Federalist and anti-Federalist debates make clear, at the moment of the constitutional founding the states were not a union or a nation but a group of local sovereignties with different laws, economies, interests, and manners.[8]

Despite the fact that Crispus Attucks, a man of mixed black and

Figure 1. "Boston Massacre." Copy of chromolithograph by John Bufford and William L. Champney, c. 1856. Crispus Attucks has been immortalized as "the first to pour out his blood as a precious libation on the altar of a people's rights." Courtesy National Archives and Records Administration.

Indian ancestry, was one of the five people killed by British soldiers in the "Boston Massacre" and thus one of the first to shed blood in defense of American liberty (Figure 1), the Constitution begins to sketch out notions of "the People" and "the Union" defined by sex (men), class (propertied men), race (white rather than Indian or black men), and territory (states but not tribes). In the ambiguous founding terms of the Constitution, women are nonexistent; indentured servants and poor white men are persons but not citizens; Indians exist in a borderline space both inside the political community as tax-paying persons and outside the United States as sovereign tribes; and slaves are constituted as mixed figures who are three-fifths person and two-fifths property or thing. The boundaries between "the People" and its others, "the Union" and its outside, are at best unstable and at worst absurd—as in the case of slaves whose mixed status as persons and things is defended by Madison through the voice of "one of our Southern brethren" in *Federalist* #54: "The federal Constitution, therefore, decides with great propriety on the case of our slaves, when it views them in *the mixed character of persons and of property. This is in fact their true character.*"[9] Here as elsewhere in "the supreme Law of the Land," there is a constitutional tension between fixity and fluidity, ambiguity and absurdity, that would make the boundaries of "the People" and "the Union" a site of perpetual and frequently violent struggle in the history of the New World and the historical emergence of the "united" states.

Against the historical prospect of an America "split into a number of unsocial, jealous, and alien sovereignties" in *Federalist* #2, John Jay, who was himself of Dutch and French rather than English descent, presents a mythic vision of the American people as a homogeneous, Anglo, and divinely anointed "band of brethren": "Providence has been pleased to give this one connected country to one united people—a people descended from the same ancestors, speaking the same language, professing the same religion, attached to the same principles of government, very similar in their manners and customs, and who, by their joint counsels, arms, and efforts, fighting side by side through a long and bloody war, have nobly established their general liberty and independence" (*FP*, 38). In Jay's formulation the "long and bloody war" for "liberty and independence" represented a means of congealing the American people and their "one connected country" around the founding ideals of the nation.

This emphasis on the blood shed in the American Revolution and the blood shared by Americans in constituting the natural boundaries of the United States receives its fullest expression in *Federalist* #14, in which Madison appeals to blood kinship and blood violence as a means of consecrating the American "Union": "[T]he kindred blood which flows in the veins of American citizens, the mingled blood which they have shed in defense of their sacred rights, consecrate their Union and excite horror at the idea of their becoming aliens, rivals, enemies" (*FP*, 104). For Jay and Madison, writing under the guise of "Publius" in *The Federalist* (1787–88), these appeals to the "kindred blood" and "mingled blood" of "American citizens" become a means of reconciling the paradox of liberty and union, of congealing the autonomous individuals of Lockean theory into an organic union by shifting what Madison calls "the cords of affection" away from the locality, region, and state toward the federal republic as national family of blood kin.

These founding appeals to the blood sacrifice of the American Revolution would become part of an ongoing national dialectics of blood union—a need to repeat the blood sacrifice of the founders as a means of consecrating the national union, the blood kinship of Americans, and their continuing commitment to the sacred ideals of liberty and independence. Writing in defense of Shays' Rebellion, an armed revolt of Massachusetts farmers against heavier taxation led by Daniel Shays in 1787, Jefferson asserted: "Let them take arms. . . . What signify a few lives lost in a century or two? The tree of liberty must be refreshed from time to time with the blood of patriots and tyrants. It is it's natural manure."[10] In "Announcement to His Soldiers," written during the War of 1812, Andrew Jackson asserted a similar need for the sons to shed blood as a means of refreshing the tree of liberty and the sacrifice of the fathers: the sons must prove that they are not "a degenerate race" and "unworthy of the blessings which the blood of so many thousand heroes has purchased for them."[11]

In his address at Gettysburg in 1863 and in his Second Inaugural Address delivered shortly before the end of the Civil War in 1865, Abraham Lincoln conjoined images of blood sacrifice in the name of Liberty, Union, and the founders' dream with eucharistic evocations of blood as a form of Christian atonement and national redemption. The Civil War was, in Lincoln's view, both the blood trial of "a new nation, conceived in Liberty, and dedicated to the proposition that all men are created equal" and a blood punishment for the national sin of slavery. If "this mighty scourge of war" continued "until every drop of blood drawn with the lash, shall be paid by another drawn with the sword," he proclaimed in his Second Inaugural Address, "so still it must be said 'the judgments of the Lord, are true and righteous altogether.'" In Lincoln's reading, the Civil War dead and the blood sacrifice of the American people are a source of national reunification, redemption from the sins of slavery, and, as he says on the field at Gettysburg, rededication to "a new birth of freedom"—"that government of the people, by the people, for the people, shall not perish from the earth."[12]

But while blood violence would become a means of affirming blood kinship and rededication to the founding ideals of liberty, equality, and national union, those others who were excluded by the Constitution—the women, blacks, Indians, poor whites, immigrants, foreigners, and outsiders against and through whom the United States defined itself—would continue to haunt the real and imaginary borders of the country with the specter of blood vengeance, blood pollution, and blood mixture. "Compared with the vital matter of pure Blood," William Benjamin Smith warned in *The Color Line: A Brief in Behalf of the Unborn* (1905), "all other matters" of contemporary America "sink into insignificance." While "the pure strain of Caucasian blood" is destined to "live and thrive and achieve great things for History and Humanity," no force is strong enough to counter "the race decadence that would surely follow in the wake of any considerable contamination of that blood by the blood of Africa."[13] As Orlando Patterson has argued in *Rituals of Blood*, Southern whites responded to this same fear of "contamination" by the blood of unmastered blacks in the post-Reconstruction South by lynching black men in elaborate rituals of blood sacrifice that unified the social community and affirmed traditional Southern values.

The Metaphorics of American Blood

"The classical myths of race, in particular the myth of Aryanism," writes Étienne Balibar, "do not refer initially to the nation but to class, and they do so from an aristocratic perspective."[14] Whereas in the Old World blood served to mark off the aristocratic body and the distinctions of a hereditary class system, in the New World blood assumed other and more mobile socially symbolic meanings as a signifier not only of class but also of bodily, sexual, racial, and cultural difference.[15] During the very years when Americans were proclaiming the rights and liberties of the British colonies and the universal rights of man, they began to deploy a metaphorics of blood to mark a boundary around whiteness, purity, virtue, intelligence, and beauty. In the Declaration of Independence and *The Federalist,* as in the Alien and Sedition acts of 1798, the Chinese Exclusion acts of the 1880s, and later efforts to regulate the flow of "alien" bodies and blood into and within the United States, blood became a national fetish, a means of affirming political community, kinship, citizenship, and union at the same time that it became the grounds for exclusion, expulsion, negation, and extermination.

Associated with the violence of the Revolution and the specter of social and national dismemberment, blood was invoked to reconstitute and rehierarchize the social body by symbolically carving into the flesh—at the very sources of human life—the distinctions of sex, race, class, and national origin. Against the pure and well-regulated blood of Anglo-Saxon men, women were defined as creatures of "volatility" and the blood of the heart and the menses; Indians were associated with the primitivism of blood rites, blood vengeance, and blood violence; Africans were depicted as beings of inferior black blood and possibly members of a subhuman species; foreigners were represented as bearers of the corrupt and "licentious" blood of the Old World; the lower classes were associated with the unruly impulses of the blood, the appetites, and the lower body parts; and Mexicans were portrayed as irrational figures of "mixed and confused blood," as John O'Sullivan wrote in his famous 1845 *Democratic Review* article on the "Annexation" of Texas in which he announced it as the "manifest destiny" of the Anglo-Saxon race to overspread the North American continent from sea to sea. By expelling emancipated Negroes from the United States into the mixed-blood "receptacle" of "[t]he Spanish-Indian-American populations of Mexico, Central America and South America," O'Sullivan seeks, like other proponents of Anglo-Saxon nationalism, to cleanse the American republic of its contaminating others—its sewage and dirt.[16]

Circulated and recirculated in its literal definition as "the red liquid circulating in the arteries and veins of man and the higher animals" (OED) and in its figurative association with the primitive, the animal body, the passions and feelings, the sensual appetites, and the fleshly nature of man, blood became a subject of fascination for a republican body committed to the Enlightenment values of mind and reason, common sense and good taste. It was in and through blood—and its real or metaphoric sources in the body and the flesh—that American culture, with the support of law, medicine, and science, defined a temperate, industrious, and chaste republican self against the bodily excesses of madmen, drunkards, onanists, sodomites, persons of color, fallen women, adulterers, mixed bloods, amalgamationists, foreigners, and other corrupters of both the individual and the political body.

And yet, while the scientific and legal establishment became increasingly precise in measuring "pure" and "impure" blood as the bodily correlates or "types" of good and bad character, citizenship, and taste, the national fetish of whiteness, manliness, purity, and virtue was dependent on the dark, low-class, bodily, and feminine other as its underlying term. What was expelled by the structures of American law, medicine, and society returned as the subject of private and public fantasy. From Charles Brockden Brown's *Edgar Huntly* (1799) and Tabitha Tenney's *Female Quixotism* (1801) in the Revolutionary period to the blood fictions of James Fenimore Cooper, Edgar Allan Poe, William Wells Brown, and Frances Harper in the nineteenth century, American literature and culture would return to scenes of mixture, crossing, inversion, and reversal as a recurrent and obsessive source of fantasy and phobia, desire and fear.

Blood and Boundaries

During the years of American national emergence, no one better embodies the paradoxes—and mobile possibilities—of American blood and boundaries than Thomas Jefferson. Jefferson was the very model of the Enlightenment man, yet he set himself against the scientific wisdom of his time in arguing that the "difference" of the black race was "fixed in nature" and perhaps attributable to "the colour of the blood, the colour of the bile, or . . . some other secretion" (*NV*, 138). He was the author of the Declaration of Independence, who proclaimed the "self-evident" truths of liberty, equality, and "inalienable rights," and yet in *Notes on the State of Virginia* (1787), he advanced it as a "suspicion" that "the blacks . . . are inferior to the whites in the endowments both of body and mind" (*NV,* 143). His election to the third presidency of the United States in 1800 was generally regarded as a reaffirmation of the principles of the American Revolution—a triumph of the forces of democracy, egalitarianism, and consensualism—and yet he continued to own and sell slaves who, with the exception of members of the Hemings family, were never freed. Jefferson appreciated the culture and social forms of Native Americans and preached their equality with whites, but he was the chief architect of an American Indian policy that led to their near extermination in the continental United States. His ideal of consensual republican government was modeled on the family and women, yet he believed that women had no place in the political body.

As I argue in Chapter 2, these contradictions are everywhere apparent in *Notes on the State of Virginia,* the only book Jefferson published during his lifetime.[17] Focusing on Jefferson's use of sex and blood to mark the biological, social, and cultural differences among the red, the white, and the black races, I examine the rituals of identification, imitation, translation, and exchange that inform the relations among Anglo, Indian, and African in the New World. I am interested in the dynamics of historical and cultural identification and exchange: the shaping presence of African slavery in the constitution of republican liberty and the impact of Native American social forms on the Constitution of the United States. But I am also interested in the symbolic and psychological processes of identification and exchange: the ways red and black mix with and underwrite the formation of "white" identity and the "white" American republic; and the ways what is prohibited by society and law gets internalized as a constitutive element of individual psyche and national fantasy.

Although Jefferson's biographers have in the past denied his sexual relationship with his mulatto slave, Sally Hemings, as "inconsistent" with Jefferson's character, what we see in his thirty-eight-year relationship with Hemings and the child—or children—he bore with her is a paradigmatic instance of the psychodynamics of white identity formation. Jefferson's social prohibitions against black blood—blacks must be "removed" from the body of the white republic "beyond the reach of mixture" to avoid "staining the blood of [the] master" (*NV,* 143)—have the effect of introjecting the black body and mixture not only as objects of the master's desire but as objects of recurrent public fantasies about the master's desire. Even if Jefferson's sexual relationship with Hemings had not been confirmed in 1998 by DNA, given the past and ongoing dialectics of blood and boundaries in the racial formation of the American republic, the story of the mixed-blood relationship between the author of the Declaration of Independence, the father of American democracy, and the third president of the United States and his mulatto slave, Sally Hemings, would continue to circulate as a story of popular fantasy, democratic desire—and fear.[18]

What Jefferson's relationship with Hemings also suggests is the ways class blood may have trumped race blood in eighteenth-century Chesapeake Virginia. Although Hemings was a woman of black "blood" in Jefferson's terms, as the offspring of Jefferson's father-in-law, John Wayles, and his mulatto slave mistress, Betty Hemings, Sally may have passed for white.[19] She was also the half-sister of Jefferson's wife, Martha Wayles, who died in 1782, seven years before Jefferson's relationship with Sally is believed to have begun, in 1789, while he was a diplomat in France. Although Hemings was of mixed blood in accord with the social and legal definitions of the time, as the half-sister of Jefferson's dead wife, she also kept their relationship within the boundaries of upper-class—and sometimes incestuous—Tidewater Virginia society, family, and blood.

In *Notes on the State of Virginia,* the enslavement of blacks and the murder of Indians are open wounds that bleed into the idyllic image of America as a republic of liberty and virtue. The flip side of Jefferson's republican pastoral is a scene of gothic excess. Like the specters of guilt, blood, inversion, and reversal that haunt and disrupt Jefferson's effort to construct a consoling republican narrative, the gothic would emerge during the Revolutionary period as a kind of political unconscious of the nation: a simultaneously psychic and social mode that registers symbolically the marginal, the mixed, the disavowed, and the taboo on the nether side of the American dream even as it anticipates and comes to shape the neuroses that would ground modern psychoanalysis and the Freudian unconscious.

Sex and Blood

A similar anxiety about blood, mixture, and crossing surrounds the representation of women during the Revolutionary period. As I argue in Chapter 3, the language and iconography of the American Revolution incited women to imagine and act on fantasies of agency, citizenship, pleasure, and power that could not and would not be controlled once the war was over. The social danger of this Revolutionary female presence called forth by the war is particularly evident in the widely circulated political cartoon "A Society of Patriotic Ladies," which was originally published in the British press in 1775 (Figure 9). Based on a declaration in support of the American policy of nonimportation signed by fifty-one women patriots in Edenton, North Carolina, in 1774, the Revolutionary scene of women transgressing the traditional boundaries of home and family to enter the public sphere of politics is satirized and demonized as a female world turned upside down and inside out. The cartoon seeks to cleanse public space of women's bodies, women's pens, and women's voices by linking the scene of women writing—and boycotting—in support of the American cause with a specter of total social collapse signified by mixture and crossing at every level: women turn into men; men turn into women; black women slaves carry pens and mingle freely with manlike women; babies mingle with animals; food mixes with excrement. What belongs outside flows in and what belongs inside flows out as dogs urinate on the floor and women empty tea into the hats of beggars.

The circulation of this and other similarly demonized and mixed images of manly women, warlike women, learned women, political women, and other cross-dressed women in the American press during the war years and after suggests that one of the most transgressive effects of the "bloody war" for American liberty was the specter of women turning into men and thus radically destabilizing the boundaries between male and female, citizen and covered woman, politics and family, and public and private space upon which the stability and health of the American republic came to depend (Figure 10).[20] Especially in the post-Revolutionary period, these images were deployed as part of a massive effort to keep women home and pure. As Jefferson wrote during the years of the constitutional founding, "[O]ur good ladies . . . have been too wise to wrinkle their foreheads with politics. They are contented to soothe and calm the minds of their husbands returning ruffled from political debate."[21] Later, in 1816, reflecting on those who could not be represented even in a pure democracy, he named "Women, who, to prevent depravation of morals and ambiguity of issue, could not mix promiscuously in the public meetings of men."[22]

Jefferson's language suggests the ways the question of female sexual and moral purity gets bound up with questions of racial purity and the purity of American national blood. These questions receive one of their earliest fictive representations in "The Panther Captivity," a brief narrative that appeared in 1787 and went through several printings in the early national period. As Jay Fliegelman observes, the story appears to be loosely based on the history of Jane McCrea, a Tory woman who was brutally killed and scalped by Indians under the command of General Burgoyne in 1777, and thus quickly emerged as a revolutionary symbol of American virtue "besmear'd with blood" at the hands of both the British and the Indians.[23] The story received visual representation in a painting titled *The Murder of Jane McCrea* (1803–1804) by John Vanderlyn, which was originally intended to illustrate Joel Barlow's *Columbiad* in 1807 (Figure 2). It was one of the first of many images of America as virginal maiden threatened with (sexual) violence, scalping, and death

Figure 2. *The Murder of Jane McCrea*, 1803–1804, by John Vanderlyn. Images of white women and children being attacked by savages in sexually suggestive acts of blood violence began to proliferate in nineteenth-century literary and pictorial representation during the same years when Natives were being forcefully "removed" beyond the banks of the Mississippi under the terms of U.S. Indian policy. Courtesy Wadsworth Atheneum, Hartford. Purchased by the Wadsworth Atheneum.

by Indians that circulated in implicit if not explicit support of the American wars against the indigenous tribes of North America throughout the nineteenth century.

Although "The Panther Captivity" begins as a story of filial disobedience about a girl who elopes with her lover and ends up being captured by Indians, it is also a story about a Jane McCrea who fights, scalps, and smears blood back. While the story ends by reinforcing the recurrent theme of post-Revolutionary writing—the providential return of the Revolutionary daughter to the home and law of the father—before she gets home she kills, decapitates, and quarters her giant captor "rather than comply with his [sexual] desire" and spends another nine years living in a cave surrounded by a cache of weapons and skulls. Written during the period of the constitutional founding, "The Panther Captivity" registers some of the culture's deepest fears about the loose, dangerous, and potentially violent female presence released by war: the specter of the daughter of liberty going savage and liking it; the horror of sexual violation by an Indian (or, in another version, a black man); and the image of the sexually transgressive woman as the medium for the corruption of American national blood.

Romancing the Border

This national dialectics of blood and boundaries, crossings and reversals, receives one of its most popular elaborations in James Fenimore Cooper's historical romance *The Last of the Mohicans: A Narrative of 1757* (1826). Set during the French and Indian Wars, and written to justify the federal policy of Indian removal that was being put in place during the 1820s, Cooper represents American prehistory as a "scene of strife and bloodshed" between tribe and tribe, nation and nation, race and race, culture and culture, class and class, sex and sex for the possession of the American continent. On the simplest level of plot, *The Last of the Mohicans* is a tale about the attempt to reunite the daughters, Cora and Alice, with their father, Colonel Munro, who is in charge of Fort William Henry at the time of the famous historical massacre of 1757. The narrative moves toward reunion and restoration of the white family and an assertion of white "mastery" and destiny in America at the same time that it symbolically enacts and in effect plays to American and European fantasies and prohibitions about blood and boundaries, mixture and crossings.

From the sacrifical killing of a colt by Hawk-eye and his Indian companions, Chingachgook and his son, Uncas, at the outset of the action to the final scenes of blood sacrifice that culminate in the death of both Cora and Uncas, blood and the threat of blood spill over the pages of the novel. This flow of blood in the contact and contest over American land is intercepted by Hawk-eye's ritualistic insistence on blood purity and blood boundaries: "I, who am a white man without a cross"; "Ye meet a man without a cross!"; "As a white man who has no taint of Indian blood"; "I am a man who has the full blood of the whites"; "being, as you'll remember, no Indian myself, but a man without a cross"; "there is no cross in my veins"; "I am a man of white blood"; "the Indians will see how a man without a cross can die."[24] These and other formulaic phrases in which Hawk-eye repeats with near-hysterical insistence that "he has no cross in his blood, although he may have lived with the redskins long enough to be suspected!" suggest the centrality of the specter of blood mixture, blood rites, and blood crossing in Cooper's historical narrative and the national fantasy (*LM*, 40).

"Miscegenation," writes Leslie Fiedler of *The Last of the Mohicans*, "is the secret theme of the world's favorite story of adventure, the secret theme of the Leatherstocking Tales as a whole."[25] But the word and the concept of *miscegenation* did not come into general usage until the period of the Civil War when it was used by David G. Croly in a pamphlet that satirized the prospect of racial mixture.[26] To use the term *miscegenation* to describe the "secret theme" of Cooper's novel tends to limit that theme to racial mixture and thus close down the multiply nuanced workings of blood mixture in the narrative. While *The Last of the Mohicans* may represent a shift in the calculus of race from skin color to the fiction of blood in the early nineteenth century, the narrative also evinces some of the more fluid cultural meanings of blood as a signifier of class, descent, manhood, sexual desire, passion, hot temper, appetite, cannibalism, carnage, and American apocalypse.

Beyond Cooper's initial use of the term to describe the headwaters of the Hudson as the "bloody arena" of his story, one of his first allusions to blood comes in his description of the "surpassingly beautiful" Cora: "The tresses of this lady were shining and black, like the plumage of the raven. Her complexion was not brown, but it rather appeared charged with the color of the rich blood, that seemed ready to burst its bounds" (*LM*, 21). Like Poe's Ligeia, Cora's ravenlike "tresses" and her "rich blood" link her with an intelligence, passion, appetite, and will that surpass traditional female "bounds." As her father observes, Cora is "of a mind too elevated and improved, to need the guardianship even of a father" (*LM*, 186). The potential danger of Cora's "charged" blood manifests itself early in the narrative when she turns an erotic and sexually transgressive gaze on the "flexible, upright" and half-naked body of Uncas: "Who that looks at this creature of nature, remembers the shade of his skin!" she says—in a remark that is followed by a "short" and "embarrassed silence" (*LM*, 62). Here, as elsewhere in the narrative,

Cora's "rich blood" is set against the pure, childlike, and bloodless figure of her sister, Alice, whose "dazzling complexion, fair golden hair, and bright blue eyes" (*LM*, 20–21) make her the ideal of whiteness, femininity, and civilization for which all races of men must bleed in Cooper's romance.

The "color" of Cora's blood is later given an explicitly racial signification when we are told that she is the mixed-blood offspring of Munro and his West Indian wife, whose mother "descended remotely from that unfortunate class who are so basely enslaved to administer to the needs of a luxurious people" (*LM*, 188). As one of the earliest fictional representations of the "tragic mulatta," Cora is the bearer of blood that is multiply crossed. She is associated not only with sexual transgression and the degradation of an "unfortunate class" and an "inferior" race. She is also associated with the corruption of Scottish blood by contact with England: "Aye, sir, that is a curse entailed on Scotland by her unnatural union with a foreign and trading people," Munro says of his mixed-blood marriage and daughter (*LM*, 188), giving voice to Cooper's notion that—contra Adam Smith's *Wealth of Nations* (1776)—commerce is a force for corruption rather than civilization.

Against the social degeneration and danger signified by Cora's mixed blood, pure blood functions in Cooper's narrative as a sign of good character between the sexes as well as among races, classes, tribes, and nationalities. Like Hawk-eye, who insists on his "unmixed blood," Chingachgook and Uncas are unmixed Mohicans. "I am an unmixed man," says Chingachgook. "The blood of chiefs is in my veins, where it must stay forever" (*LM*, 37). Chingachgook is a Delaware chief, and his son, Uncas, is "the pride of the Delawares; the last of the high blood of the Mohicans" (*LM*, 314). So important are bloodlines, family descent, and class to Cooper's narrative that Munro literally interrupts the battle for Fort William Henry against the French forces of Montcalm to explain to Major Heyward, who is a suitor for Alice's hand, that as descendants of ancient and noble Scottish families he and Heyward share the same class and blood and that his daughter Alice, unlike Cora, is the offspring of pure Scottish blood. Within Cooper's carefully calibrated symbolics of blood, even Hawk-eye knows his place—perhaps especially in the forest. When he, Heyward, Alice, and Cora appear as captives before the Delaware chief Tamenund, "Hawk-eye had placed himself a little in the rear, with a deference to the superior rank of his companions, that no similarity in the state of their present fortunes could induce him to forget" (*LM*, 349).

The survival of the high-blood white family emblematized by the marriage of Alice Munro and Duncan Heyward and the promise of their pure progeny in America is the historical end toward which action and character move in *The Last of the Mohicans*. This narrative movement is threatened throughout by Magua, the "mongrel Mohawk" and exile of the Huron tribe who seeks to avenge his public shaming at the hands of Munro by terrorizing his daughters, Alice and Cora, whom Magua holds captive for most of the story. In accord with the blood logic of Cooper's narrative, it is not Alice but Cora—Magua's "mixed" double—who evokes Magua's lust. "Let the daughter of the English chief follow, and live in his wigwam forever," Magua proposes at the outset of the narrative, a proposal to which Cora responds with "powerful disgust" (*LM*, 122). Uncas, the last of the Mohicans, also wants Cora and tries to rescue her from Magua's possession. Neither can have her. But the threat of blood violence, rape, penetration, and the mixture of red and white blood hangs over the narrative from beginning to end as the ultimate threat to the future of white civilization on the American continent.

This threat receives its most horrific physical embodiment in the scene of promiscuous bloodletting and blood drinking that—as Cooper tells it—sets off the historical massacre at Fort William Henry. When a mother with a child in her arms refuses to give up her "gaudy" shawl to "a wild and untutored Huron" during the British retreat from William Henry, "the savage relinquished his hold of the shawl, and tore the screaming infant from her arms. . . . [H]e dashed the head of the infant against a rock, and cast its quivering remains to her feet. . . . [E]xcited at the sight of blood, the Huron mercifully drove his tomahawk into her own brain. The mother sank under the blow, and fell, grasping at her child, in death, with the same engrossing love that had caused her to cherish it when living" (*LM*, 207). Like the sexually prurient image of the dark savage laying "his soiled hands" on the hair, shoulders, skin, and bodies of white women in Cooper's border romance, the image of the white mother "grasping at her child" under savage attack became a standard icon in nineteenth-century written and pictorial representations of the American frontier. As in John Mix Stanley's painting *Osage Scalp Dance* (1845), the specter of the white mother and child being surrounded, penetrated, and absorbed by wild and irrational savages allegorized the threat to white womanhood, family, religion, civilization, and future generations on the borders of white settlement in America.

Immediately following the fall of the white mother under the blow of a tomahawk, Magua raises a "fatal and appalling whoop" that unleashes "two thousand raving savages" onto hundreds of unsuspecting women, children, and soldiers on the plain outside Fort William Henry. "We shall not dwell on the revolting horrors that succeeded," Cooper writes: "Death was everywhere, and in his most terrific and disgusting aspects. Resistance only served to inflame the murderers, who inflicted their furious blows long after their victims were beyond the power of their resentment. The flow of blood might be likened to the outbreaking of a torrent; and as the natives became heated and maddened by the sight, many among them even kneeled to the earth, and drank freely, exultingly, hellishly, of the crimson tide" (*LM*, 207–8). This melodramatic scene of savages literally drinking the blood of the whites they have killed in a kind of heathen reversal of the Christian sacrament vividly embodies the white cultural fear of incorporation and absorption by red blood. Inverting Hawk-eye's image of an organic society ordered and ranked by the boundaries of blood difference and blood purity, the torrential "flow of blood" is associated with blood mixture and an "outbreaking" of bounds in acts of cannibalism, unreason, appetite, passion, and the fulfillment of sexual desire. This conflation of blood shed and blood mixture is underscored when Magua repeats his marriage proposal to Cora at the end of the massacre, raising his "reeking hand" in savage triumph. "It is red, but it comes from white veins!" he says, in words that evoke both the specter of white incorporation by red blood and the interdependency of "red" and "white" in defining the fiction of blood.

For all of Cooper's prohibitions against blood mixture, *The Last of the Mohicans* acts out the taboos and fears of white American culture in a fantasy of crossings and reversals. Hawk-eye is himself a figure of the borders, a man of "superstitious terror" who admits that his frontier past is a "trail of blood" strewn with the corpses he has killed in order to make American "civilization" possible (*LM*, 160, 216). From his participation in the blood sacrifice of a colt at the beginning of the narrative, to his practice of codes of blood violence and vengeance, to his avowed preference for Indian heaven and the eroticized male world of the forest and the Indians over the feminized world of the settlements and white women, to his culminating retreat back into the forest with Chingachgook, Hawk-eye engages in the very acts of mixture and crossing he ritualistically condemns.

Like a *Midsummer Night's Dream* in the American forest, in which the erotics of American blood is substituted for Puck's love juice, several of the characters exchange, change, reverse, or cross identities and roles at some point in the narrative. In an act of phallic inversion, Hawk-eye, the manly man of the forest, exchanges his gun "Kill deer" for a "tooting we'pon" as he turns himself into David Gamut, the feminized New England singer of psalms (*LM*, 315, 323); Gamut becomes Uncas; Uncas and Hawk-eye become bears; Heyward becomes a medicine man; Alice becomes an Indian squaw; and Chingachgook disguises himself as a beaver. It is all carnivalesque and make-believe, but the ease with which the characters slip into and out of their sexual and social opposites and doubles suggests the instability rather than the fixity of New World identity, boundaries, and blood.

It is this apocalyptic specter of a New World "confusion" of bloods (*LM*, 233) that underlies Cooper's reassertion of the absolute distinctions of nature and blood in the concluding pages of his narrative. As members of a "cursed" race, both Cora and Uncas must die for the survival of Alice, the pure white flower of Anglo-American civilization. "Like thee and thine," Cora tells Tamenund, "the curse of my ancestors has fallen heavily on their child. But yonder is one [Alice] who has never known the weight of Heaven's displeasure until now" (*LM*, 362). Protect this "treasure," Cora admonishes Hawk-eye and Heyward as she prepares for her own sacrificial death: "'Abandon her not until you leave her in the habitations of civilized men. . . . She is kind, gentle, sweet, good, as mortal may be. There is not a blemish in mind or person at which the proudest of you all would sicken. She is fair—Oh! How surpassingly fair!' laying her own beautiful but less brilliant hand in melancholy affection on the alabaster forehead of Alice, and parting the golden hair which clustered about her brows. 'And yet, her soul is pure and spotless as her skin!'" (*LM*, 374). With her "alabaster forehead," "golden hair," and "pure and spotless" skin, Alice is the fetishized object of white desire for which not only Cora and Uncas but all other races and nations must continue to kill, bleed, and die in the Americas.

The Indian maidens imagine that Cora, who "was of a blood purer and richer than the rest of her nation," will be reunited with Uncas in "the blessed hunting grounds of the Lenape" (*LM*, 406), and even Colonel Munro envisions them as the democratic emblem of a time when all peoples might assemble around the throne of "the Being we all worship . . . without distinction of sex, or rank, or color" (*LM*, 411). But Hawk-eye shakes his head in absolute negation. "To tell them this," he says, "would be to tell them that the snows come not in the winter, or that the sun shines fiercest when the trees are stripped of their leaves" (*LM*, 411). For Hawk-eye as for Cooper, the mixture of bloods is against nature. The natural distinctions "of sex, or rank, or color" will endure unto and beyond death in separate red and white heavens.

As in Thomas Cole's magisterial painting of the final scene of *The Last of the Mohicans* (Figure 3), which depicts the frontiersman with rifle in hand standing between the white body of Cora and the dark body of Uncas as he prepares to rid the American landscape of the savage Magua, Cooper's novel ends by prophesying white mastery and the inevitable death of the Indian. "The palefaces are masters of the earth, and the time of the Red Men has not yet come again" (*LM*, 415), Cooper writes, ventriloquizing the fantasy of white mastery through the voice of Chief Tamenund himself.[27] But while whiteness triumphs over redness,

Figure 3. *Landscape with Figures: A Scene from "The Last of the Mohicans,"* 1826, by Thomas Cole. Hawk-eye stands between the white body of Cora and the dark body of Uncas, insisting on the natural distinctions "of sex, or rank, or color" as he prepares to rid the American landscape of the savage Magua. Photography courtesy of Terra Foundation for the Arts.

and America over Britain and France at the end of the narrative, unlike the new dawn on the westward horizon of Cole's America in *Landscape with Figures: A Scene from "The Last of the Mohicans"* (1826), the America that Cooper imagines is reminiscent of Boucher's "field of blood"—a devolution into a state of brute nature rather than a revolutionary ascent toward progress and freedom. Cooper's American landscape is, in effect, a graveyard—"a vast and deserted charnel house" (*LM*, 225)— haunted by a past of blood violence among races, tribes, and nations and spooked by the prospect of a collapse in the distinctions of sexual, racial, and class blood in the America of the future.

The irony is that the one boundary that remains open—the erotically charged cross-race and same-sex bond among Hawk-eye, Uncas, and, by extension, Chingachgook—is the bond that might seem least threatening by the normative sexual and racial standards of Cooper's time. While the white man and the Indians might share in the phallic rites of guns and blood and sleep with each other in the forest, they would not reproduce a mixed-blood progeny: the love triangle of Hawk-eye, Uncas, and Chingachgook enables the fantasy of blood mixture—of sex and rank and color—without the threat of generation.

At the close of the narrative, Hawk-eye casts a final wistful and desiring gaze on the formerly "erect, agile, and faultless" (*LM*, 363) and now dead body of Uncas: "Deserted by all of his color, Hawk-eye returned to the spot where his own sympathies led him, with a force that no ideal bond of union could bestow. He was just in time to catch a parting look of the features of Uncas, whom the Delawares were already inclosing in his last vestments of skin. They paused to permit the longing and lingering gaze of the sturdy woodsman, and when it was ended, the body was enveloped never to be unclosed again" (*LM*, 413). The love that binds Hawk-eye to Uncas unto and beyond death is grounded in an eroticization of blood as a signifier of manliness and the rituals of blood violence they have shared together. While Hawk-eye continues to speak of the differences of "nature" and "blood"—"it may be your blood was nearer," he tells Chingachgook (*LM*, 414)—the erotic "force" and blood "sympathies" that propel his "parting look," his "longing and lingering gaze" at the body of Uncas, belie these distinctions. In the end, Hawk-eye chooses redness over whiteness, man over woman, as he retreats back into the forest hand in hand with Chingachgook: "Chingachgook grasped the hand that, in the warmth of feeling, the scout had stretched across the fresh earth, and in that attitude of friendship these two sturdy and intrepid woodsmen bowed their heads together, while scalding tears fell to their feet, watering the grave of Uncas like drops of falling rain" (*LM*, 414). Whatever meanings this final "burst of [male] feeling" (*LM*, 414) may have had for Cooper's time, its potential subversiveness for contemporary audiences is suggested by the fact that in the Hollywood movie version of *The Last of the Mohicans* (1992), the love triangle among Hawk-eye, Uncas, and Chingachgook literally drops out of the picture: the movie focuses throughout on the primary romance between Hawk-eye and Cora.

The Poetics and Politics of Blood

"Poe has no truck with Indians or Nature," writes D. H. Lawrence in *Studies in Classic American Literature*. "He makes no bones about Red Brothers and Wigwams. He is absolutely concerned with the disintegration-processes of his own psyche."[28] Lawrence's response is characteristic of a critical tradition that has tended to cordon Poe off from history by emphasizing the primarily personal and psychological meanings of his art. In Chapter 4, I read against this tradition by locating Poe's poetics of whiteness and purity in the context of the historical struggles over blood and boundaries, mixture and crossing, that ground the emergence of white subjectivity and Western aestheticism. I connect Poe's concept of beauty, his aesthetics, his writing, and especially his poetry to Jefferson's reflections on the difference of white and black blood,

Andrew Jackson's Indian policy, and the writings of James Fenimore Cooper. While Cooper was a Northern Democrat and Poe a Southern Whig, they shared their culture's anxiety about sexual and racial purity and the collapse of a settled order of hierarchy and subordination in the ascent of the commercial marketplace and the democratic masses. This anxiety underwrites Poe's ideals of whiteness and womanhood, his notion of the "poem written solely for the poem's sake," and his desire to create a cultural aristocracy of taste and distinction.[29]

The themes of paranoia, schizophrenia, incest, necrophilism, vampirism, addiction, and compulsion at the center of Poe's work are no merely personal affair. Rather, Poe's work reveals the social markings of the Freudian unconscious. In Poe's poems and tales, what has been expelled and disavowed by the founding ideology and the rationalism of the Western Enlightenment returns as the black phantasms, savages, spooks, madmen, ghosts of women, and body parts that haunt his work.[30] The cultural ideal of sexual purity produces fantasies of defilement; the social subordination of dark to light produces a cultural fascination with amalgamation and reversal. Far from being removed from their world, Poe's poems and tales may be the most powerful artistic representation we have of the traumatic psychic and cultural effects of the social crisis and political breakdown that marked the post-Enlightenment not only in the United States but, as the later response of Baudelaire, Mallarmé, and other modernist and postmodernist writers to Poe's work suggests, in the West more generally.

In Whitman's view, Poe was the "demoniac" brother of his age and time, the "dim man" whose "lurid dreams" revealed the "sub-currents" of pathology—"the terror, the murk, and the dislocation"—beneath the surface of "the perennial and democratic concretes at first hand."[31] "I wanted, and still want for poetry, the clear sun shining, and fresh air blowing—the strength and power of health, not of delirium, even amid the stormiest passions" (*PW,* 1:232), Whitman said on the occasion of the public reburial of Poe's bones in Baltimore in 1875. And yet, while Whitman seeks to define a democratic poetry of sunshine and "health" against the "morbidity, abnormal beauty" and "sickliness" of Poe's verse, he shared some of what he called Poe's "incorrigible propensity toward nocturnal themes" (*PW,* 1:231–32), especially in his early years, before he transformed himself from Walter Whitman into Walt.

Whitman's early temperance novel, *Franklin Evans; or the Inebriate: A Tale of the Times* (1842), along with several of his short stories focus on some of the same themes of addiction, compulsion, and irrational desire that preoccupy Poe.[32] But whereas the "delirium" of Poe's characters tends to be mental, spiritual, and even ratiocinative—the perverse impulse that impels humans to act "for the reason that we should *not*," as Poe says in "The Imp of the Perverse"—the delirium of Whitman's characters has its sources in the body and the blood.[33] In *Franklin Evans*, the effort to control bodily compulsion and desire is compared to the experience of having the skin cut away from the body: "But what if the beginning be dreadful?" says the protagonist Franklin Evans of his struggle to abstain from drink. "What if a process comparable to flaying alive, have to be endured?"[34]

Although *Franklin Evans* is framed by the rhetoric of temperance reform, as Michael Moon and Michael Warner have argued, the language of temperance functions as a fluid medium for voicing at the same time that it condemns a seductive urban underworld of male desire, pleasure, cruising, dissipation, same-sex eroticism, fluid identities, and border crossings that penetrate the illusory boundaries of class and identity, sex and blood.[35] "A wretched scene!" Franklin Evans exclaims as he reflects on his former dissolution with "Half-a-dozen men, just entering the busy scenes of life, not one of us over twenty-five years . . . benumbing our faculties, and confirming ourselves in practices which ever too surely bring the scorn of the world" (*EPF*, 167–68). As a signifier of the seductions of drink and other forms of male desire and abjection, "The Demon of Intemperance" (*EPF*, 167)—or "The Snake-Tempter" (*EPF*, 221)—is associated with the corruption of both masculine and national "blood." "To know that the blood is poisoned," Evans moralizes, "and that the strength is to be broken down, and the bloom banished from the cheek, and the lustre of the eye dimmed, and all for a few hours' sensual gratification, now and then—is it not terrible!" (*EPF*, 168). Here as elsewhere in the narrative the physiognomy and "blood" of the drunkard merges with the typology of the onanist, or masturbator, and other kinds of "sensual gratification" among and between men that became the target of the male purity movement and the antimasturbation tracts during the Age of Jackson.[36]

The story of *Franklin Evans* is driven by a narrative urge to kill off all the women characters as the men pursue their desire for pleasure and each other. This urge toward male bonding and eroticism becomes bound up with the experience of cross-race sexual desire when Evans marries a creole slave named Margaret after a drinking binge in the South with Bourne, a gentleman planter of French descent vaguely associated with the radicalism of the French Revolution. Almost "clear white" but with "some hue of African blood in her veins" (*EPF*, 204), Margaret is both a border figure and a representative of the social prohibition against racial mixture onto which Whitman displaces the "strange infatuation" and "disgust" with same-sex male desire that drives his narration.[37] "What had I to do with such as she?" Evans asks: "Every feeling of prudence and self-respect, spoke loudly in opposition to my allowing any sentiment akin to love for the girl in my bosom, or to express it by my conduct. And yet, strangely enough, I thought nothing of all this; but in my wine-drinking interviews with Bourne, frequently alluded to the subject, and spoke of the regard I had for *his slave*" (*EPF*, 206). The word Whitman invents to describe this "strange infatuation" is *obfusticated*, a word that signifies the breakdown of the boundaries between mind and body, "right" and wrong, black and white, male and female, upper and lower class, "self-respect" and boundlessness experienced in a state of "intemperance" (*EPF*, 206).

While Margaret is the manifest object of Evans's erotic gaze, it is his *obfusticated* relationship with the "bachelor" Bourne that frames and enables this gaze. "So intimate did we at length become, and so necessary to one another's comfort, that I took up my residence in his house" (*EPF*, 203), Evans writes of his "companionship" with Bourne—whose very name denotes stream and boundary, the erotic flow and social limit that both draws them together and keeps them apart. It is Bourne himself, Evans tells us, who as "a justice of the peace, united myself and the creole in matrimony" (*EPF*, 207). This "strange" triangulation of cross-race and same-sex desire in *Franklin Evans* is further suggested by the fact that on their wedding night, Evans spends the night not with Margaret but with Bourne: "A couple of apartments in the homested were assigned to her use—and I signalized this crowning act of all my drunken vagaries, that night, by quaffing bottle after bottle with the planter" (*EPF*, 207). Not surprisingly, it is through the agency of Margaret that the light-haired and blue-eyed Mrs. Colman—the ideal of womanhood and the proper object of male desire within the white heteronormative symbolic—gets killed off. Whereas Margaret ends by killing herself, Evans moves on to become a bachelor, an "'unincumbered' person" (*EPF*, 232), in pursuit of further "companionships" with men.

As later critics have noted, there is more to the creole Margaret than meets the eye. And yet, these critics have been quick to locate her story safely within the heteronormative narratives that have dominated past and recent accounts of Whitman's life and work. Commenting on Whitman's fictional "entanglement with an octoroon, whose chief recommendation is her voluptuous appeal to his senses," Emory Holloway writes: "And as to this last, there are those who will see in it a strange adumbration of what happened to Whitman in New Orleans less than six years later."[38] Holloway repeats the "myth" of Whitman's New Orleans romance with a dark-skinned, high-born woman of the creole class which, as Henry Binns originally told it, liberated Whitman's senses and made him a poet.[39] But, as Holloway had himself discovered, the poem that became the main evidence for this "romance," "Once I

Pass'd through a Populous City," was originally addressed to a man rather than a woman.[40] If this cross-gendered "Children of Adam" poem continues to elicit the possibility that Whitman had an affair in New Orleans with a man rather than a woman, then the creole Margaret— who "was of that luscious and fascinating appearance often seen in the south, where a slight tinge of the deep color, large, soft voluptuous eyes, and beautifully cut lips, set off a form of faultless proportions" (*EPF*, 204)—might also provide "a strange adumbration" of a New Orleans romance that was not only cross-race but same-sex. In other words, if there was a creole "Margaret" at the sources of Whitman's erotic fantasy and his art, the evidence suggests that she may have been a black man rather than a black woman.[41]

Whereas in *Franklin Evans* the sexual underworld of the musical drinking shops, "where the mind and the body are both rendered effeminate together" (*EPF*, 239), is represented as a possible threat to the republican legacy and "blood" of the founders, in the 1855 edition of *Leaves of Grass*, it is through the erotic force of sexuality and the same-sex gaze that Whitman reimagines the politics of national blood. Thus, for example, in the poem later titled "I Sing the Body Electric," the poet's loving evocation of the "goodsized arms and legs" (and, more furtively, phallus) of a slave at auction prompts a refiguration of the blood not as a sign of racial difference or sexual impurity but as a democratic and erotic flow that "swells and jets" and unites men and races—"red black or white"—across the socially proscribed boundaries of race and sex:

Exquisite senses, lifelit eyes, pluck, volition,
Flakes of breastmuscle, pliant backbone and neck, flesh not flabby, goodsized
    arms and legs,
And wonders within there yet.
Within there runs his blood . . . . the same old blood . . the same red running
    blood;
There swells and jets his heart . . . . There all passions and desires . . all reachings
    and aspirations.[42]

Similarly, in poem 12 of "Live Oak, with Moss," the unpublished sequence of twelve poems written in the late 1850s in which Whitman recounts the story of his love affair with a man, the temperance and antionanist discourses of blood corruption and blood impurity are rearticulated in the image of "the blood of friendship—hot and red" as a symbol of both same-sex love and democratic comradeship.[43] The poem was published as "Calamus" 42 (later "To a Western Boy") in the 1860 edition of *Leaves of Grass,* with the more emphatically corporeal allusion to the blood "hot and red" of homoerotic desire toned down to the (perhaps) more ambiguous "blood like mine":

To the young man, many things to absorb, to engraft, to develop, I teach, to help
    him become élève of mine,
But if blood like mine circle not in his veins,
If he be not silently selected by lovers, and do not silently select lovers,
Of what use is it that he seek to become élève of mine?[44]

In "Calamus" 15 (titled "Confession Drops" in the manuscript and
later "Trickle Drops"), the "blood" that "silently" binds the poet to his
lovers is associated with the pain of repression and the open wounds
(perhaps self-inflicted) that bleed into his poems from every part of his
body:

O drops of me! Trickle, slow drops,
Candid, from me falling—drip, bleeding drops,
From wounds made to free you whence you were prisoned,
From my face—from my forehead and lips,
From my breast—from within where I was concealed—Press forth, red
    drops—confession drops,
Stain every page—stain every song I sing, every word I say, bloody drops. (*LG*
    1860, 361)

Transgressing the distinctions between body and mind, private and public, feeling and reason, sex and politics that structure the print public
sphere, the poet breaks out of the prison of the body, privacy, and same-
sex desire by bleeding—or more properly hemorrhaging—into public
song. This scene of homosexual bloodshed embodies the violence of
repressive social and sexual codes at the same time that it makes the
homerotic male body present, visible, and "felt" as part of the political
body of the republic. The poet's wounds—whether self-inflicted or
socially imposed—become a source of freedom by bleeding openly into
speech, print, and song.
    "[A]ll ashamed and wet," Whitman also draws on nineteenth-century
medical theory of semen as a form of blood to represent his poems as a
kind of masturbatory flow into print and publicity:

Let them know your scarlet heat—let them glisten,
Saturate them with yourself, all ashamed and wet,
Glow upon all I have written or shall write, bleeding drops,
Let it all be seen in your light, blushing drops. (*LG* 1860, 361)

Saturating a "them" that encompasses the printed page, "every song I
sing," and the public he addresses with the blood, semen, and tears of
homosexual passion, Whitman's poetic act of making the private public
is part of a political struggle for freedom and justice. As the political
theorist Seyla Benhabib observes: "All struggles against oppression in
the modern world begin by redefining what had previously been consid-

ered private, nonpublic, and nonpolitical issues as matters of public concern, as issues of justice, as sites of power that need discursive legitimation."[45]

In Chapter 5, I argue that Whitman's rise to national and international prominence as *the* poet of American democracy has been accompanied by a critical effort to close down the relations among homosexual love, poetic utterance, and political vision that remain open and fluid in Whitman's work. Reading across the critical lines of distinction between high art and low, poetry and politics, private and public, homosexuality and democracy that have structured the discipline of literary study and past and recent approaches to Whitman's work, I argue that the erotic pleasures of the body, sex, and urban cruising and the socially taboo bonds of attraction and love between men are at the very sources of his democratic verse and vision.

Although critics have acknowledged the importance of Whitman's visionary democracy as vision, few have been willing to cross the traditional boundary between poetry and political theory, vision and history, by reading him as a serious philosopher of democracy. In recent years, however, political philosophers such as George Kateb have turned to Whitman with renewed attention as "perhaps the greatest philosopher of the culture of democracy."[46] But while Kateb and others have emphasized the importance of Whitman's reflections on the democratic individual, it was the political tension between individual liberty and social union—what Whitman called the "separate person" and the "En-masse"—that constitutes the central paradox of American democracy and the overarching concern of Whitman's life, art, and political vision. Whitman's attempt to resolve the paradox of democracy and the political crisis of the nation on the level of the body, sex, and homosexual love not only breaks the traditional boundaries among poetry, sexuality, and politics. His emphasis on the role of affection, sexual passion, and desire as opposed to reason, law, or guns in achieving political union also has an important contribution to make to current discussions among political philosophers and theorists about the role of affect, the emotions, and the body in the formation of democratic and global community.[47]

White Election

"Of all dangers to a nation," Whitman writes in *Democratic Vistas* (1871), "there can be no greater one than having certain portions of the people set off from the rest by a line drawn—they not privileged as others, but degraded, humiliated, made of no account" (*PW* 2:382). Whereas in Whitman's visionary poetics "the same red running blood" (*LG* 1855,

121) becomes a signifier of the erotic and democratic flow that "fuses, ties and aggregates" humanity across the boundaries of race, sex, class, region, and nation (*PW* 2:381), in the life and art of Emily Dickinson the blood functions as a marker of class distinction, a national, social, and cultural "line drawn" between those of *pure* and *impure* blood. "Amalgams are abundant, but the lone student of the Mines adores Alloyless things," Dickinson wrote.[48]

In the past, the difference between Whitman and Dickinson has been defined as the difference between *male* and *female*, between what Sandra Gilbert calls Whitman as "the supreme patriarch," "an acolyte of healthful masculine blood-brotherhood" and "virtually ontological maleness," and Dickinson as the "exemplar of a cult of purity," "an Angel in the House" and "devotee of female renunciation."[49] Gilbert presents Whitman and Dickinson as "the father and mother of American poetry" whose psychosexual differences give birth to "two different (male and female) traditions in modern American poetry, even while they reflect, and reflect back upon, a history of sexual difference in poetry."[50] In Chapter 6, I seek to complicate this ontologically sexed American poetics by examining not only the gendered but the social and specifically racial and class locations of Dickinson's art.

With a family lineage that extended back to the Great Migration of religious dissidents to America in the 1630s, the Dickinsons were "pure bloods" who resisted the widespread democratization, amalgamation, and "fusion" that marked nineteenth-century American society.[51] When in 1856 Dickinson's brother, Austin, married Susan Gilbert, the daughter of a local tavern keeper, their troubled marriage was seen as a cautionary tale about the danger of mixing bloods: "The whole situation was another illustration of the impossibility of a marriage between different grades of society ever becoming a perfect fusion," wrote Mabel Loomis Todd. "In those early days the democratic mixing of upper and lower classes was, to be sure, much more easily accomplished than in these later and stricter days of preserving family and training carefully."[52] Within this "stricter" order of late nineteenth-century class relations, Austin carried on a thirteen-year love affair with Todd, who became the editor (with Thomas Higginson) of Dickinson's first volumes of poems published in the 1890s. Emily Dickinson, in her turn, formed a passionate love relationship with her putatively abject sister-in-law, Susan Gilbert Dickinson: "Where my Hands are cut, Her fingers will be found in side—" (*LD*, 2:430), she wrote, in language that sensuously embodies the erotics of intimacy, pain, and blood that marked their lifelong relationship. As in Poe's "Fall of the House of Usher," the seemingly odd pairing of class and race purity with incestuous longing suggests the ways *incest*—either symbolic or real—often shadows the fear of blood mixture as its underlying logic and double.[53]

The thematic of *spatial enclosure*—first within New England, then within Amherst, then within the house, and ultimately within her room and the space of her own mind—was at the center of Dickinson's life and work. "The Soul selects her own Society — / Then — shuts the Door — / To her divine Majority — / Present no more —," she wrote, in a poem that reaffirms an aristocratic order of divine right and hereditary entitlement against the majoritarian rule of democracy.[54] But while Dickinson held herself aloof from the political and social struggles of her time, this does not mean that she had no politics or no public attitude toward the political events of her time. In fact, Dickinson lived and wrote in a more political house than did Whitman. Her father, Edward Dickinson, was actively involved in local and state government over many years, and in 1853, at a time of intensified struggle over slavery, he was elected to a two-year term as a conservative Whig representative to the national Congress. During his first year in Congress, he voted with other antislavery Whigs to oppose the Kansas-Nebraska bill; and, when the bill was passed, some thirty congressmen met in his rooms to discuss the formation of a new antislavery party that would be called the "Republican party." Edward Dickinson refused to join. Resisting what his friend Otis P. Lord called the new parties of "fusion," he chose to remain loyal to "the true Republicanism" of the Whig Party, which had been formed in 1833–34 to oppose Jacksonian tyranny.[55]

Although Dickinson did not share her father's public political commitment or his faith in what Henry Clay called the "American System"—a progressive, business-oriented, and national Whig agenda grounded in a strong military, a federal tariff, a national bank, and internal improvements—as I argue in Chapter 6, she shared many of his class values and social fears in response to Jacksonian democracy, the masses, foreigners, the Irish, Negroes, labor, reform, and western expansion at a time when the aristocratic class-based values of the past were being eroded under the pressure of an increasingly democratic and industrial capitalist society of new money and new men.

Against the modernizing, democratizing, and politically diversifying forces of her time, Dickinson turned to art as a higher order of power—a power she associated with *whiteness* and a purity so pure that, during her lifetime at least, she resisted print publication. "Publication — is the Auction / Of the mind of man —," she wrote in a poem that associates publication with blackness, wage slavery, and the degradations of both the slave auction and the capitalist marketplace:

Poverty — be justifying
For so foul a thing

Possibly — but We — would rather
From Our Garret go
White — unto the White Creator —
Than invest — Our Snow — (*Fr* 788)

Deploying the language of antislavery protest and artisan republican protest against wage labor as a new form of slavery to constitute herself and her writing as part of an elect community of whiteness, Dickinson resists the "foul" values of the commercial marketplace: "reduce no Human Spirit / To Disgrace of Price —." Written at the time of the Emancipation Proclamation when the war to save the Union had become in the eyes of many, including Edward Dickinson, an unconstitutional executive war to abolish slavery, Dickinson's poem suggests that her refusal to publish was not so much a private act as it was an act of social and class resistance to the commercial, democratic, and increasingly amalgamated and mass values of the literary marketplace.[56]

When Dickinson wrote to Thomas Higginson in 1862 that she had "never read [Whitman's] Book but was told that he was disgraceful," she may have been thinking of a review titled " 'Leaves of Grass'—Smut in Them," which appeared in the *Springfield Daily Republican* on 16 June 1860. The review, which was probably written by her friend Josiah Gilbert Holland, who was associate editor of the *Republican*, presents the 1860 edition of *Leaves of Grass* as an "obscene book," a source of "impurity," "libertinism," and "filth" that threatens "Christian marriage," revealed truth, and "virtuous community." Written against the view that Whitman is "the poet of sexual purity," the review suggests the ways that attitudes toward the social and sexual body continue to inhabit and invest aesthetic judgment and literary value in the nineteenth century. Questions of social and sexual mixture—of "men in masses" and "promiscuous intercourse of the sexes"—ooze into matters of *taste,* aesthetics, and what counts as a poem. Whitman's "smut" is "about as much like poetry as tearing off a rag, or paring one's corns." Only those of impure bodies—"lewd women," "prurient boys," and "lechers"—can respond positively to Whitman's *Leaves* as a "pure book" and as "poetry." Men and women of "higher affinities," "the pure in society," will "shun it" and "be led straight away."[57]

For Dickinson, as for Holland, Higginson, and other members of her class during the Civil War years and after, art becomes a new form of social and class distinction, a higher realm of culture, value, and truth through which an older New England elite seeks to maintain its power against the rising forces of democracy, mixture, modernity, and the masses signified by Whitman's "disgraceful" book. The fusion of social with sexual and aesthetic purity in the *Springfield Daily Republican* review

of Whitman might be compared with a later response to Dickinson written by Samuel G. Ward, a patron of the arts and one of the founders of
the Metropolitan Museum of Art, who emphasized Dickinson's *pure blood*
as the site and source of her poetic value. "I am, with all the world,
intensely interested in Emily Dickinson," Ward wrote to Higginson, who
edited the first edition of Dickinson's *Poems* with Todd in 1890: "No wonder six editions have been sold, every copy, I should think to a New Eng-
lander. She may become world famous, or she may never get out of New
England. She is the quintessence of that element we all have who are of
the Puritan descent *pur sang*. We came to this country to think our own
thoughts with nobody to hinder. Ascetics of course, & this our Thebaid.
. . . It was *awfully* high, but awfully lonesome."[58] Ward's emphasis on the
purity of Dickinson's New England "descent" and blood suggests the
ways her works were used to empower and canonize a particular region,
class, and race as the *pur sang* of America. Whereas Whitman is associated with "the dregs of the social and moral world,"[59] Dickinson comes
to signify the "*awfully* high" moral and ultimately "ascetic" and Puritan
ideals of New England and America.

In the words of one of Dickinson's earliest reviewers, William Dean
Howells, writing as editor of *Harper's Monthly* in 1891: "If nothing had
come out of our life but this strange poetry we should feel that in the
work of Emily Dickinson America, or New England rather, had made a
distinctive addition to the literature of the world, and could not be left
out of any record of it; and the interesting and important thing is that
this poetry is as characteristic of our life as our business enterprise, our
political turmoil, our demagogism, our millionarism."[60] Against the
apparent crassness of both the new money and the new masses, "the
work of Emily Dickinson" is invoked as a figure of what Perry Miller
would later call "the New England Mind" assuming its rightful and culturally dominant position as a representative not only of the American
mind but of All Mind on the stage of world literature.

Dickinson's status as a New England "pure blood" underwrites her
later emergence as a New Critical icon of noncontingent aesthetic value.
In his important 1932 article, "New England Culture and Emily Dickinson," Allen Tate begins by setting Dickinson as a poet of New England
mind and culture against the "intellectual chaos" of Marxian criticism
and the kinds of political writing associated with the Depression: Dickinson's poetry is "a poetry of ideas," he says, "and it demands of the
reader a point of view—not an opinion of the New Deal or of the League
of Nations, but an ingrained philosophy that is fundamental, a settled
attitude that is almost extinct in this eclectic age."[61] Deployed as a
weapon against the political, ideological, and popular approaches to literature associated with the Left, the masses, and the 1930s, in the criti-

cism of Tate, R. P. Blackmur, Yvor Winters, and others, Dickinson's poems became both the exempla and occasion for modernist and New Critical definitions of the *literary*—grounded in distinctions between poetry and history, aesthetics and politics, high art and mass culture, form and feeling—that came to dominate academic criticism and literary studies in the United States during the cold war years and after.[62]

Culture and Miscegenation

The relations among blood, purity, culture, and national representation that would continue to frame not only Dickinson studies but literary studies more generally in the post-World War II period lend credence to Toni Morrison's observation that the passions aroused by the canon wars arise out of a fear of "miscegenation" as previously marginalized groups seek to make incursions "into a Eurocentric stronghold." "Canon building is Empire building," she says; "Canon defense is national defense."[63] What Morrison's formulation suggests is the ways contests over *literature* and *culture*—over what counts as literature and who gets to speak for or represent a given culture—get intimately bound up with questions of *blood,* of *consanguinity,* of what bodies and texts appear to belong or not belong within an always already pure and consanguineous European or specifically national American literary tradition.[64]

As the relation between Dickinson's "pure" New England blood and her emergence as the representative of transcendent literary and cultural value suggests, in the post-Civil War years and especially in the years following the World Wars, debates about differences of class, race, sexual, and national blood get displaced onto debates about cultural tradition, Kantian assertions of universal aesthetic value, and the superiority of the *masterworks* of the West. As I have argued elsewhere, it is not entirely coincidental that a triumvirate of white male European theorists—Michel Foucault, Jacques Derrida, and Jacques Lacan—came to dominate the academy and literary criticism at the very moment when previously excluded ethnic, gay, and women writers were asking for a voice, a representation, and a presence in the American academy, the canon, the curriculum, and in American literary and social history.[65] The struggle between European and particularly French poststructuralist theory and various forms of American "identity" studies has played itself out as a struggle between *discourse* and the *flesh,* between the structures of language and what Cherríe Moraga and Gloria Anzaldúa call "theory in the flesh" to denote the "flesh and blood experiences" of lesbian and feminist women of color.[66] For Anzaldúa, Moraga, and other minority, gay, and women writers, poststructuralist theory appears to function as a new form of intellectual colonization that puts down the uprisings of women, gays, blacks, Chicanos, Native Americans, and other minorities at the very moment when they are seeking to constitute themselves as legitimate subjects in history.

Whereas Roland Barthes and Foucault have declared that in the future the author will be for all intents and purposes *dead,* several African American women critics—including Mary Helen Washington, Barbara Christian, Claudia Tate, Gloria Hull, and Frances Foster, to name only a few—have spent the last few decades struggling to bring into voice, visibility, and circulation the works of previously obscure, anonymous, or socially *dead* African American women writers in order to change what Stuart Hall has called the "relations of representation."[67] In other words, while Foucault, Barthes, and other poststructuralist theorists have dismissed traditional notions of voice, authorship, and historical subject as matters of indifference, many African Americanists still place issues of voice, authorship, and historical agency at the center of discussions of such texts as Harriet Jacobs's *Incidents in the Life of a Slave Girl.*[68]

One way of responding to the potential contradiction between poststructuralist theory and multicultural practice in the United States might be to criticize African Americanists, and black women critics in particular, for being hopelessly enmeshed in historical, textual, and essentially bourgeois modes of analysis.[69] But I believe something more is at stake. In Jacobs's *Incidents in the Life of a Slave Girl,* as in writings by women, gays, and others minorities that are being discovered or recovered by feminist, Latino/a, and gay critics in the United States, it *does* matter who is speaking for reasons that have to do with the historical experiences and alternative cultural and political practices of minority cultures in America. For Harriet Jacobs, as for Olaudah Equiano and Frederick Douglass, the unstopped black mouth, the black subject who thinks, speaks, writes, and creates *back,* is integral to the process of transforming the black person's material and symbolic status as "cargo," slave, and other within the imperialist narratives and representational practices of white Euro-American history.

"Reader, be assured this narrative is no fiction," writes "the Author" and narrator, Linda Brent, in the preface to *Incidents in the Life of a Slave Girl.*[70] In Brent's narrative, it does matter who is speaking because against a cultural economy that equates literacy and writing with whiteness and maleness, Brent/Jacobs demonstrates the ability of a "slave girl" to write, to create, to narrate, and (in the words of Brent) to engage in a "Competition in Cunning" with the master himself. It does matter who is speaking because against the freely circulating national fictions of freedom and equality, *Incidents in the Life of a Slave Girl* bears witness to a black girl's actual experience of enslavement and brutalization at the hands of a white Southern lady and a white Christian slave master. It does matter who is speaking because by testifying to the physical violation of mothers and children—the rape, incest, child abuse, and daily assault on the parent-child bond that are part of the everyday practice of slavery—*Incidents in the Life of a Slave Girl* erodes the sacred national myth of a true and pure womanhood and motherhood and thus the fundamental social, sexual, and religious categories (motherhood, sexual purity, republican virtue, the home, the family, Christianity) that ordered mid-nineteenth-century American society. Finally, it does matter who is speaking because against the master's attempt to stop her mouth and thereby usurp her power to speak for, represent, and write herself, Brent/Jacobs seeks to give voice to her historical experience as a slave woman in order to resist and change the material—and not merely fictive or discursive—relations of power and dominance in the United States.

And yet, as we move toward a new phase of what Hall has called "New Ethnicities"—a shift "from a struggle over the relations of representation to a politics of representation itself"—there is a need to complicate the politically and historically sedimented notions of identity, subjectivity, authorship, writing, culture, and difference that have come to constitute the fields of ethnic, gay, and women's studies.[71] What does it mean to speak of a white author or a Native American author, a woman subject or a man subject, a straight culture or a gay culture? What does it mean to say that an author, a text, or a tradition inscribes "an authentic black voice" or that "the Afro-American critic ought to be committed to exploring the blackness of black texts"?[72] Or, to return to the example of *Incidents in the Life of a Slave Girl*, what does it mean to "authenticate" Harriet Jacobs as the author of this text? Doesn't the focus on "authentic authorship" in this, as in any text, tend to reinforce privatized and aestheticized notions of authorship set in place by capitalist and bourgeois individualist modes of production and thus remove *Incidents in the Life of a Slave Girl* from the complicated network of power relations—racial, sexual, textual, literary, and political—that are part of its publication history?

Although Linda Brent's *Incidents in the Life of a Slave Girl* was "written by herself," the copyright and the contract of the book, which was published by Thayer and Eldridge of Boston in 1861, were owned by Lydia Maria Child, who is named as editor on the title page of the book.[73] Just as Jacobs's attempt "to give a true and just account of my own life in Slavery" was published as part of the antislavery struggle in nineteenth-century America, so a new and still pseudonymous edition, with introduction and notes by Walter Magnes Teller, was published in 1973 in the context of the ongoing political and cultural struggle of blacks to gain visibility, voice, and representation in American literature and history. Whereas the first edition of *Incidents in the Life of a Slave Girl* was authenticated by two "highly respected" white women, Lydia Maria Child and Amy Post, and "a highly respected colored citizen of Boston," George W. Lowther, it was not until 1981 that Jacobs's authorship was verified by a white woman, Jean Fagan Yellin, who edited an "authenticated" version of the book for Harvard University Press in 1987. This edition includes a "Cast of Characters" and a documentary apparatus that tends to literalize Jacobs's creative narration—what she calls her "Competition in Cunning"—as direct transcription. Before the text was authenticated by Yellin, its validity as a slave narrative had been questioned by several prominent black writers and critics—including Sterling Brown, Arna Bontemps, and John Blasingame, who, in *The Slave Community* (1972), judged *Incidents in the Life of a Slave Girl* to be "not credible."[74]

The authentication of Jacobs's authorship of *Incidents in the Life of a Slave Girl* has shifted the focus away from disputes over the text's complicated and hybrid genealogies (is it black or white, fiction or history, literature or politics?) toward critical approaches that tend to play down or erase the collective and "mixed" nature of the text signified by the simultaneously interactive and resistant relationships not only between Jacobs as "author" and Child as "editor" but also among Jacobs, Harriet Beecher Stowe, and an entire tradition of domestic sentimental fiction. Does life follow art or does art follow life in the intertextual relation between Jacobs's "Loophole of Retreat" in *Incidents in the Life of a Slave Girl* and Cassy's garret enclosure in *Uncle Tom's Cabin*? Moreover, Jacobs was herself of mixed blood, the *mulatta* offspring of a putatively illegal sexual relation between a white man and a black slave girl. The feminist emphasis on the essentially maternal and domestic nature of *Incidents*, with Linda Brent as heroic slave mother and the grandmother as the ultimate heroine of the story, tends to gloss over the fact that Jacobs may not have been a good mother (at least in the conventional terms in which the problem has been posed). As Hortense Spillers argues in "Mama's Baby, Papa's Maybe," "[U]nder a system of enslavement . . . the customary lexis of sexuality, including 'reproduction,' 'motherhood,' 'pleasure,' and 'desire' are thrown into unrelieved crisis."[75] By inserting *Incidents in the Life of a Slave Girl* into the customary white, middle-class lexis of "reproduction" and "motherhood," Child's "edition," like recent feminist accounts of the narrative, erases Jacobs's sexuality and thus the whole question of her own "pleasure" and "desire" in the text, a pleasure and desire that may be inseparable from her decision to write about her illicit mixed-blood relationship with a white man who is not her master.

It is important to note that it was the white woman editor, Child, who suggested that a concluding focus on the death of Jacobs's grandmother would be a more "appropriate" and "natural" end to her story. "I think the last Chapter, about John Brown, had better be omitted," Child wrote Jacobs in August 1860. "It does not naturally come into your story, and the M. S. is already too long. Nothing can be so appropriate to end with, as the death of your grandmother."[76] But while the text's conclusion with the "tender memories of my good old grandmother" confirms the feminist emphasis on familial and specifically mother-daughter bonds among women, by concluding with the death of Jacobs's grandmother (Child's suggestion) rather than with the aborted slave insurrection led by John Brown at Harper's Ferry (Jacobs's original manuscript), *Incidents in the Life of a Slave Girl* is in some sense more fully inscribed within a sentimental, domestic, maternal, and "quietest" tradition associated with Child rather than within the more stridently political, insurrectionary, violent, and contemporaneous narrative suggested by John Brown.

What the publication history of *Incidents in the Life of a Slave Girl* suggests is the complex network of economic, social, political, and cultural relationships in which black authors and texts, like all authors and texts, are implicated. By complicating the notion of a purely "individual" authorship, a purely "black" text, and a purely "factual" narration, *Incidents in the Life of a Slave Girl* is in some sense representative of the fluid boundaries, hybrid textualities, and politically situated "identities" and "traditions" that have come to constitute not only ethnic, gay, and women's studies but also, as Toni Morrison argues in *Playing in the Dark*, the formation of "white" identity and "white" American literature and culture.

Whereas in the past, American culture has been conceived as some unified idea or ideal *into* which the works of ethnic minorities, women, gays, and other "others" can be absorbed or incorporated, *Mixed Bloods and Other Crosses* seeks to rethink American literature and culture as a fluid and contested field of contact, struggle, and exchange across borders that are themselves historically constituted, permeable, and in flux. As I argue in Chapter 7, this future of American literary and cultural studies was already imagined over a half-century ago by the black West Indian Marxist intellectual C.L.R. James in *Mariners, Renegades and Castaways: The Story of Herman Melville and the World We Live In* (1953). Beginning with an epigraph from Melville's *Redburn* in which the narrator reflects on the mixture of American bloods—"You can not spill a drop of American blood without spilling the blood of the whole world"—James's study redirects the symbolism of American blood away from its association with singularity and difference—national or otherwise—toward its global and potentially more democratic meanings as a signifier of the historical movement, mixture, and flow of people and culture across the borders.[77] For James, the Melvillean figure of America as "the blood of the whole world" comes to signify both a mode of interpretation that reads American literature and civilization beyond the boundaries of the nation-state and the possibility of a future New World democracy of blood kin—of "America being in future years a society of liberty and freedom, composed of all the races of the earth" (*M*, 91).

Like "Notes on American Civilization," the prospectus for a longer study of American civilization from which *Mariners* was drawn, James's reading of Melville's *Moby Dick* represents a multiply crossed model of literary criticism that resists linear, disciplinary, and national boundaries and that links the realms of culture and society, literature and history, aesthetics and politics, art and the masses that were driven apart by the founding terms of American literary studies during the cold war years. Forming connections with cultural formations and political practices across the boundaries—with Toussaint L'Ouverture and Herman Melville, cricket and reggae, American gangster films and black nationalism—James imagines an American future and a future of American literary and cultural studies in which the creative and productive power of both labor and culture, the worker and the writer, will bring about what he calls "a new conception of democracy beyond anything we have known."[78]

Chapter 2

Mixed Bloods
Jefferson, Revolution, and the Boundaries of America

> *Next to the case of the black race within our bosom, that of the red on our borders is the problem most baffling to the policy of our country.*
> —*James Madison to Thomas L. McKenney, 10 February 1826*

> *Two human groups never meet but they mingle their blood.*
> —*Melville J. Herskovits*, The American Negro

In the preface to his 1956 publication of *Errand into the Wilderness*, Perry Miller recounts the origins "on the edge" of the African Congo of his own "errand" to expound "the massive narrative of the movement of European culture into the vacant wilderness of America." "It was given to me," he says, "on the edge of a jungle of central Africa, to have thrust upon me the mission of expounding what I took to be the innermost propulsion of the United States, while supervising, in that barbaric tropic, the unloading of drums of case oil flowing out of the inexhaustible wilderness of America."[1] Against the exceptionalist vision of America as a world apart, this "origin" of Miller's "errand" in "a jungle of central Africa" reveals the worldly location of both America and the American as part of a global system of commerce, circulation, and exchange that moves across the geopolitical spaces of Africa, Europe, and the New World. This "origin" of Miller's "errand"—and in some sense the entire American studies "mission"—on the boundaries of the "barbaric" African jungle also lends support to Toni Morrison's observation that the intensity and turbulence of disputes over the canon suggest an underlying fear of "miscegenation" as "third-world or so-called minority literature" makes incursions "into a Eurocentric stronghold."[2]

Over the last few decades, critics have come to recognize the centrality of race in the political and cultural constitution of the United States and in the formation of American national identity. But while race has moved from invisibility to the foreground in American literary and cultural studies, until quite recently American cultural critics have tended to keep traditional racial categories intact (white, black, Indian, Hispanic, Asian) and, at least among white critics, to stress the imperial politics of what *we did to them*, rather than the considerable amount of cultural exchange and transformation across racial bounds that has taken place, and is still taking place, in American history and literary history.

In this chapter, I want to bring Morrison's notion of the underlying fear of "miscegenation" in the formation of American culture to an analysis of what I shall call the "erotics of race": the simultaneous constitution of a sexualized body, a racialized sexuality, and an ideology of sexual, racial, and national difference in revolutionary America. Focusing on Jefferson's *Notes on the State of Virginia* (1787), which was originally written as a response to twenty-two queries posed by a Frenchman, François Marbois, on the American states,[3] I want to examine the centrality of sex and race and blood in the cultural constitution of American national identity and, correspondingly, the amount of exchange—sexual, cultural, and political—that took place despite the desire of white Americans to keep sexual, racial, cultural, and geographical boundaries rigidly intact. Without discounting the blood violence and violation that were part of the history of the encounter of white people and people of color in the New World, I want to argue that for all Jefferson's efforts to map and define the limits of body, race, and nation, *Notes on the State of Virginia* reveals the impossibility of eluding contact, mixture, and exchange across borders that are themselves fluid, contested, and subject to change.

The Erotics of Race in Revolutionary America

On 18 June 1779, Jefferson was one of a "Committee of Revisors" who submitted a "Report" to the Virginia Assembly aimed at "reforming the entire structure of the law so as to strip it of all vestiges of its earlier monarchical aspects and to bring it into conformity with republican principles" (*PTJ*, 2:305). In an attempt to, in Jefferson's words, "proportion crimes and punishments" (*NV*, 143), the committee proposed that "Rape, Sodomy, Bestiality . . . be punished by Castration" rather than by death (*PTJ*, 2:325). This localization of sexuality in a particular and punishable part of the body is symptomatic of an increasing juridical and scientific focus on the body as the site of what Jefferson called "unbounded licentiousness" (*NV*, 85) and the emergence of technologies of bodily and social control that, ironically, went hand in hand with the emergence of a republican discourse of individual rights, liberty, and equality.[4] It is, indeed, to bring the penal code into "conformity with republican principle" that Jefferson suggests that acts of sodomitic excess—which, in accord with the definitions of the time, might include men copulating with men, women copulating with women, or either sex copulating with animals—be punished with sexual "Dismemberment" rather than death (*PTJ* 2:305; *NV*, 144–45).[5]

This increasing focus on the body as a potential source of excess within the body politic corresponds with a revolutionary transformation in the concept of the person in the eighteenth century. For Jefferson as for other colonists, the American Revolution represented a profound break in the social order, as power and sovereignty were shifted from the external authority of God and king to the internal authority of the subject. "[L]et the crown . . . be demolished, and scattered among the people whose right it is," Tom Paine had proclaimed in *Common Sense* (*CS*, 1:29). At its most radical, the Revolutionary language of reason, rights, liberty, and independence empowered everybody. This relocation of power and authority among the people corresponded with an increasing anxiety about a potentially unruly body and an increasing juridical and scientific emphasis on "natural" differences among men, women, bodies, classes, races, nations, and bloods.

Not coincidentally, Jefferson's discussion of his attempt to bring the Virginia legal system into conformity with "republicanism" in Query XIV of *Notes on the State of Virginia* (titled "Laws") also occasions his "scientific" attempt to map the difference of color—of white from black blood—onto an eroticized black body that is more sexual than rational, more sensation than imagination, more heart than head, more body than mind. In his effort to tease out the difference between the black and white races, Jefferson associates blacks with what Bakhtin has called the grotesque body—with bodily fluids, odors, and secretions, the lower body parts, and the animal.[6] Jefferson is one of the first in America to assert the Negro-ape connection: blacks prefer the "superior beauty" of whites as "uniformly" as "the Oran-ootan" prefers "the black women over those of his own species" (*NV*, 138).[7] Advancing it "as a suspicion only, that blacks . . . are inferior to the whites in the endowments both of body and mind," Jefferson calls for the emancipation of "all slaves born" after the passage of the proposed republican revisions of Virginia laws; at the same time, he calls for the colonization of blacks elsewhere (*NV*, 137–38).[8] "Among the Romans emancipation required but one effort," writes Jefferson. "The slave, when made free, might *mix with, without staining the blood of his master*. But with us a second is necessary, *unknown to history*. When freed, he is to be removed *beyond the reach of mixture"* (*NV*, 143; emphasis added). Fearing mixture with and blood pollution by an inferior and eroticized black body, Jefferson proposes that the offending member be, in effect, castrated from the social body of the American republic in much the same way that those who commit rape, sodomy, and bestiality are to be punished—in accord with "republican principle"—not by death but by dismemberment.

Jefferson's comments on Native Americans in *Notes* are similarly focused on the erotics of race but in a different register. Whereas Jefferson constitutes blacks as an inferior race that must be expelled from the classical body of the republic, he represents Indians as the same as the white man and defends them against the "imputation of impotence" made by the French naturalist Buffon, the Abbé Raynal, and others, who argued that America was the site of natural, human, and moral degeneration.[9] Jefferson, in effect, uses his response to Marbois's queries as an occasion to respond to the colonial notion of America—and the Virginia slaveholder in particular—as the abject, impotent, and degenerate *other* of European imperial fantasy.[10] His response to Buffon's charges of American inferiority reveals the complex triangulation and underlying instability of American New World identity as Jefferson seeks to disavow the bodily and the African, embrace the savage and the Native, and affirm the essential superiority of New over Old World man.

If, as Benedict Anderson has argued, the New World represents the origins of a "new form of imagined community" that is the nation-state, Jefferson's *Notes* reveals the pervasive presence of sex and race—or the erotics of race—in the formation of this new "creole" consciousness.[11] From Jefferson's lyrical and orgasmic evocation of the waters of the "Patowmac" and Shenandoah rushing through the Blue Ridge ("the riot and tumult roaring around"), to his detailed account of the Indian legend of "the Mammoth, or Big Buffalo," to his impassioned defense of the size and potency of the Indian's sex organs, *Notes on the State of Virginia* is, on the most fundamental level, an early nationalist narrative of New World sexual virility, or "MINE'S BIGGER THAN YOURS."

As quoted by Jefferson, Buffon's comments in *Histoire naturelle* (1779) foreground the relations among sexuality, the body, race, and the emergence of New World creole nationalism. "All living nature has become smaller" in the "new world," writes Buffon:

The *savage is feeble,* and has *small organs of generation;* he has neither hair nor beard, and *no ardor whatever for his female.* . . . [T]he most precious spark of the fire of nature has been refused to them; they lack ardor for their females, and consequently have *no love for their fellow men* . . . the most intimate of all ties, *the family connection,* binds them therefore but loosely together; between family and family there is no tie at all; hence, they have *no communion, no commonwealth, no state of society.* Physical love constitutes their only morality. . . . Everywhere the original defect appears; they are indifferent because *they have little sexual capacity, and this indifference to the other sex is the fundamental defect* which weakens their nature, prevents its development, and—destroying the very germs of life— uproots society at the same time. Nature, by refusing him the power of love, has treated him worse and lowered him deeper than any animal. (*NV*, 59; emphasis added)

Rather than questioning Buffon's assumption that male-female sexual desire is central to the definition of race and the constitution of the individual, the family, and the social body, Jefferson, too, focuses centrally on the sexual and reproductive power of Indians in responding to Buffon's charges of sexual, racial, and national inferiority. Himself a transplanted New World man—indeed a "creole" in Anderson's terms[12]—Jefferson identifies with the Indian against Buffon's charge of sexual impotence. His detailed discussion of the size of the American Indian's sex organs, his sexual and reproductive capacity, and his ardour for his female is not only a defense of America against Europe; it is also an impassioned nationalist and republican defense of the sexual potency of New World manhood, "whether aboriginal or transplanted" (*NV*, 58). Drawing on his "own knowledge" and the "information of others better acquainted with him," Jefferson argues that the "Indian of North America . . . is neither more defective in ardor, nor more impotent with his female, than the white reduced to the same diet and exercise" (*NV*, 59). Arguing that the "defective" sexual and reproductive capacity of the Indian is circumstantial rather than a sign of racial and New World inferiority, Jefferson concludes that although "more facts are wanting . . . we shall probably find that they are formed in mind as well as in body, on the same module with the 'Homo sapiens Europaeus'" (*NV*, 62).

Jefferson's conclusions about Indians reverse his conclusions about blacks. Unlike his "suspicion" of black inferiority, which stands apart from its time in appearing to endorse polygenesis, undermine the Bible, and anticipate the scientific racism of the nineteenth century, his view of the sameness of Indian nature accords with the environmental and culturalist theories of his time.[13] Whereas he wants to prohibit the mixture of black and white blood by removing blacks from the country, he appears to approve of the marriage of Indian women and white trappers (and thus the mixture of red and white blood) as a sign that Indians have the same sexual and reproductive capacity as Europeans.[14] Here again, Jefferson's comments reveal the ways black, Indian, and female sexuality become entangled with early republican definitions of white (heterosexual) manhood. "The same Indian women," he says, "when married to white traders, who feed them and their children plentifully and regularly, who exempt them from excessive drudgery, who *keep them stationary and unexposed* to accident, produce and raise as many children as the white women" (*NV,* 61; emphasis added). Jefferson's entire argument about Indian sexuality ends by underwriting what would become, during his presidency, an increasingly central tenet of American Indian policy. Although Indians were, in Jefferson's view, "formed in mind as well as in body, on the same module" as whites, they were still "savages" who needed to move from the hunter to the agricultural stage in order to survive historically.

It is only through incorporation by and assimilation to white culture that "savages" could be "civilized" and thus saved from the prospect of extinction. Or, as Jefferson wrote the Creek agent Colonel Benjamin Hawkins in 1803: "In truth, the ultimate point of rest and happiness for them [the Indians] is to let our settlements and theirs meet and blend together, to intermix, and become one people. Incorporating themselves with us as citizens of the United States, this is what the natural progress of things will, of course, bring on, and it will be better to promote than to retard it."[15] Here the image of bodily incorporation—of whites literally absorbing Indians into their blood—encodes white mastery and the peaceful appropriation of Indian lands through sexual intercourse.[16] In Jefferson's Indian policy, history—"the natural progress of things"—moves in only one direction. Whites do not become Indians: Indian men must incorporate themselves as farmers and "citizens of the United States"; and Indian women, like white women, must be taken out of the field of agricultural labor and production and relocated in the home—"stationary and unexposed"—in order to protect their reproductive capacity and thus the propagation of the American race. Unlike Crèvecoeur's farmer James, who trembles at the prospect of producing a "mongrel breed" through the mixture of European and Indian blood in the borderlands of America, Jefferson embraces the intermixture of red and white as the best and most peaceable means of acquiring Indian lands.[17]

Mapping the Social Body

In *Notes on the State of Virginia,* mapping the boundaries of the land is inseparable from the process of mapping the boundaries of the body, race, nation, and blood. Jefferson included in early editions of *Notes* a map of Virginia and other surrounding states and territories, based in part on a map drawn by his father, Peter Jefferson, in collaboration with Joshua Fry. This map, which Jefferson liked to say was more valuable than his book, is not only a means of staking Virginia's claims to disputed western lands; it is also a cognitive sign of print culture and a new way of organizing space, subjectivity, knowledge, and the body through the demarcation of lines, limits, and boundaries.

Jefferson's analytic focus on a sexualized body, a racialized sexuality, and questions of sexual, racial, and national difference as central to the operations of the social body is part of a more general structure of knowledge in *Notes* that seeks to regulate and control the potentially turbulent and unruly impulses of nature and the body, culture and the body politic, by fixing, rationalizing, and systematizing them in accord with republican principle and scientific law. Beginning with a precise geographical mapping of "the limits and boundaries of the state of Virginia" in Query I, titled "Boundaries of Virginia," *Notes on the State of Virginia* moves through an ever-expanding analytics of investigation, differentiation, and delimitation toward a mapping of the "limits and boundaries" of the entire social order (3). Geography, the body, laws, and politics intersect with and reinforce each other in an intricate web of limits and controls, suggesting the ways that, in the words of Peter Stallybrass and Allon White, "the body cannot be thought separately from the social formation, symbolic topography and the constitution of the subject."[18]

Fearing what he calls the "unbounded licentiousness" of foreigners who will "warp and bias" the republican direction of America and "render it a heterogeneous, incoherent, distracted mass" (*NV*, 85), Jefferson proposes that "the importation of foreigners" be banned in order to preserve the republican harmony, "common consent," and homogeneity of Virginia (*NV*, 84). He seeks to write over the ongoing historical struggle over the "undefined boundaries" of Indian languages, tribes, and nations by treating them as a bygone site of linguistic, anthropological, archaeological, and statistical analysis. In an effort to make the legislative, executive, and judiciary functions of government "separate and distinct" and to protect republican Virginia from both corrupt human nature and the tyranny of corrupt rulers, Jefferson calls for "a convention *to fix the constitution*, to amend its defects, and *to bind up* the several branches of government by certain laws" (*NV*, 120, 129; emphasis added). He proposes a massive revision of the Virginia code of laws in order to "strip" the law of its monarchical "vestiges" and bring it into accord with "republican principles" (*NV*, 137–49).

To regulate the volatile and unruly body of the masses, he further proposes "to diffuse knowledge more generally through the mass of the people" with a system of mass education that would operate via rigorous networks of selection, hierarchy, and exclusion to, in Jefferson's words, rake "the best geniuses . . . from the rubbish annually" (*NV*, 146). It is within this same Enlightenment taxonomy of knowledge that Jefferson articulates a system of human and cultural value in which black is to white as "Oran-ootan" is to "black women," and "the compositions" of "a Phyllis Whately" [*sic*] are, as he says in one of the earliest acts of republican and nationalist canon formation, "below the dignity of criticism" (*NV,* 138, 140). It is in accord with this same scientific and republican logic of separation, exclusion, and difference that Jefferson concludes that blacks must be sent out of the country, foreigners must be kept out of the country, and Indians must "intermix" or die.

Intermixture and the National Fantasy

Jefferson's prohibitions against black and white mixture proved impossible. The "country swarms with mulatto bastards," wrote Peter Fountaine of Virginia in 1757, in a comment that suggests that despite legal prohibitions and social taboos against racial mixture, the mixture of blacks with whites was widespread during the colonial period.[19] Contrary to traditional notions that the French and Spanish amalgamated, and the Anglos segregated, recent historians have suggested that before the nineteenth century, white men and women of all classes were mixing with blacks, sexually as well as culturally, all over the state of Virginia.[20] As Joel Williamson observes, with its large and almost equal population of blacks and whites, the upper South, especially Virginia, "supported conditions nearly ideal for the proliferation of a large mulatto population."[21]

Jefferson's Monticello, where blacks outnumbered whites by about ten to one, was itself a mixed household that troubled the distinctions between whiteness and blackness, master and slave. When the French writer Volney visited Monticello in 1796, he wrote that he was "astonished" (*étonné*) to see slave children "as white as I am called blacks and treated as such."[22] Jefferson was, in effect, surrounded by instances of racial mixture and white (or near-white) slavery. His father-in-law, John Wayles, fathered six children with his mulatto slave Elizabeth ("Betty") Hemings. Jefferson's wife, Martha Wayles, brought all six Hemings children to Monticello as part of her inheritance. After his wife's death, Jefferson formed what appears to have been a long and monogamous relationship with Betty's youngest daughter, Sally Hemings, with whom he fathered at least one and possibly six or seven children.[23]

According to James Callender, who first published an account of the relationship in the *Richmond Recorder* in 1802, Hemings's eldest son, who was named Tom, bore such a "striking though sable resemblance" to the President that Callender called him "President Tom," "our little mulatto president."[24] Jefferson's nineteenth-century biographer, Henry S. Randall, reported that one of Jefferson's grandsons, Thomas Jefferson Randolph, told him that Hemings "had children which resembled Mr.

Jefferson so closely that it was plain that they had his blood in their veins"; "the likeness between master and slave was blazoned to all the multitudes who visited this political Mecca."[25]

Whether or not the story of the six or seven mixed-blood children and the thirty-eight-year relationship Jefferson had with his slave—and half sister-in-law—Sally Hemings is true, this story of racial mixture, "incest," and transgression has continued as a kind of shadow figure, or racial double, of the American republic and the Jeffersonian legacy, suggesting the complicated interdependencies of black and white in America, as well as a complex racial psychology in which what is excluded, disavowed, and taboo on the overt social level—the black body in the white American republic—erupts in the national imaginary as a forbidden source of desire, a recurrent fantasy, and an obsessive set of representations. Despite attempts by historians to deny the Hemings relation as inconsistent with Jefferson's "character,"[26] the story continues to produce and reproduce itself in oral and written, fictive and autobiographical, journalistic and filmic form—from Callender's report of Jefferson's relationship with his slave "concubine" Sally and their many mulatto children in the Federalist press in 1802, to William Wells Brown's novel *Clotel; or, The President's Daughter: A Narrative of Slave Life in the United States* (1853), to Madison Hemings's autobiographical account in the *Pike County (Ohio) Republican* (1873), to Barbara Chase-Riboud's best-selling novel, *Sally Hemings* (1979), to the film *Jefferson in Paris* (1995), to the recent proliferation of headlines, special reports, and docudramas in the national and international media following the 1998 revelation that Jefferson fathered at least one of Hemings's children, Eston Hemings.[27]

Just as Jefferson could not—and did not—prevent the mixture of white and black "bloods" within his own family of slaves and just as historians have been unable to prevent the endless proliferation of stories of the "mixed-blood" relationship between Sally and Tom, so in *Notes on the State of Virginia* the discourse of racial difference produces fantasies of penetration, mixture, violence, and reversal, black and red mix with and underwrite the constitution of whiteness, and the distinct boundary between US and them, America and its "others," becomes unclear. For all Jefferson's seemingly rational and scientific effort to map and define sexual, racial, cultural, and national bounds between red, white, and black, savage and civilized, foreign and native, monarchical and republican, Europe and America, *Notes on the State on Virginia* reveals the impossibility of avoiding contact, mixture, and exchange across boundaries that are never finally fixed or settled.

Implicitly questioning later genealogies of American history that begin with the English and the Puritans in New England, Jefferson's history of America begins with the first European—and Catholic—settlement of the Spanish in San Domingo in 1493 and proceeds through the failed attempts of Walter Raleigh to establish a settlement in North America, which, he notes, may have been "incorporated with the savages" (*NV,* 111), to the founding of Jamestown in 1607. During this early period of settlement, the land grants issued by Queen Elizabeth suggest that the primary distinctions between the English and the Natives were cultural rather than racial: not between white and nonwhite as in the late eighteenth and nineteenth centuries, but between Christian and heathen.[28]

The documents, memorials, land grants, treaties, and state papers that make up Jefferson's "history" of Virginia are a record of continual contact between Europeans and Natives and continual struggle and negotiation over boundaries that are always open to question. Query XIII on the Constitution of Virginia and its ancient charters is also a history of disputes over territorial boundaries within the British Empire, with Natives, and among the states themselves. Jefferson's inability to map and define the boundaries of Indian tribes is suggested textually and materially by the fact that the first edition of *Notes* contains a foldout chart—a list of Indian tribes native to Virginia—which literally exceeds the boundaries of the book form and the republican narrative that seeks to contain them. There is an underlying tension in Jefferson's narrative not only between state bounds and what he calls the "undefined bounds" of Indian tribes and nations but also among river, mountain, and place names that often bear the multiple names of Indian, English, and local inhabitants: geography as cultural palimpsest. Registering this ambiguity of names and boundaries, Jefferson refers to "the *Tanissee,* Cherokee, or Hogohege river" and the "*Cumberland,* or Shawanee river" (*NV,* 11). "At Fort Pitt," he writes, "the river Ohio loses its name, branching into the Monongahela and Alleghaney" (*NV,* 14).[29]

Although we tend to read back into Revolutionary history the eventual triumph of the colonists over Great Britain, Jefferson's references to "the present contest" throughout *Notes* draw attention to the fact that at the time he was composing his *Notes* in the early 1780s, the war had not been settled, the future of the American republic remained uncertain, and Virginia still maintained claims to extensive tracts of western lands that encompassed large parts of the continent.[30] Like the fluid and contested territorial boundaries of Virginia itself, Jefferson's *Notes* moves almost imperceptibly from a more local focus on the state of Virginia to a more nationalist focus on the state of America, with Virginia enacting the republican and continental destiny of the nation.

A similar fluidity of perspective and bounds is evident in Jefferson's discussion of racial difference. Although Jefferson's attempt to distinguish between the white and the black races comes to us as hard fact, his actual discussion of race is more tentative, advancing it "as a suspicion only" that blacks are inferior to whites in mind and body. Jefferson himself calls attention to the apparent feebleness of a scientific method applied to faculties such as the imagination and reason, which "bid defiance to calculation" and cannot in any literal sense be observed, tested, measured, or known. Thus, he writes, "the opinion, that [blacks] are inferior in the faculties of reason and imagination, must be hazarded with great diffidence," especially "where our conclusion would degrade a whole race of men from the rank in the scale of beings which their Creator may perhaps have given them" (NV, 143).

For all of Jefferson's attempts to represent blacks as different, other, and outside the American social body, blacks are, in effect, already "inside" the social body and thus inseparable from the republican and ultimately national story he seeks to tell. In arguing against the future "importation of foreigners" into the state of Virginia, Jefferson includes the black population in his statistical calculation of the increase of the native population—what he calls "our single stock"—that would take place through "natural propagation" without further emigration from abroad. In this formulation, blacks are inside rather than outside Jefferson's attempt to constitute the common ground of a republican and American nationality. This is further borne out by the fact that in Virginia, according to Jefferson's calculations, the number of slaves (270,726) almost equals the number of free inhabitants (296,852). The black population is in fact increasing faster than the white population; or, as Jefferson says, in a passage that appears to undermine the affirming republican rhetoric of his narrative, "Under the mild treatment our slaves experience, and their wholesome, though coarse, food, this blot in our country increases as fast, or faster, than the whites" (NV, 87).

What Jefferson calls the "blot" of slavery suggests at once a moral stain on the republican ideal of "temperate liberty," the possible obliteration of the American republic under the contradiction of slavery, and an American future in which blacks will erase, or at least "blot" out, whites.[31] Indeed, if "those who labor in the earth" really are "the chosen people of God," as Jefferson asserts in what has become the classic formulation of the "agrarian myth" and American republican ideology,[32] it might also be argued that insofar as blacks rather than whites are the primary laborers and cultivators in the fields of the South, it is the black laborers rather than their white slave masters who represent a "peculiar" site for what Jefferson calls "substantial and genuine" republican "virtue" (NV, 165). In accord with the republican and agrarian logic of Jefferson's argument, slaves rather than masters represent the true citizens and the future of the American republic.

"How is it that we hear the loudest *yelps* for liberty among the drivers of negroes?" Samuel Johnson once asked, in a comment that suggests the ways white freedom comes to depend on black enslavement in the constitution of American national identity.[33] As Edmund S. Morgan has argued, an economy of slavery made the assertion of republican freedom easier and less risky than an economy of free laborers that might produce an angry working class: "Slaves did not become leveling mobs," Morgan observes.[34] But the relation between slavery and freedom was more than economic: the colonists also identified with the slave as part of the American cause. "[T]he Crisis is arrivd," wrote George Washington to Bryan Fairfax in 1774, "when we must assert our Rights, or Submit to every Imposition that can be heap'd upon us; till custom and use, will make us *as tame, & abject Slaves, as the Blacks we rule over with such arbitrary Sway.*"[35] As in the original version of the Declaration of Independence, in which slavery is represented as part of the "assemblage of horrors" imposed on the American people by the enslaver king, the "abject" presence of slavery—its horror and its excess—underwrites the logic of both republicanism and revolution during the period of the founding. Like the Africans who—in the words of the original Declaration—were captured and carried "into slavery in another hemisphere," the colonists, too, were the "distant people" whose "most sacred rights of life and liberty" were being violated by the British king (*WTJ*, 1:34).[36]

In *Notes on the State of Virginia*, it is America's identification with the slave that propels what Jefferson calls "our present resistance" (*NV*, 125) and the ideology of republicanism he seeks to affirm. Over and over in the narrative, Jefferson returns to the figure of the slave in his attempt to define fundamental American rights and principles. The American colonists did not expend their "blood and substance for the wretched purpose of changing this master for that" (*NV*, 126), he declares as part of his argument for a revision in Virginia laws in accord with republican principle. While Virginians have been willing to sacrifice "their lives and their fortunes for the establishment of their civil freedom," they remain in "religious slavery," he asserts (*NV*, 159). Unless Virginia passes a law declaring "unbounded tolerance," he predicts a future of continued enslavement and possible apocalypse: "The shackles," he writes, "which shall not be knocked off at the conclusion of this war, will remain on us long, will be made heavier and heavier, till our rights shall revive or expire in a convulsion" (*NV*, 161).[37] Advocating a future of peace, free trade, and "cultivation of the earth," Jefferson once again invokes the figure of America as a slave knocking off shackles as an embodiment of its commitment to a republican economics of laissez-faire: "Our interest will be to throw open the doors of commerce, and to knock off all its shackles, giving perfect freedom to all persons for the vent of whatever they may chuse to bring into our ports, and asking the same in theirs" (*NV*, 174).

The interdependencies of slavery and freedom, master and slave—and their possible convertibility—reach a crescendo and a crisis in Query XVIII ("Manners"), as Jefferson's membership in and loyalty to a planter class committed to an economic system of slavery come into explosive conflict with the ideals of revolutionary freedom and equality that he set forth in the Declaration of Independence and that underwrite his republican narration. It is in "Manners" that the contradictions of both text and culture load up: between Jefferson's republican identification with the slave and his identity as a Southern slave master; between the ideal of "temperate liberty" and the everyday "intemperance" of slavery; and between an idyllic vision of an American republic of virtuous farmers and a recognition that "of the proprietors of slaves a very small proportion indeed are ever seen to labour" (*NV*, 163).

Responding to a query about "the particular customs and manners that may happen to be received in that state" (*NV*, 162), "Manners" is wholly taken up with the disastrous effects of the slave-master relationship on the entire population. "There must doubtless be an unhappy influence on the manners of our people produced by the existence of slavery among us," Jefferson observes. Once again, "our people" includes both masters and slaves, who are engaged in an unrepublican "exercise of the most boisterous passions, the most unremitting despotism on the one part, and degrading submissions on the other" (*NV*, 162). Particularly troubled by the ill effects of slavery on children, "who are nursed, educated and daily exercised in tyranny" and the "worst of passions," Jefferson is led, in a moment of self-revelation and self-loathing, to reflect on his own inability to act historically against slavery: "And with what execration should the statesman be loaded, who permitting one half the citizens thus to trample on the rights of the other, transforms those into despots, and these into enemies, destroys the morals of the one part, and the amor patriae of the other" (*NV*, 162–63).[38] No longer the grotesque Others—or "moveables"—of the American republic, whose "difference is fixed in nature" (*NV*, 137, 138), blacks are here represented not only as citizens with certain rights but also as citizens in whom Jefferson wants to inspire a love of country.

In Jefferson's anxious evocation of the rituals of identification, imitation, and exchange that inform "the whole commerce between master and slave" (*NV*, 162), the master needs the slave to define both his mastery and his freedom. As Hegel suggests, master and slave are engaged in a dialectics of struggle, exchange, and possible reversal: in the slave the master sees the limits and instability of his freedom, the specter of his own possible future and desire as slave.[39] Reflecting on the ways the daily practice of slavery in America violates the republican principle of liberty as a God-given right and thus erodes the moral base of the American republic, Jefferson predicts a revolution of blacks against their slave masters: "Indeed I tremble for my country when I reflect that God is just: that his justice cannot sleep for ever: that considering numbers, nature and natural means only, a revolution of the wheel of fortune, an exchange of situation, is among possible events: that it may become probable by supernatural interference! The Almighty has no attribute which can take side with us in such a contest!" (*NV*, 163). In this self-flagellating passage Jefferson identifies with the slave—and with the republican logic of revolution—against the economic interests of his own class.[40] His prediction of "supernatural interference" represents a supreme moment of cultural recognition—a moment that registers the force of racial and ideological contradiction as formal rupture and narrative break.

Under the pressure of the contradiction between the republican ideal of revolutionary freedom and equality and an actual dependence on black slave labor, the hitherto rational narrative breaks into a prediction of supernatural intervention, catapulting the narrative out of the realm of reason, science, and natural law into a magical realm of unpredictability, unreason, and the unknown.[41] In this realm, nothing is fixed or stable, especially the relation of white to black, master to slave: "[A]n exchange of situation, is among possible events." To avert the bloody specter of slave insurrection and a reversal of the master-slave relation, Jefferson concludes with an anxiously voiced prospect of gradual emancipation. "I think a change already perceptible, since the origin of the present revolution," he asserts: "The spirit of the master is abating, that of the slave rising from the dust, his condition mollifying, the way I hope preparing, under the auspices of heaven, for a total emancipation, and that this is disposed, in the order of events, to be with the consent of the masters, rather than by their extirpation" (*NV*, 163).[42]

Propelled by racial and ideological contradiction, *Notes on the State of Virginia* hesitates between alternative stories and contradictory modes: a republican logic of rights, consent, and voluntary emancipation or a gothic apprehension of supernatural intervention, black insurrection, and the extirpation of the masters. Neither story includes slavery. Like Jefferson's myth of the ideal American republic—"Those who labour in the earth are the chosen people of God"—both stories suggest that the American future may indeed belong to black labor.

Crossing the Border

"Next to the case of the black race within our bosom, that of the red on our borders is the problem most baffling to the policy of our country,"

James Madison wrote in 1826.[43] Although Madison made this comment at a time when the Jeffersonian policy of Indian incorporation had failed and a national policy of removing Indians west of the Mississippi was being put into place, it reveals the ongoing presence of race—"within our bosom," "on our borders"—as a crisis and struggle over the body, boundaries, and blood of the United States.[44] As Jefferson's *Notes* suggests, whereas the presence of the black race within the body of the American republic erupted into conflicts over the "problem" and contradiction of black slave labor, the presence of the red race on the borders of the republic manifested itself in contests over the land. Just as Jefferson's "suspicion" of the natural distinction between the black and white races might be used to justify black enslavement and eventual removal—"beyond the reach of mixture"—so the distinction Jefferson poses between savagism and civilization might be used to justify the incorporation of Natives and their territories into the American body and, if that failed, removal and possible extinction.

Among critics, *Notes on the State of Virginia* is commonly regarded as one of the ur-texts in outlining what Roy Harvey Pearce calls "an American theory of savagism," a theory that led to the "Removal" and "virtual death" of the Indian by the 1830s. In the work of Jefferson and other American writers, Pearce argues, the savage is defined in opposition to civilization: "he showed civilized men [what] they were not and must not be."[45] While Jefferson emphasizes "the savage's essential humanity," writes Pearce, he also demonstrates the ways "circumstance" accounts for "the savage's essential inferiority, the final inferiority of even his savage virtues" (95). More recent critics, including Ronald Takaki and Richard Drinnon, have added a Lawrentian twist to Pearce's savagism in presenting Jefferson as the archetypal white Enlightenment man who seeks to kill off the body, nature, the instincts, and the Indians through a republican regime of order, reason, and control.[46]

Nowhere is this version of Jefferson more evident than in his study of Native barrows or "repositories of the dead," in which we see him in the role of a protomodern archaeologist digging among the dead, carefully measuring and counting bones, as he violates the sacred burial ground of the Natives.[47] His catalogs of Native bones and body parts are macabre and unrelenting: "The bones of which the greatest numbers remained, were sculls, jaw-bones, teeth, the bones of the arms, thighs, legs, feet, and hands. A few ribs remained, some vertebrae of the neck and spine, without their processes, and one instance only of the bone which serves as a base to the vertebral column. The skulls were so tender, that they generally fell to pieces on being touched" (*NV*, 98–99). Whatever the occasion for these barrows, Jefferson notes, "they are of considerable notoriety among the Indians": he remembers that some thirty years before a party of Indians went directly to the barrow in his neighborhood and "staid about it some time with expressions which were construed to be those of sorrow" (*NV,* 100). The entire sequence presents a ghoulish image of the ways an Enlightenment canon of numbers—of what Max Horkheimer and Theodor Adorno have called an "identification of the wholly conceived and mathematized world with truth"—appears to suppress or write over the sacred, the mythic, and the animistic in older systems of belief.[48] Jefferson's concluding observation that "within these dozen years" the barrows in his neighborhood have been "cleared of trees and put under cultivation . . . by the plough, and will probably disappear in time" presents a disturbing image of America—and its idyllic dream of a republic of small farms—as a grave site quite literally "cultivated" out of the bones of dead Indians.[49]

And yet, for all Jefferson's effort to present Natives as a doomed site of archaeological, philological, and anthropological analysis, even his own statistics reveal that at the time he was writing, there were thousands of Natives still present on the continent, and their doom, or death, or ultimate incorporation into whiteness was not at all settled or inevitable. Despite the tendency of past and recent critics to emphasize the savage-civilized binary as the fundamental form of American history, and the "inexorable" triumph of whiteness as the end of Native history in the New World, I want to argue that this is not the story that Jefferson's *Notes on the State of Virginia* tells; or, at least, it is not the only story it tells.

There is in *Notes* a dialectical tension between the abstract, classifying, and boundary-building imperatives of Enlightenment reason and science and a more provisional—and radical—recognition of flux, instability, and alterability in climate, skin color, human society, constitutions, and what Jefferson calls "the rise and fall of towns" (*NV,* 109).[50] These moments of instability and alterability in the narrative are often prompted by the experience of contradiction—especially racial contradiction—in the body of the American republic. As in "Manners," in which the repressed other of the Revolutionary Enlightenment appears to break through the narrative in the form of magic, myth, spirit, and God, so Jefferson's attempt to speak for and as a *native* American in *Notes* triggers similar moments when his Enlightenment narrative swerves from its course, revealing both the limits of reason and the possibility of other stories and alternative points of view.

Like the fluctuation in the narrative among the state of Virginia, the territorial boundaries of the United States, and the "undefined boundaries" of "the nations and numbers of Aborigines which still exist in a respectable and independant form" (*NV,* 102), there is an alternation and a slippage in *Notes* not only among the terms *Aborigine, Indian, barbarian,* and *savage* but also within the term *native* itself, which is sometimes used to refer to Indians as the original inhabitants of the continent and sometimes used to refer to the local inhabitants of the state of Virginia. This slippage and alternation suggests that in *Notes*, as in the culture at large, the boundaries between red and white, Indian and Anglo, Native and American are not at all settled or secure. Indeed, rather than presenting *savage* and *civilized* as hard-bound oppositions as Pearce and other critics have argued, *Notes* suggests the ways Native and European have bled into each other—literally on the borders and figuratively within the body of America—in the constitution of American New World identity.

Jefferson's fullest comments on Native Americans appear in two sections: "Productions Mineral, Vegetable and Animal" (Query VI) and "Aborigines" (Query XI). Although his identification of Natives with the land and the movement of his narrative from a description of the physical landscape and its resources in Queries I-VII, to an account of the original inhabitants in Queries VI and XI, to a discussion of the constitution, laws, society, and histories of the state in Queries XIII–XXIII appears to encode a progression from savage to civilized, red to white, nature to law, there is a residual or counternarrative in *Notes* in which the New World narrator is, in effect, instructed and "enlightened" by his contact, both direct and indirect, with Native American story, ritual, and cultural practice. Thus, for example, as part of his "mine's bigger than yours" defense of New World potency, Jefferson expends considerable effort presenting evidence for the existence in North America of "the Mammoth, or big buffalo, as called by the Indians," which is "the largest of all terrestrial beings" (*NV*, 43, 47).

As his key piece of evidence in countering Buffon's charge that animals in the New World are smaller, Jefferson presents a direct transcription of a sacred story of the Delawares—"a tradition handed down from their fathers"—which, when he was governor of Virginia, was delivered to him orally by the "chief speaker" of the tribe, "with a pomp suited to what he conceived the elevation of his subject." The story tells of how "in the antient times" these "tremendous animals" provoked the wrath of "the Great Man above" when they began to destroy the bear, deer, buffalo, and other animals "created for the use of the Indians." He "seized his lightning" and "hurled his bolts among them till the whole were slaughtered, except the big bull, who presenting his forehead to the shafts, shook them off as they fell; but missing one at length, it wounded him in the side; whereon, springing round, he bounded over the Ohio, over the Wabash, the Illinois, and finally over the great lakes, where he is living at this day" (*NV*, 43). Jefferson's use of this story, which is one of the first tales of the Natives of the Ohio Valley to be recorded or preserved in printed form,[51] once again reveals the cross-cultural mix of voices, forms, and modes in *Notes* as Jefferson's appeal to the sacred stories, myths, and traditions of the Indians intersects with his more scientific and Western approach to the geography and history of America. Coming as it does in the very section in which Jefferson seems most intent on displaying his own scientific skills to the European intellectual community through a reasoned appeal to facts, experience, numbers, and tables, the story suggests the ways his experience of contact and exchange with Native American tribes complicates rather than affirms any simple Enlightenment opposition between savage and civilized, oral and written, sacred and scientific, "traditionary testimony" and truth.[52]

Just as the colonists, in one of the inaugural acts of the American Revolution, dressed up as Indians and dumped tea into Boston Harbor to protest British imperialism in the New World, so Jefferson frequently identifies with Native American customs and rituals in his critique of the government and institutions of the Old World. At a time when the Americans were attempting to address the fundamental paradox of the American republic—how to reconcile the desire for liberty with the need for social order—Jefferson appears to have found an appealing model of social organization among the tribes of the Powhatan confederacy, which, in his view, had "never submitted themselves to any laws, any coercive power, any shadow of government." "Their only controuls are their manners," Jefferson observes, "and that moral sense of right and wrong, which, like the sense of tasting and feeling, in every man makes a part of his nature" (*NV*, 93). Noting the role of social pressure rather than law in making "crimes very rare among them," he chooses the "savage Americans" rather than the "civilized Europeans" as a model of New World social order: "[W]ere it made a question, whether no law, as among the savage Americans, or too much law, as among the civilized Europeans, submits man to the greatest evil, *one who has seen both conditions of existence* would pronounce it to be the last" (*NV*, 93; emphasis added). Here, as elsewhere in *Notes,* it is not *against* but *in* and *through* the "savage" that Jefferson identifies what is "estimable" about America and the American.[53]

While Jefferson's embrace of "savage" over "civilized" social forms is conditional and hypothetical ("were it made a question"), his appendix on Indians by Charles Thomson,[54] the secretary of the Continental Congress who was himself an adopted member of the Delaware tribe, suggests that as "a kind of patriarchal confederacy" (*NV*, appendix 1, 202), Indian local, tribal, and national organization served as a model not only for the formation of state governments and the confederacy but, at a time when America was still in the process of constituting itself as a federal union, also for what would become the Constitution of the United States.[55] This exchange across borders is suggested textually by the fact that Jefferson's own "Draught of a Fundamental Constitution for the Commonwealth of Virginia" (1783) directly follows Thomson's comments on Native tribal organization in the appendices to early editions of *Notes*.

Thomson's comments further reveal the ways Native customs and social forms, which still subsist "among the Indian nations bordering upon the United States" (*NV*, 203), offered alternative and resistant modes of social organization. The communal organization and kinship practices of the Indian tribes he describes implicitly challenge and pose an alternative to the rhetorics of innate rights, private property, and possessive individualism that Sacvan Bercovitch has called "the American consensus."[56] Thomson's defense of the "seeming frigidity" of the Indian warrior against the "those excesses" and "that fondness which is customary in Europe" (*NV*, 200) evinces a nostalgia for a model of masculinity different from the civilized and increasingly domesticated man of the Old World. His description of Indian women, whose "province" is "labour or the culture of the soil" and whose sociosexual behavior "judged of by Europeans, would be deemed inconsistent with the rules of female decorum and propriety" (*NV*, 202, 201), presents both "modes of acting" and models of social organization that challenge the ideologies of sexual difference, the sexual division of labor, and the separation of male and female spheres that began to emerge during the Revolutionary period.

"They are all equal—the only precedence any gain is by superior virtue, oratory, or prowess," wrote James Adair in his *History of the American Indians* (1775), in a comment that suggests the impact of Native American social and cultural forms on debates about the precise form that American culture and society would take during the Revolutionary period.[57] This impact is evident throughout *Notes on the State of Virginia* in Jefferson's conceptions of time, history, human nature, religion, constitutions, government, the power of oratory, and the importance of "good sense" in creating forms of social cohesion and "fair play" outside the "coercive power" of the law and "the state" (93, 161).

In his defense of what he calls "unbounded tolerance" in religion, Jefferson appears to speak not only *for* the Indians but *as* an Indian. Arguing in support of the separation of church and state and the need for a provision in the Virginia Constitution guaranteeing the free exercise of religion in accord with the dictates of conscience, Jefferson writes: "The legitimate powers of government extend to such acts only as are injurious to others. But it does me no injury for my neighbour to say *there are twenty gods, or no god*" (*NV*, 159; emphasis added). Here again one is struck by the mixture of voices and tones—legalistic and pagan, rational and animistic—that reveals the impact the many gods of Jefferson's own neighbors, the Indians, had on his notions of religious freedom and tolerance. The statement, which provoked much heated controversy in Jefferson's lifetime and beyond, suggests the ways living among and within Native American belief structures would continue to shape not only *Notes on the State of Virginia* and its afterlife but also ongoing debates about the fundamental meanings and values of America.

These circuits of identification, exchange, and seepage across racial and cultural boundaries are particularly evident in Jefferson's presentation of a speech by the Mingo warrior Logan as an instance of Native American eloquence that counters Buffon's charge of New World degeneration. Reflecting Jefferson's own admiration for the Indian use of "personal influence and persuasion" to resolve controversy in a society "forbidding all compulsion," Logan's speech is, he asserts, "comparable to the whole orations of Demosthenes and Cicero, and any more eminent orator, if Europe has furnished more eminent" (*NV*, 62). His identification with the voice and eloquence of Logan is here so complete that Jefferson was later accused of having forged the speech himself: "But wherefore the forgery?" he responded with apparent nonchalance about authorial and racial bounds: "Whether Logan's or mine, it would still have been American" (*NV*, 230). While Jefferson continued to name Logan as the "author" of the speech—"But it is none of mine; and I yield it to whom it is due" (*NV*, 230)—his insistence on its *Americanism* suggests the origins of American national creation in forms of cultural exchange, collaboration, and mixture across the borders. This is different from the absorption, or incorporation, of Natives into whiteness: it is not ac-culturation but inter-culturation, a transformation of both cultures into something different by *contact*.[58]

Logan's speech, which he originally delivered in his native tongue to his brother-in-law, General John Gibson, at the end of Lord Dunmore's War in 1774, is itself a product of what Richard White has called the "middle ground," a "place in between: in between cultures, peoples, and in between empires and the nonstate world of villages."[59] Logan was himself a mixed figure, an Iroquois warrior who had left his tribe and lived on the borders between Native and European peoples in the Yellow Creek area of the Ohio River. The speech reflects this in-betweenness, as does Jefferson's transcription of the speech in *Notes,* which represents one of the earliest appearances of Native oratory in printed form and the textual space in which two cultures, Iroquois and Anglo, two forms, oral and written, and two voices, Logan and Jefferson, come into contact.[60]

Beginning with an invocation to white men—"I appeal to any white man to say, if ever he entered Logan's cabin hungry, and he gave him not meat"—the speech, as it is recorded in *Notes,* encapsulates the dynamics of Native-European relations in the New World: hospitality, exchange, betrayal, blood vengeance, defeat, peace, mourning. At first there is friendship and accomodation: "Such is my love for the whites . . . I had even thought to have lived with you." But this relation is destroyed by the rituals of blood violence on the frontier: "Col. Cresap, the last spring, in cold blood, and unprovoked, murdered all the relations of Logan not sparing even my women and children." Logan seeks revenge: "I have killed many: I have fully glutted my vengeance." The Indians are defeated and peace is restored, but Logan is left alone: "There runs not a drop of my blood in the veins of any living creature. . . . Who is there to mourn for Logan?—Not one" (*NV,* 63).

As his words are translated by Gibson and transcribed by Jefferson, Logan appears to speak the values of Iroquois culture in the language and rhythms of the King James Bible. His emphasis on the loss of blood relations and his concluding question—"Who is there to mourn for Logan?"—invokes the Iroquois ritual of condolence, the need for communal mourning, grief, and replenishment, at the same time that it adumbrates the melancholic figure of the dying Indian that would be popularized in the nineteenth century by Cooper's *Last of the Mohicans* (1826) at the very moment when the government was carrying out a policy of Indian removal. While Logan appears to give voice to the Iroquois values of kinship, tribal loyalty, and clan revenge, his speech also registers some of the mixed impulses of terror, desire, fascination, nostalgia, and guilt that surround the representation of Native Americans in *Notes* and in the culture at large. On the one hand, they are "savages" whose possession of the land stands in the way of the progress of civilization westward and the continental designs of the American nation; on the other hand, they are superior beings whose social organization, culture, and native eloquence evoke identification, envy, and reverence.

These mixed impulses probably explain the popularity of Logan's speech, which was widely circulated in the American and British presses during the Revolutionary period and used as a recitation piece for American schoolchildren in the eighteenth and nineteenth centuries.[61] But while Logan's speech appears to enforce the myth of the dying Indian and the future direction of American Indian policy, as Jefferson frames the speech in early editions of *Notes,* it is not about Indians offering to die off so whites can possess the country but about evoking *sympathy* for Indians who resist their white killers. This is what Jefferson would later call "the moral view of the subject" (*NV,* 228).

In the 1787 Stockdale edition of *Notes,* as in earlier editions, Jefferson presents Logan not as the historically troubled figure he may have been—a warrior whose retaliatory actions were carried out against the wishes of the Shawnee and Mingo chiefs—but as a celebrated chief and "friend of whites" whose family was brutally murdered by a hostile party of white men.[62] Following the robbery and murder of "an inhabitant of the frontiers of Virginia, by two Indians of the Shawnee tribe," Jefferson writes: "Col. Cresap, *a man infamous for the many murders he had committed on those much-injured people,* collected a party, and proceeded down the Kanhaway *in quest of vengeance.* Unfortunately, a canoe of *women and children, with only one man,* was seen coming from the opposite shore, *unarmed and unsuspecting an hostile attack from the whites.* Cresap and his party concealed themselves on the bank of the river . . . and, at one fire, *killed every person in it.* This happened to be *the family of Logan,* who had long distinguished himself as *a friend of the whites."* (*NV,* 275; emphasis added). Like Logan's speech, Jefferson's account of "the incidents necessary for understanding it" (*NV,* 62) reverses the savage-civilized binary. It is not about red savages but about *white savages*: white savages who kill Indian friends of the whites in acts of blood vengeance, white savages who kill "unsuspecting" Indian women and children "in cold blood, and unprovoked" (*NV,* 63). It is this murderous image of white savagery that, like the moral contradiction of slavery in the American republic, threatens to erode Jefferson's republican narration.

When in 1797 Luther Martin, a Maryland Federalist and son-in-law of Michael Cresap, accused Jefferson of forging both Logan's speech and the story of the murder of his family that frames it in order to slander the good name of Cresap, Jefferson responded with *Appendix to the Notes on Virginia Relative to the Murder of Logan's Family,* published separately in Philadelphia in 1800, in which he reaffirmed the authenticity of Logan's speech, revised his account of Cresap's murders for "any future edition of *Notes"* (*NV,* 275), and added some thirty pages of new material to his original narrative.

Along with later contests about the "authenticity" of Logan's speech and the "truth" of Jefferson's narration, these revisions reveal red-white relations in the New World as an enduring site of historical struggle rather than a grave site for archaeological analysis.[63] In fact, in a further formal instance of what might be called the return of the Native American repressed, the appendix on the murder of Logan's family threatens to engulf the original narrative of *Notes* in the ongoing border struggles between whites and Natives on the Virginia and Pennsylvania frontiers.[64] Growing as a kind of textual appendage to the 1787 edition of *Notes,* the "fragments of evidence" that Jefferson presents to the public in the form of letters, extracts, certificates, testimonials, declarations, and as-told-to accounts, complete with "a small sketch or map of the principal scenes of these butcheries" (*NV,* 231), suggests the experimental forms, textual indeterminacies, multiplicity of voices, and conflicting stories to which the attempt to tell the historical "truth" about Native-white relations in the New World would give rise.[65]

In the advertisement to *Notes on the State of Virginia,* Jefferson refers to "the circumstances" of their composition as "open wounds that have already bled enough" (*NV,* 2). For all of Jefferson's efforts to suture and heal the wounds both personal and political that accompanied the composition of his *Notes,* race remained—and would remain—one of the open wounds that continued to bleed into his attempt to construct a consoling narrative of national and rational restoration. The "murder" of Indians and the "enslavement" of blacks convulse Jefferson's narrative with a darker vision of human corruption, sexual excess, dictatorial ambition, blood violence, and the inevitable decline of the American republic. Beneath the "enlightened" vision of America as a republic of virtue, balance, and "temperate liberty" is a gothic vision of America as an economy of masters and slaves grounded in scenes of excess and "a perpetual exercise of the most boisterous passions" (*NV,* 162). Beneath the idyllic vision of an American republic of virtuous farmers is a corrosive vision of America as a savage nation carved out of the butchered bodies of dead Indians.

Like the gothic figure of Edgar Huntly, who bleeds into and with the bloody corpse of the Indian he has killed in Charles Brockden Brown's *Edgar Huntly; Or, Memoirs of a Sleep-Walker* (1799), the specter of whites *going* savage, the specter of whites *being* savage, haunts the political imaginary of the new nation and the republican story Jefferson seeks to tell.[66] It is this disturbing figure of white savagery that closes the 1800 *Appendix Relative to the Murder of Logan's Family* and thus all future authorized editions of *Notes on the State of Virginia.* In this concluding scene, Cresap receives a scalp, "a very fine large one," as a form of intimate exchange among white "gentlemen." "This scalp, I think he told me, was the scalp of Logan's brother," writes the recorder; "though as to this *I am not absolutely certain*" (*NV,* 258; emphasis added). Rather than achieving textual resolution or closure, these last words of Jefferson's narrative underline the rituals of exchange, blood violence, and reversal and the "uncertainty" that would continue to mark both the history of Native American and Euro-American cultures and the boundary between them in the frontier "settlements" of the New World.

Notes Unbound

In his 1954 introduction to the standard modern edition of *Notes on the State of Virginia,* William Peden describes the book as "an American classic," "one of America's first permanent literary and intellectual landmarks" (*NV,* v, xxv). As "an American classic," *Notes on the State of Virginia* entered the American canon as a bounded text, with a single white male author, vision, voice, genre, and nationality. But it was not until the post-

World War I period—and the emergence of the American studies movement—that *Notes* was read as what Gilbert Chinard in 1929 called "one of the first masterpieces of American literature."[67] Before that time *Notes* was, as Peden observes, "favorably regarded as a popular handbook of natural science and geography" (*NV*, xxv). Like the title and the state of Virginia itself, which fluctuated between the mapped but still contested boundaries of the state of Virginia and the as yet undecided boundaries of the continental United States, the textual boundaries of *Notes on the State of Virginia* are themselves fluid, in process, and never finally settled.

Called forth by the queries of a Frenchman, François Marbois, in 1780 and written in the early 1780s to garner French support for the American cause at a time when Tidewater Virginia had been invaded by the British and the outcome of the Revolution was uncertain, *Notes on the State of Virginia* is more a negotiation among Native American, Anglo-American, Spanish, French, and British contestations over the terrain of America than it is a distinctively American text. Although Jefferson sent his response to Marbois's twenty-two queries on 20 December 1781, he continued to add new material to the manuscript and later published editions of *Notes*. The first edition of two-hundred copies was printed for private circulation only in France in 1785, with no author's name. Jefferson collaborated on a French translation, by Abbé André Morellet, which was published in France in 1787 with no translator's name and Jefferson's initials. The first edition bearing Jefferson's full name was published in England by John Stockdale in 1787. While this is commonly regarded as Jefferson's "definitive text," he emphasized its "imperfections" in an advertisement (*NV*, 2), and, for the remainder of his life, he continued to make insertions in the margins and the body of the text, and he continued to revise his "notes" based on materials sent to him by friends or informants. He added several appendices to the first French and English editions, including the observations of his friend, Charles Thomson, regarding the "nations of Indians of North America" (*NV*, 202); and, as we have seen, in 1800 after a controversy arose regarding his account of the murder of Logan's family and his report of Logan's speech to Lord Dunmore, he published an appendix "in the form of letters, certificates, and affidavits" (*NV*, 231) from several informants regarding "the Murder of Logan's Family" (*NV*, 226–58), which was to be incorporated into "any future edition of *Notes*" (*NV*, 275).

When in the early nineteenth century the publisher John Melish expressed interest in bringing out a new edition of *Notes on the State of Virginia*, Jefferson responded in 1814: "I consider . . . the idea of preparing a new copy of that work as no more to be entertained. The work itself indeed is nothing more than the measure of a shadow, never stationary, but lengthening as the sun advances, and to be taken anew from hour to hour. It must remain, therefore, for some other hand to sketch its appearance at another epoch, to furnish another element for calculating the course and motion of this member of our federal system" (10 December 1814, *WTJ*, 14:220–221). Jefferson's comment suggests both the fluid, processual, and unfinished state of his *Notes* and a more fluid and collaborative notion of authorship that still prevailed at the time he was writing. Rather than being the work of a single American author, *Notes on the State of Virginia* might be read as a richly collaborative work that draws on a multiplicity of sources, cultures, voices, and nationalities—Native American, Anglo-American, Hispanic American, Portuguese, Italian, Spanish, French, English, Roman, Greek—in constructing its "American" story. By insisting on its status as an "American classic" by a single canonical author and by translating into English the multiple quotations from Spanish, French, Portuguese, Italian, Latin, and Greek that appeared in the original editions of *Notes on the State of Virginia*, modern editors and interpreters, in an attempt to construct and bound *Notes* as a distinctively American book, have in some sense silenced and written over the richly comparative and multilingual dynamics of Jefferson's "never stationary," intercultural, and ultimately transnational narrative.[68]

The final section of the 1787 edition of *Notes on the State of Virginia*, titled "Histories, Memorials, State-Papers," suggests this fluid and unfinished state not only of Jefferson's *Notes* but also of the American Revolution, the American republic, and what Jefferson calls the "present contest" over the geopolitical bounds of the United States.[69] At this point in *Notes*, Jefferson's relatively formal narrative account breaks into a list, a "chronological catalogue of American state-papers," which focuses centrally on boundary disputes and settlements between Euro-Americans and Natives over the physical space of America. This "catalogue" and the entire *Notes* conclude with a "Deed from the six nations of Indians to the crown for certain lands and settling a boundary" dated 5 November 1768. Beginning with an attempt to map the still contested boundaries of the state of Virginia as a metonymic figure for the continental destiny of the American republic and ending with a "Deed" that figures the ongoing struggles between Euro-Americans and Natives over territorial boundaries in the New World, *Notes on the State of Virginia* has as its central, unsettled, and unsettling problematic the question of boundaries—sexual, racial, cultural, national, and otherwise. For all Jefferson's attempt to constitute and fix men, bodies, sexualities, races, laws, and nationalities, *Notes on the State of Virginia* is itself a *mixed blood*—a cross-fertilized text, whose "never stationary" boundaries continue to project the fluid, unsettled, and still contested meanings of the America and the American that Jefferson seeks to represent.

Chapter 3
Revolutionary Women

Where liberty dwells, there is my country.
—Anonymous

In a letter written to John Adams during the Revolutionary War, Abigail Adams described the appearance of a new phenomenon in America: the female mob. Angry at "an eminent, wealthy, stingy Merchant," who was hoarding coffee and refusing to sell at a reasonable price, "A Number of Females some say a hundred, some say more assembled with a cart and trucks, marchd down to the Ware House and demanded the keys, which he refused to deliver, upon which one of them seazd him by his Neck and tossd him into the cart. Upon his finding no Quarter he deliverd the keys, when they tipd up the cart and dischargd him, then opend the Warehouse, Hoisted out the Coffe themselves, put it into the trucks and drove off." The incident is remarkable both in its display of female physical force and violence and the seeming abandon with which the women break bounds and overturn traditional orders of masculine authority. Abigail Adams tells the story with obvious relish, noting in conclusion, "A large concourse of Men stood amazd silent Spectators of the whole transaction" (31 July 1777, *AFC*, 2:295).[1] As told by Adams to her husband, who was at that very moment at the Continental Congress constituting a new form of republican government that would exclude women, the female uprising has the quality of a cautionary tale: frustrated by conditions of injustice and deprivation, the female rioters take the law into their own hands as the men stand by in mute horror, gazing upon the scene of revolutionary destruction.

The rioting women of Boston were not unique. During the severe inflation of the war years, there were a number of instances in which "a corps of female infantry" attacked merchants as a form of what Joan Hoff Wilson has called "popular price control."[2] These female uprisings were legitimized by both the antipatriarchal rhetoric of the Revolutionary years and the many instances of mob action—most notably the Boston Tea Party—engaged in and abetted by the Sons of Liberty. The female mobs of Boston and elsewhere illustrate almost paradigmatically the radicalizing effect Revolutionary rhetoric and action had on traditional female behaviors. For the founding fathers, the American Revolution became a kind of Pandora's box, releasing transgressive and potentially violent female energies that would not and could not be controlled once the war was over. Despite the attempt to silence and disembody women politically by depriving them of citizenship and legal rights under the terms of the Articles of Confederation and the new Constitution approved by the states in 1788, a revolutionary female presence would continue to make itself felt in the political and cultural struggles and literary imaginary of the new republic.

In his important essay "The Transforming Radicalism of the American Revolution," Bernard Bailyn traces the changes in the concepts of representation and consent, constitutions and rights, as well as the challenge to the institution of slavery, the religious establishment, and traditional social orders brought by the American Revolution. While the American Revolution was not intended to be a social revolution, he argues, society was changed not as a result of the economic displacements brought by the war but because of "changes in the realm of belief and attitude." "For a decade or more," writes Bailyn, "defiance to the highest constituted powers poured from the colonial presses and was hurled from half the pulpits of the land. . . . Defiance to constituted authority leaped like a spark from one flammable area to another, growing in heat as it went."[3]

The invisibility of women in past historical accounts is suggested by the fact that in tracing "the Democracy Unleashed" by the American Revolution, Bailyn says nothing of its transforming effect on the lives of women. In this chapter, I shall argue that it is precisely in mounting a challenge to the "constituted powers" of man, father, husband, and king and to traditional conceptions of male and female nature that we find the American Revolution at its most radically transforming. I shall begin by tracing the effects that Revolutionary rhetoric and action had on American women, focusing in particular on the lives and writings of Abigail Adams and Phillis Wheatley. I will then look at the ways the political constitution and cultural creation of the postwar period sought to restore a loose, "manly," and potentially dangerous Daughter of Liberty to her traditional role as wife and mother under the law of the father. I shall conclude by suggesting the long-term "flammable" effects of the American Revolution in giving women the language, the knowledge, the power, and the moral and political ground to renew their assault on the constituted orders of masculine authority in the nineteenth century and beyond.

At the height of the agitation for independence from Britain, the Virginia clergyman Jonathan Boucher preached a sermon titled "On Civil Liberty, Passive Obedience, and Non-Resistance" (1775) in which he defended the divine right of kings and the notion of "authority, settled subordinations, subjection, and obedience." "The first father was the first king," he argued, enjoining a policy of obedience and nonresistance in the relationship between America and England: "from the obedience due to parents, wisely derives the congenial duty of *honoring the king and all that are put in authority under him.*" The concepts of *equality* and *consent* were, in Boucher's view, "particularly loose and dangerous" notions. Recognizing and indeed advocating the close relationship between the orders of father and king, family and state, Boucher feared the potentially far-reaching social consequences of Revolutionary rhetoric: "you are encouraged to resist not only all authority over us as it now exists, but any and all that it is possible to constitute."[4]

Those who advocated a break with England did so in the language of two primary social tropes: the family and slavery. The position of America was figuratively represented as the natural right of the son or daughter to revolt against a tyrannical parent and the natural right of the slave to revolt against a master. Through a masterful deployment of these parent-child and master-slave tropes in *Common Sense,* which was published in January 1776, Tom Paine galvanized popular support for the formal political break with England that would occur six months later. In his attempt to "divest" the king and monarchy of its traditional authority, Paine represented the king as a slave master seeking to deprive Americans of their natural liberties: "[W]hen republican virtues fail, slavery ensures. Why is the Constitution of England sickly, but because monarchy has poisoned the Republic; the crown has engrossed the Commons" (*CS,* 1:16). Pleading the cause of "final separation" from Britain in the language of "the violated unmeaning names of parent and child" (*CS,* 1:23), Paine says: "No man was a warmer wisher for a reconciliation than myself, before the fatal nineteenth of April 1775 [Battle of Lexington], but the moment the event of that day was made known, I rejected the hardened, sullen-tempered Pharoah of England for ever; and disdain the wretch that with the pretended title of FATHER OF HIS PEOPLE can unfeelingly hear of their slaughter, and composedly sleep with their blood upon his soul" (*CS,* 1:25).

In a political economy in which the rights of women were absorbed and legally "covered" by the constituted authority of white men and in which blacks were held as property under the institution of slavery, the widespread rhetorical representation of America as a Daughter of Lib-

Figure 4. "Brittannia Mutilated, or the Horrid (but true) Picture of Great Brittain, when Depriv'd of her Limbs by her enemies," 1774. This newspaper cartoon represents the violent effects of British colonial policies in the image of Britannia as stripped and mutilated female body. Courtesy the Library Company of Philadelphia.

erty or enchained slave oppressed by the tyranny of father/master had a particularly potent social appeal. This appeal was heightened by the violent and bloody visual iconography that accompanied the written representations of the American cause.

In the newspaper cartoon "Brittannia Mutilated" (1774), for example, Britain appears as a naked female figure, enchained, amputated, and deprived of her former power by the aggressive colonial policies of king and Parliament (Figure 4). In "The able Doctor, or America Swallowing the Bitter Draught" (1774), America is figured as a half-clad Indian woman who is violated by a number of male figures who force her to submit to the "bitter draught" of the Boston Port Bill and other British policies while Britannia turns away in distress (Figure 5). In the etching "Liberty Conquers Tyranny" (1775), Liberty leans on a pillar with her foot on the neck of a man whose crown and chain represent the oppressions of Britain as monarch and enslaver. The old order of the patriarch is represented as a barren landscape of war and violence in which a female appears to be at the mercy of an aggressive male figure. The New

Figure 5. "The able Doctor, or America Swallowing the Bitter Draught," 1774. America is depicted as a half-clad Indian woman being raped and violated by the "Bitter Draught" of the Tea Act and other British colonial policies as Britannia covers her eyes in distress. Courtesy the Library of Congress, Prints and Photographs Division, LC-USZ61–77.

World order of female liberty is represented as a pastoral landscape of abundance, fertility, and peace where male and female dance in apparent harmony (Figure 6). In "Columbia Trading with All the World," Columbia as a figure of the United States takes her sovereign place among the four sister continents: America, Africa, Asia, and Europe. Liberated from the oppressions of patriarch and slave master, she freely engages in commerce and exchange with the entire world (Figure 7).

While these images draw on a classical and allegorical tradition of representing abstractions and countries as feminine, by identifying the Revolutionary and republican cause with women, including Indian and enslaved women, these emotionally charged images could—and did—have the effect of soliciting women to imagine and act on a revolutionary vision of themselves as historical actors and makers on the stage of the world.

Abigail Adams and the Rights of Women

The radicalizing effect that Revolutionary rhetoric and iconography could have on women's self-conceptions and traditional relations thofe who are delegated to *devife* and appointed to *execute* public meafures, be directed to fuch, as thou in thy fovereign goodnefs fhalt be pleafed to render effectual for the falvation of a great empire, and reuniting all its members in one facred bond of harmony and public happinefs! Grant this, oh Father, for thy Son Jefus Chrift's fake; to whom, with thee and the holy Spirit, one God, be Glory, Honour and Power now and for ever! A M E N.

IfaacTaylor del. et fculp.

Figure 6. "Liberty Conquers Tyranny," 1775. Liberty with her foot on the neck of the monarch as patriarchal enslaver of women and Africans. Courtesy the Library of Congress, Prints and Photographs Division, LC-USZ62–45534.

Figure 7. "Columbia Trading with All the World," c. 1800. Columbia as a figure of the United States trading with her sister continents: America, Africa, Asia, and Europe. Courtesy the Library Company of Philadelphia.

between male and female is particularly evident in the correspondence between Abigail and John Adams during the Revolutionary years. Abigail Adams was one of the first to note and draw out the Revolutionary implications of the analogy between the political position of the American colonies and the position of women within the family and the state. "I long to hear that you have declared an independancy," she wrote John on 31 March 1776, urging a declaration of political independence and threatening a revolt of women against men some three months before the official Declaration of Independence and break with England took place: "[A]nd by the way in the new Code of Laws which I suppose it will be necessary for you to make I desire you would Remember the Ladies, and be more generous and favourable to them than your ancestors. Do not put such unlimited power into the hands of the Husbands. Remember all Men would be tyrants if they could. If perticular care and attention is not paid to the Laidies we are determined to foment a Rebelion, and will not hold ourselves bound by any Laws in which we have no voice, or Representation." Drawing on Revolutionary appeals to common sense, plain truth, and natural law, she asserts: "That your Sex are Naturally tyrannical is a Truth so thoroughly established as to admit of no dispute. . . . Why then, not put it out of the power of the vicious and Lawless to use us with cruelty and indignity with impunity. Men of Sense in all Ages abhor those customs which treat us only as the vassals of your Sex" (*AFC*, 1: 370).

In this justifiably famous passage Adams not only challenges the laws of coverture and presses for expanded female rights both within and outside marriage; her masterful deployment of the rhetorics of representation and consent, self-sovereignty and natural law, liberty and the right of revolution, also illustrates the fluidity and volatility of the Revolutionary moment as women extended and transformed the meanings of the American Revolution by reiterating and revising its terms.[5] While Adams's threat of female "Rebelion" is framed by an affirmation of women's dependence on men, "as Beings placed by providence under your protection" (*AFC*, 1:370), her translation of the language of political revolution into a reinterpretation of power relations between men and women within the home, marriage, and the family is crucial in suggesting the mobile circuits of exchange between public and private, political and domestic, and male and female "spheres" during the Revolutionary years as the political challenge to patriarchal kingship led to a renegotiation of traditional gender boundaries and roles both within and beyond the household.

Whereas John Adams and the founding fathers wanted a change of masters, Abigail Adams was asking for a "new Code of Laws" and a change of world. Like such male satirists as Alexander Pope in England

and John Trumbull in America, John Adams seeks to diffuse the logic and power of Abigail Adams's revolutionary appeal through humor. "As to your extraordinary Code of Laws, I cannot but laugh. We have been told that our Struggle has loosened the bands of Government every where. That Children and Apprentices were disobedient—that schools and Colledges were grown turbulent—that Indians slighted their Guardians and Negroes grew insolent to their Masters. But your Letter was the first Intimation that another Tribe more numerous and powerfull than all the rest were grown discontented." Recognizing the dangerous loosening of traditional bonds of rank and subordination brought by the Revolutionary situation, John reasserts the absolute power of patriarchy: "Depend upon it, We know better than to repeal our Masculine systems" (*AFC*, 1:382). His bantering tone does not disguise his self-contradiction and fear. While he was advocating the right of rebellion in the political sphere, asserting that "the people have a right to revoke the authority that they themselves have deputed and to constitute abler and better agents, attorneys, and trustees," he was attempting to suppress the rebellion in his own household by maintaining the absolute authority of a "Masculine" system that was hereditary, divinely sanctioned, and beyond repeal.[6]

Abigail Adams refused to be silenced. She pointed out the contradiction between the anti-authoritarian rhetoric of the Revolution and her husband's insistence on maintaining the divine right of the father as king: "I can not say that I think you very generous to the Ladies," she wrote, "for whilst you are proclaiming peace and good will to Men, Emancipating all Nations, you insist upon retaining an absolute power over Wives. But you must remember that Arbitrary power is like most other things which are very hard, very liable to be broke" (7 May 1776, *AFC*, 1:402).

To her friend Mercy Otis Warren, Adams confided that she had tested the "Disinterestedness" of her husband's republican "Virtue" and "found it wanting": "He is very sausy to me in return for a List of Female Grievances which I transmitted to him. I think I will get you to join me in a petition to Congress" (27 April 1776, *AFC*, 1:398). Adams's war letters, especially the ones she wrote in the years immediately preceding and following the formal Declaration of Independence on 4 July 1776, are remarkable in revealing "the changes in the realm of [female] attitude and belief" (to reformulate Bailyn) and the powerful new female voice that had been released by the Revolution. Adams's fantasy of joining her friend in submitting a "List of Female Grievances" to Congress suggests a level of raised political consciousness, a heightened imaginative desire and aspiration, and a radically utopian will that refused to be quelled once the physical combat with Britain ended.

Like other Revolutionary women, Abigail Adams took advantage of the Revolutionary moment to press for political reform both within and outside marriage. Alarmed by a "conspiracy of the Negroes" in Boston, who had agreed to fight on the side of the royalist governor in return for arms and liberation, she expressed her sympathy with the slaves' demand for liberation: "I wish most sincerely there was not a Slave in the province," she wrote John in 1774, pointing out the contradiction between the rhetoric of liberty and the fact of slavery in the American colonies. "It allways appeard a most iniquitous Scheme to me—fight ourselfs for what we are daily robbing and plundering from those who have as good a right to freedom as we have. You know my mind upon this Subject" (*AFC,* 1:162). Unlike the Revolutionary founders who noticed and then dropped the logical connection between republican calls for colonial liberty and the emancipation of African slaves, Abigail Adams criticized the decision to "expunge" the antislavery passage from the Declaration of Independence as a failure of manliness on the part of the founders: "I cannot but feel sorry that some of the most Manly Sentiments in the Declaration are Expunged from the printed coppy," she wrote John on 14 July 1776 (*AFC,* 1:46).

Only a few weeks after the revolt against England was formalized in the Declaration of Independence, Adams also complained of the "deficiency of Education" in America. "The poorer sort of children are wholly neglected, and left to range the Streets without Schools, without Busniess, given up to all Evil. . . . If you complain of neglect of Education in sons, What shall I say with regard to daughters, who every day experience the want of it." In making her case, Adams mounted a defense of female education that would become public policy for the next one hundred years. "If we mean to have Heroes, Statesmen and Philosophers, we should have learned women," she said (*AFC,* 2:94). But while Adams grounded her argument for female education in the political importance of women as wives and mothers of the future sons of the republic, like Mary Wollstonecraft and Judith Sargent Murray later in the century, she insisted on the essential equality of male and female mental capacities. For all three, mind was, in effect, nongendered. Reflecting on the "difference of Education between the male and female Sex" in a letter to her cousin John Thaxter, she observed: "Pardon me Sir if I cannot help sometimes suspecting that this Neglect arises in some measure from an ungenerous jealousy of rivals near the Throne—but I quit the Subject or it will run away with my pen" (*AFC,* 2:391–92). Adams's comment suggests that the social construction of an inferior and dependent female subject had more to do with anxieties about manhood than it did with female nature.

During the Revolutionary years, Adams's pen frequently ran away with its female "Subject," leading her to warlike fantasies of violence not only against Britain but against patriarchy itself as she imagined a larger field of action for women in the political constitution of the new republic. "My pen is always freer than my tongue," she wrote to John in 1775; "I have wrote many things to you that I suppose I never could have talk'd" (*AFC*, 1: 310). For Adams as for many women who turned to letters during the Revolution as a place to carry on frank and at times radical *talk* about affairs both public and private, writing became not only a means of ordering and interpreting the disruptive events of the war but also a form of self-exploration, self-creation, and self-enlargement at a time when traditional social roles and relations were being eroded. "[M]y *Pen is* my only pleasure" (*AFC*, 2:133; emphasis added), Adams wrote to John shortly after the war began, in a phrase that inadvertently connects *pen, pen-is,* and *pleasure* to letter writing as a form of sexual cross-dressing, a place where women might speak in the traditionally male voice of mind, politics, history, and war.

While John Adams served as a delegate to the Continental Congress and later as ambassador to France, he relied on Abigail Adams's letters as a primary source of information about political happenings in America. He shared her correspondence with other delegates and even cited one of her letters in a speech to Congress.[7] "I think you shine as a Stateswoman," he wrote. "Pray where do you get your Maxims of State, they are very apropos" (*AFC*, 1:420). Comparing her with the British republican historian Catharine Macaulay and the French classical scholar Anne Dacier, he came to see her letters as a kind of history of the war (*AFC*, 3:122).

Abigail Adams was conscious of the pen as a form of political power. "What a politician you have made me," she wrote John of the elections under the new Massachusetts Constitution of 1780. "If I cannot be a voter upon this occasion, I will be a writer of votes," she said, ironizing female disenfranchisement under the new state constitution at the same time that she broached the question of voting rights for women as the logical next step to writing votes for men (*AFC*, 3:372). Reflecting the eighteenth-century transatlantic interest in the "epistle," or letter, as a form of literary and political discourse, Adams's correspondence enabled her to become, in effect, a woman of letters, trespassing on traditionally masculine terrain as she wielded the pen as weapon and power in the world.[8] At a time when the writing woman was still an anomaly, Adams's self-consciously literary correspondence represented an affirmation of female mind and an assertion of female agency in the process of cultural and national creation. Along with the many selves she invented and lived during the war, Adams's letters became a means of writing herself into history.

In 1773, as part of her aspiration as a woman of letters, Adams entered into an extensive correspondence with Mercy Otis Warren, the Massachusetts writer, poet, and patriot, who had already moved from letters to print with the anonymous publication of her political satires, *The Adulateur* (1772) and *The Defeat* (1773), and who would write during the war a three-volume history that was published in 1805 as *The Rise, Progress, and Termination of the American Revolution*.[9] "Thus imbolden'd I venture to stretch my pinions," Adams wrote in her first letter to Warren, in words that associate their "correspondence" with "pleasure" and "improvement," a stretching of mental wings, and the opportunity for flight beyond what Warren called "the Narrower Circle of Domestic Care" to which women were "Confined" (*AFC*, 1:182). The letters that Adams and Warren wrote to each other during the American Revolution read like an alternative female committee of correspondence—an exchange of women's intelligence—in which commentary on books, writing, politics, and the public events of war intermingles with talk of their day-to-day struggle to manage farm and family amid the boycotts, inflation, shortages, deprivations, and constant threat of violence brought by the war. By the beginning of 1775, while most men in the Continental Congress and elsewhere were still talking about reconciliation, both women had become strong advocates for a break with Britain. "[I]t seems to me the Sword is now our only, yet dreadful alternative, and the fate of Rome will be renued in Brittain," Adams wrote Warren on 3 February 1775 in response to a speech given by George III to Parliament that she had read in the *Massachusetts Spy* (*AFC*, 1:183).

Concerned about the proper representation of the American cause in the British press and in history, Warren and Adams agreed to send their own accounts of events in America to the republican historian Catharine Macaulay. Although Warren's was never sent, Adams sent a letter to Macaulay in 1774, presenting an heroic account of "the complicated misiries and distresses" brought upon America by Britain, with "all the Horrours of a civil war threatning us on one hand, and the chains of Slavery ready forged for us on the other" (*AFC*, 1:177).[10] Drawing on the language of transatlantic republicanism and the classical models of the past, Adams and Warren work out for themselves, their husbands, and their country a personal and political ethos of virtue and self-sacrifice for the public good as they try out the new roles for women made possible by the war.

The fantasy of a world without men—of woman alone—is part of the horror and the possibility of the Revolution as it is staged in the letters of Adams and Warren. Even before the formal declaration of war, Warren notes that their husbands, James Warren and John Adams, might be "Marked out as Early Victims to successful Tyrany." "And Which of us should have the Courage of an Aria or a Portia in a Day of trial like theirs," Warren asks, hoping she can rise to the challenge with these "Celebrated Ladies" as her model (*AFC* 1:182). Perhaps in response to Warren's classical republican call, when Boston was occupied by British troops a few months later, Abigail Adams began signing her letters with the name Portia, whose husband, Brutus, had famously opposed the tyranny of Julius Caesar in the Roman republic. Her assumption of the identity of Portia was a means at once of asserting the continuity of the American struggle with the republican struggles of the past and scripting herself into a starring role in the political drama of the nation. The figure of Portia enabled Adams to reimagine herself historically as a rational, educated, independent, virtuous, and politically minded citizen of a new republican country. As the "Good Portia," Warren wrote, aiding her in the process of self-creation, Adams's "Mind" was "Agitated by A Variety of passions of the Noblest kind: A Sense of Honnour, of Friendship, of parental and Conjugal affection, of Domestick Felicity And public Happiness" (7 February 1776, *AFC*, 1:343–344).

The discourse of republicanism—which stressed political citizenship as the highest form of existence and sacrifice for the *patria* as the highest form of virtue—placed both John and Abigail Adams in an anomalous position. The overarching irony of their relationship during the Revolutionary years is that while they played at being the ideal republican couple, the republican ethos of civic virtue led them to spend much of their early married life apart. In the ideal republican household, the father was, in effect, absent serving his country while the mother assumed traditionally male functions as a form of self-sacrificial service to the state.

The Revolutionary situation gave Adams a chance to play the man she had always in some sense wanted to be. "Had nature formed me of the other Sex," she wrote her cousin Isaac Smith when he departed for England in 1771, "I should certainly have been a rover" (*AFC*, 1:76). While John served as a delegate to the Continental Congress between 1774 and 1777, Abigail Adams, like many women during the war years, assumed full responsibility for family, farm, crops, tenants, and accounts.[11] "I find myself dear Marcia . . . doubled in Wedlock," she wrote Mercy Otis Warren in April 1776, referring to her assumption of both masculine and feminine roles in the Adams household. "I find it necessary not only to pay attention to my own in door domestick affairs, but to every thing without, about our little farm &c." In the absence of male support, she imagines herself in the role of a ship captain navigating a wartime economy of scarcity, rising prices, and absence of goods: "Frugality, Industery and ecconomy are the Lessons of the day—at least they must be for me or my small Boat will suffer shipwreck" (*AFC*, 1:377).

When John departed to serve as a diplomat in France in 1778, Abigail Adams rented their farm to tenants and started an international import business, first through John's mediation and ultimately by corresponding directly with the French "House of Joseph Guardoqui and Sons." As a female merchant, she traded various goods—tea, china, dishes, fabric, handkerchiefs, ribbons, shoe binding, thread—with townspeople, and she engaged her friends, including Mercy Otis Warren, to serve as agents for her business. For all her emphasis on rural virtue and republican self-sacrifice, Abigail Adams was in fact an ambitious and successful entrepreneur, at war with the same self-interested and individualistic impulses in herself that she and John feared. "[H]ow hard is it to devest the Humane mind of all private ambition, and to sacrifice ourselves and all we possess to the publick Emolement," she wrote to Warren in the summer of 1775 (*AFC*, 1:255).

Recognizing the value of property and hard money during the inflationary war years, Adams also invested in real estate and engaged in land speculation with property that she could not legally possess as a woman under Massachusetts law. When John objected to her buying land in Vermont with the idea of eventually "retiring" to farm there, she bought the land anyway. "Nothing venture nothing have," she quipped, once the deal had been closed, in language that sounds closer to venture capitalism than classical republicanism (*AFC*, 4:345).

A little over a month after the Declaration of Independence and the outbreak of hostilities between Britain and the colonies, Adams began to dream of a revolutionary free space in which she might have the liberty to write, to think, and to choose alone. "I do not covet my Neighbors Goods," she wrote John from her aunt's study in Boston, "but . . . I always had a fancy for a closet with a window which I could more peculiarly call my own" (*AFC*, 2:112). Throughout the war years there was a growing gap between her rhetoric of domesticity and dependence and her actual transgressions of traditional female bounds. "Whilst you are engaged in the Senate your own domestick affairs require your presence at Home, and . . . your wife and children are in Danger of wanting Bread," she wrote John in September 1776; but she concluded the same letter with an Amazonian fantasy of power in a female land: "We are no ways dispiritted here, we possess a Spirit that will not be conquerd. If our Men are all drawn of[f] and we should be attacked, you would find a Race of Amazons in America" (*AFC*, 2:128–29).

Even before the war, Abigail Adams expressed anxiety about constituting a new form of government in America. "I am more and more convinced that Man is a dangerous creature," she wrote John in November 1775, "and that power whether vested in many or a few is ever grasping" (*AFC*, 1:329). Toward the close of the war she suffered from "a dejection of Spirits" as she took note of the new breed of moneyed and self-interested men who were eroding the republican ethos of virtue and self-sacrifice for the public good. "You are loosing all opportunities for helping yourself," she wrote John in March 1782, "for those who are daily becomeing more and more unworthy of your Labours and who will neither care for you or your family when their own turn is served—so selfish are mankind. I know this is a language you are unwilling to hear. I wish it was not a truth which I daily experience" (*AFC*, 4:296). Ambiguously positioned between the "truth" of her "daily experience" of the American economy and the republican language that John wanted to hear her speak, Abigail Adams marks the growing gap between the self-sacrificial rhetoric of the founding fathers and the fact of an increasingly self-interested market economy.[12]

But the anxiety and depression that Adams suffered toward the close of the war was at least in part provoked by her discovery of similarly "grasping" impulses in herself. There were times when she seemed to want to give up the language of republicanism and the mask of public virtue and take what she could get. "Desire and Sorrow were denounced upon our Sex; as a punishment for the transgression of Eve," she wrote John in 1782; "I never wonderd at the philosopher who thanked the Gods that he was created a Man rather than a Woman" (*AFC*, 4:306). Adams's depression about the prospects of the American republic were linked with her uncertainty about the putative virtue of the republican woman upon whom the health of the new nation was said to depend. The new breed of self-interested men she saw in the external landscape of the republic were in fact uneasy reminders of the ambitious and transgressive new impulses she had discovered in herself during the war years.

If at the close of the war and in her later roles as wife of the second president, John Adams, and mother of the sixth, John Quincy Adams, Abigail Adams appears to embody and foster the ideal of republican womanhood as a socially acceptable model of American womanhood that locates the political consciousness women learned during the Revolution within the traditional boundaries of the home and family, she also reveals the limits, contradiction, and instability of republican womanhood as both social formation and a category of historical analysis.[13] Adams's experience of the Revolution and the multiple roles she played in it—as republican patriot, advocate of women's rights, politician, farmer, merchant, wife, husband, mother, rover, writer, Amazon, and woman alone—marked a radical transformation in women's self-conception and a major rethinking of the relationship between subject and state, woman and man, private and public, brought by the war. Like Abigail Adams, during the war years and after, women began to conceive of themselves not merely as subjects of God, King, State, and Man but as historical agents, makers, and citizens of the world with certain inalienable liberties and rights. The multiple forms and fantasies of female being that were released by the war would continue to redefine, contest, and press beyond the socially proscribed bounds of the terms *republican, woman, citizen, polity,* and *revolution* itself.

Phillis Wheatley and the Black American Revolution

During the American Revolution, the challenge to constituted authority came not only from privileged and high-born white women like Abigail Adams but, as John Adams had grudgingly noted, from apprentices, Indians, and Negroes who "grew insolent to their Masters." The potential danger of this challenge is evident in the life and work of the poet Phillis Wheatley, who was abducted from Africa and sold as a slave in Boston in 1761, during the very years when the contest over the rights of the North American colonists within the British Empire was beginning to intensify. Whereas Abigail Adams compared the condition of women in America to "Egyptian bondage," for Wheatley, drawing upon the Old Testament image to describe the captivity of African people to "our Modern Egyptians," the language of bondage and freedom was no longer metaphoric but real. Knowing the truth of slavery as part of her daily experience as the slave of a prosperous Boston merchant, John Wheatley, and his wife, Susanna, Phillis Wheatley, too, pointed out the contradiction between the rhetoric of liberty and the reality of slavery in America. In a letter to the Mohegan preacher Samson Occom, which was first published in the *Connecticut Gazette* on 11 March 1774 and widely circulated in New England newspapers, Wheatley noted ironically "the strange Absurdity of their Conduct whose Words and Actions are so diametrically opposite. How well the Cry for Liberty, and the reverse Disposition for Exercise of oppressive Power over others agree,—I humbly think it does not require the Penetration of a Philosopher to determine."[14] Positioning herself in the breach between trope and truth, between the rhetoric of republican liberty and her experience of African enslavement, Wheatley transformed the Revolutionary discourse on liberty, natural rights, and human nature into a subtle critique of the color code and the oppressive racial structures of republican America.

It is no coincidence that Wheatley's *Poems on Various Subjects, Religious and Moral* (1773), which was the first book published by an African American, appeared during the Revolutionary period. According to her "Master," John Wheatley, "Phillis was brought from *Africa* to *America,* in the Year 1761, between Seven and Eight Years of Age. Without any Assistance from School Education, and by only what she was taught in the Family, she, in sixteen Months Time from her Arrival, attained the English Language" (*PPW*, 1). By age twelve she was reading and translating Ovid, at age fifteen she published her first poem, and she was twenty when *Poems* was published. Wheatley and her book were, in effect, a Revolutionary and a transatlantic phenomenon.

Her volume of *Poems* was accompanied by the authenticating documents—a picture and a "Notice to the Public" signed by several local authorities—that would frame later African American writing (Figure 8). Wheatley's politically fraught position as a black woman slave in Revolutionary America is suggested by the fact that the signatures of the royalist governor of Massachusetts, Thomas Hutchinson, and the leader of Boston resistance, John Hancock, were joined for a brief moment over the body of her *Poems*.[15] But while Wheatley was the "property" of John Wheatley and the authenticating male figures who "notice" her text, she was possessed by the insurrectionary "Goddess of Liberty" who stalks her poems as she was at that very moment stalking the political landscape of Revolutionary America.

In *Home*, LeRoi Jones criticizes what he calls Wheatley's "ludicrous departures from the huge black voices that splintered southern nights."[16] But in his emphasis on an authentic vernacular black male voice, Jones misses the revolutionary implications of Wheatley's verse. Within the discourse of sexual and racial inequality in the eighteenth century, the fact of a black woman reading, writing, and publishing poems was itself enough to splinter the categories of male and female, white and black, and undermine a social order grounded in notions of sexual and racial difference. The potential danger of her enterprise is suggested by the doubleness of the authenticating picture that represents her in the revolutionary figure of a black woman reading, thinking, and writing at the same time that it enchains her in the inscription: "Phillis Wheatley, Negro Servant to Mr. John Wheatley" (Figure 8).

Even before Wheatley's book was published, the Philadelphia physician and antislavery advocate Benjamin Rush cited her poetry as a sign of black humanity, sexual and racial equality, and the sameness of human nature. In his antislavery tract, *An Address to the Inhabitants of the British Settlements in America, Upon Slave-Keeping* (1773), he wrote: "There is now in the town of Boston a Free Negro Girl, about 18 years of age, who has been 9 years in the country, whose singular genius and accomplishments are such as not only do honor to her sex, but to human nature. Several of her poems have been printed, and read with pleasure by the public."[17]

In the Revolutionary contest between Britain and the American colonists, loyalist and patriot alike laid claim to Wheatley's voice: for the loyalists she served as a possible means of garnering slave support for the

Figure 8. Phillis Wheatley. This frontispiece from *Poems on Various Subjects, Religious and Moral* (1773) aptly represents Wheatley's contradictory location as African, American, woman, and slave in Revolutionary America. The volatile figure of an African American woman slave writing and thinking is encircled and framed by her captor's inscription: "Phillis Wheatley, Negro Servant to Mr. John Wheatley, of Boston." Courtesy the Library Company of Philadelphia.

cause of Britain in America; for the patriots she represented a sign of human progress rather than degeneration in America. But while Wheatley seemed to utter the ideals of her time in the ordered and allusive heroic couplets of Pope and the neoclassical writers, she also knew how to manipulate language, image, and phrase in a manner that destabilized while it appeared to reinforce the categories of the dominant culture. Although Wheatley criticism has tended to divide between those who criticize her for writing wholly within white culture and those who have sought to identify an authentic black voice outside whiteness, it is important to bear in mind that it was only through her traumatic experience of the transatlantic slave trade and the institutions of slavery that Wheatley assumed an identity as "African" and "American."[18] By focusing on Wheatley's doubled relation to both skin color and mask, I want to suggest that her power as a poet resides not so much in her ability to get wholly outside whiteness or fully inside blackness but in the subtlety and art with which she "puts on the white world" so as to hybridize, reaccent, and revolutionize some of its key religious, moral, and political terms.[19]

From the dedication to the Countess of Huntington that opens her *Poems on Various Subjects, Religious and Moral* to her tribute titled "To the Right Honourable William, Earl of Dartmouth" enclosed within, Wheatley's book is enmeshed in a web of Revolutionary associations. Margaret Burroughs exaggerates only slightly when she says: "If the Continental Congress had possessed an intelligent counter-intelligence service, Phillis Wheatley might have been interned for the duration as a security risk, on the principle of guilt by association."[20] The Countess of Huntington was a well-known supporter of both the evangelical and the antislavery movement in England. Her friend and associate, the Earl of Dartmouth, supported the British policy of inciting slaves to revolt against rebel masters when he served as secretary of state for North America between 1772 and 1775.

As a book of poems by a woman slave celebrating the cause of American liberty, Wheatley's *Poems* is loaded with the irony and contradiction of a cause and a country at odds with itself. While Wheatley was in London in 1773, where she met several supporters including the Earl of Dartmouth, Benjamin Franklin, and Granville Sharpe, one of the leaders of the British antislavery movement, no less than five petitions for freedom were presented to the Massachusetts General Council by Boston slaves: "We have no Property. We have no Wives! No Children! We have no City! No Country!" one exclaimed. In February 1774 an article in the *Massachusetts Spy* signed by an "African" patriot invoked the rhetoric of natural rights and consent to point out the analogy between America's defiance of Britain and the slaves' defiance of their masters in America: "Are not your hearts also hard, when you hold them in slavery who are intitled to liberty, by the law of nature, equal as yourselves? If it be so, pray, Sir, pull the beam out of thine eye."[21] Toward the close of the war, in February 1782, a Boston slave woman named Belinda presented a petition to the Massachusetts General Council in which she draws on the languages of both republicanism and evangelicalism to make her case for remuneration for fifty years of unpaid labor given to a master who had fled to England. Reading the "present war" as an instance of the ways "nations must be agitated, and the world convulsed, for the preservation of that freedom, which the Almighty Father intended for all the human race," Belinda pleads her case "to a body of men, formed for the extirpation of vassalage, for the reward of virtue, and the just returns of honest industry."[22] Although none of these petitions for black rights, freedom, and citizenship was ever granted, they suggest the more radical transatlantic contexts of black republicanism, evangelicalism, and antislavery activity out of which Wheatley's poems emerged.

At the time Wheatley's *Poems* was published, there was widespread fear of slave revolt. Abigail Adams's September 1774 letter to John on the conspiracy of Boston Negroes is only one of a number of signs that fear of slave insurrection was spreading from the South to New England. Perhaps because of this growing fear of blacks, whether free or enslaved, Wheatley's book, having failed to receive an adequate subscription in the American colonies, was sponsored and published in England. Wheatley eliminated several explicitly patriot poems from the English edition, including a nonextant poem, "On the Arrival of the Ships of War, and Landing of the Troops," and another on the Boston "Massacre" titled "On the Affray in King-Street, on the Evening of the 5th of March, 1770." She also suppressed a poem titled "America" (1768), in which Britannia's imposition of taxes on the colonies is associated with the figure of a monstrous mother and cruel enslaver, and another titled "On the Death of Mr Snider Murder'd by Richardson" (1770), in which she laments the death of a young boy—"first martyr" of "fair freedom's" cause—who was accidentally shot in one of the popular uprisings of patriots against Tory merchants in Boston at the time of the boycotts in protest against British taxation.

In these poems, which may have been circulated in broadside and print, Wheatley reveals herself as a public commemorator and popularizer of the local colonial struggle against Britain's attempt to tighten the "Iron chain" of slavery on her "virtuous" American children ("America," *PPW*, 125–26). Despite Wheatley's efforts to tone down the political and insurrectionary markings of *Poems* in favor of more properly feminine "subjects, religious and moral," her sympathy with the republican, colonial, and African cause of freedom continues to make itself felt. Even in her poem addressed "To the King's Most Excellent Majesty. 1768," she celebrates the king's repeal of the Stamp Act in language that associates his policy with a broader emancipatory design that will banish "evil" and "in each clime with equal gladness" "set his subjects free!" (*PPW*, 53).

Like others who have lived and written in politically dangerous times of social breakdown and crisis, Phillis Wheatley knew the art of speaking with a double tongue. "Sometimes by Simile, a victory's won," she wrote in "America," affirming the political power of art—of simile—at the same time she locates the sources of her voice and vision in the Revolutionary figure of Liberty: "Thy Power, O Liberty, makes strong the weak / And (wondrous instinct) Ethiopians speak" (*PPW*, 125). In her poetry, Wheatley makes subtle use of ambiguity and irony, double meaning and symbolic nuance, to speak what was otherwise unspeakable from her position as an African woman slave in Revolutionary America.

Poems on Various Subjects, Religious and Moral opens with an address titled "To Maecenas," the patron of Horace and Virgil, who appears to represent Wheatley's image of an ideal patron and audience for her poems. The poet enters the literary community by invoking the classical tradition of Homer and Virgil, but she ends with an invocation to Terence, the Roman slave of African descent who was able to use his literary talent to attain freedom:

The happier *Terence* all the choir inspir'd;
His soul replenish'd, and his bosom fir'd;
But say, ye *Muses*, why this partial grace,
To one alone of *Afric's* sable race;
From age to age transmitting thus his name
With the first glory in the rolls of fame? (*PPW*, 50)

Self-consciously locating herself and her poems in relation to one "of *Afric's* sable race" writing in republican Rome, Wheatley registers her own ambitious desire to share—or perhaps transcend—the "first glory" of her African republican forebear in a poetics of liberation and ascent "That fain would mount, and ride upon the wind" (*PPW*, 50).

Wheatley's most anthologized poem, "On Being Brought from Africa to America," is formally split, like the title, between Africa and America, embodying the speaker's own split relation to herself as African and American. In the opening quatrain, the poet speaks as an American, representing slavery as a paradoxical Christian deliverance, a necessary stage in the black person's advance toward redemption and civilization; in the second quatrain, the poet speaks as an African, turning the terms of Christian orthodoxy into a critique of white hypocrisy and oppressive racial codes:

'Twas mercy brought me from my *Pagan* land,
Taught my benighted soul to understand
That there's a God, that there's a *Saviour* too:
Once I redemption neither sought nor knew.
Some view our sable race with a scornful eye,
"Their colour is a diabolic die."
Remember, *Christians, Negros,* black as *Cain,*
May be refin'd, and join th'angelic train. (*PPW,* 53)

As in "To the University of Cambridge," in which the African speaker's status as saved soul empowers her to instruct the male students to shun the serpent's egg of sin, the poet's "redemption" becomes the source of her moral and poetic authority, signaling her transformation from being passively "brought" and "taught" by God's Providence to being an active black subject who speaks and instructs as a kind of female preacher in the second quatrain of the poem.

The poem operates on what Maya Angelou has called the "Principle of Reverse": "Anything that works for you can also work against you."[23] Speaking as a black woman slave, Wheatley turns the racial codes of the dominant culture back upon themselves, giving them an ironic inflection. What appears to be repetition is in fact a form of *mimesis* that mimics and mocks in the act of repeating. This process is particularly evident in the final lines of the poem in which Wheatley challenges and destabilizes the white discourse of racial difference by placing this discourse in quotation marks—"Their colour is a diabolic die." Wheatley's words ventriloquize whiteness, literally mimicking the white view of "our sable race" in a manner that recasts the discourse of racial difference in an ironic mode.

The use of italicization in the poem has a similarly destabilizing effect: the italicized terms *Pagan, Christians, Negros,* and *Cain* are simultaneously underscored and marked for interrogation. The slipperiness of these terms is evidenced in the final lines of the poem, where through punctuation and italicization the phrase "Remember, *Christians, Negros,* black as *Cain*" might be read doubly as an address to Christians about black humanity and an address to Christians *and* Negroes that links them both in the figurative image "black as *Cain.*" Both readings undermine the color code by emphasizing the equality of spiritual condition shared by whites and blacks alike as sinful descendants of Adam and potentially "redeemed" heirs of Christ.

Wheatley's most overt criticism of the institution of slavery occurs in "To the Right Honourable William, Earl of Dartmouth, His Majesty's

Principal Secretary of State for North-America, &c." Here again the poet speaks doubly as an American patriot and an African slave, celebrating "Fair Freedom" as the cause of New England patriots and "the *Goddess* long desir'd" by enslaved blacks. She associates the 1772 appointment of Dartmouth as secretary of state for North America with the return of *Freedom,* "long lost to realms beneath the northern skies":

Elate with hope her race no longer mourns,
Each soul expands, each grateful bosom burns,
While in thine hand with pleasure we behold
The silken reins, and *Freedom's* charms unfold. (*PPW,* 82)

Wheatley's Enlightenment abstractions—"her race," "*Freedom's* charms"—continually slip into more local and material allusions to her status as an enslaved African in British North America. The meaning of her poem in praise of Dartmouth comes to turn on the instability and contest around the term *race* in the eighteenth century, which fluctuates between an older and more common reference to "the human race" and an emergent reference to geopolitical location (North America or New England), nationality (English or American), and skin color (black, red, or white). When one remembers that as secretary of state for the colonies and president of the Board of Trade and Foreign Plantations between 1772 and 1775, the Earl of Dartmouth actively participated in the British policy of inciting American slaves to revolt against their patriot masters, the poet's "hope" of freedom for "her race" takes on a particularly black and insurrectionary meaning.

Wheatley draws on the Revolutionary rhetorics of tyranny and enslavement to promote the American cause, but as the language of an African slave her words also give voice to the cause of black liberation:

No more, *America,* in mournful strain
Of wrongs, and grievance unredress'd complain,
No longer shalt thou dread the iron chain,
Which wanton *Tyranny* with lawless hand
Had made, and with it meant t'enslave the land. (*PPW,* 83)

The poet's exhortation suggests her double location, both *outside* and *inside* America: as an African slave she speaks both *to* America and *as* America, projecting a revolutionary future in which, under Dartmouth's "silken" reign, "her race"—Africans as well as Anglos in British North America—will be liberated from the yoke of "wanton *Tyranny*" and enslavement.

Wheatley further materializes the slave metaphor by calling attention to her own condition as an African slave:

Should you, my lord, while you peruse my song,
Wonder from whence my love of *Freedom* sprung,
Whence flow these wishes for the common good,
By feeling hearts alone best understood,
I, young in life, by seeming cruel fate
Was snatch'd from *Afric's* fancy'd happy seat:
What pangs excruciating must molest,
What sorrows labour in my parent's breast?
Steel'd was that soul and by no misery mov'd
That from a father seiz'd his babe belov'd:
Such, such my case. And can I then but pray
Others may never feel tyrannic sway? (*PPW,* 34)

Literalizing the Revolutionary trope of enslavement in a firsthand account of the traumatic psychic and social effects of African slavery and the slave trade, Wheatley authorizes her voice as the poet of freedom in her historical experience as an African slave. Her most direct personal statement about her African past becomes as well her most direct protest against the tyranny of African enslavement—a protest that extends beyond the boundaries of British North America to include the transatlantic slave trade and its sorrowful effects not only on Africa and its people but on the "Steel'd" souls of the enslavers themselves.

Wheatley's reference to her "seeming cruel fate" has been read as a sign of the mutilating influence of slavery, the mark of the black poet's capitulation to the codes of the dominant culture.[24] But her words are self-protectively ambiguous. Read within the context of Wheatley's ardent Christian faith and her involvement with the more radical wing of the evangelical movement in America and Britain, her words also suggest a moving attempt to make sense of her fate and the fate of her people as slaves within a "seeming cruel" providential order.[25] The poet is not "brought" but "seiz'd" and "snatch'd from *Afric's* fancy'd happy seat," a phrasing that represents her enslavement as a kidnapping and Africa as a site not of illusory but of *still* imagined happiness.[26] Bearing witness to slavery and the slave trade as a cold-blooded violation of the fundamental social unit—the familial bond between father and child—Wheatley turns her personal history into an emotionally charged "case" against the slave trade and the institution of slavery. Her prayer that "Others may never feel tyrannic sway" is a prayer that encompasses not only American patriots but the "Others" of her own African race.

According to her nineteenth-century biographer, Margaretta Matilda Odell, Wheatley's only memory of her African homeland was the daily sunrise ritual of her mother, who "poured out water before the sun at his rising."[27] In Wheatley's writings, the memory of African sun worship merges with the rhetorics of evangelical Christianity and Revolutionary freedom to produce a poetics of ascent and liberation. In this poetics the sun/Son is the central figure in a constellation of images that moves from dark to light, white to black, sin to redemption, bondage to deliverance.

The intersection of these languages is particularly evident in the poem "On Imagination," in which Wheatley imagines herself mounting on the silken pinions of *Fancy* toward the sun, toward God, and toward liberation:

Soaring through air to find the bright abode,
Th'empyreal palace of the thund'ring God,
We on thy pinions can surpass the wind,
And leave the rolling universe behind:
From star to star the mental optics rove,
Measure the skies, and range the realms above.
There in one view we grasp the mighty whole,
Or with new worlds amaze th'unbounded soul. (*PPW*, 78–79)

Like Memory (*Mneme*) in "On Recollection" and Liberty ("the *Goddess*") in "To the Right Honourable William, Earl of Dartmouth," "To His Excellency General Washington," and "Liberty and Peace, A Poem," Wheatley's *Imagination* is a potent female figure, an "imperial queen" whose wings carry the poet into "new worlds" of the "unbounded soul." These "new worlds" are at once the heavenly world of biblical Revelation and the poet's own "raptur'd" vision of an alternative world order. In the last stanza of the poem, the "rising fire" of Wheatley's poetic aspiration fuses with the rhetorics of revelation and revolution and her memory of the African sunrise, leading her to an insurrectionary vision of deliverance out of the "iron bands" of an oppressive white order—figured in the poem as the "frozen deeps" of *Winter*—into the "radiant gold" of a new dawn on earth. The poet's voice and vision "cease" in the final lines of the poem: "*Winter* austere forbids me to aspire, / And northern tempests damp the rising fire; / They chill the tides of *Fancy's* flowing sea" (*PPW*, 80). But the poet's closing image of herself as "rising fire" and "flowing sea" suggests that she will continue to sing against and beyond the chill of Northern white oppression.

Wheatley's belief in the millennial promise of evangelical Protestantism enabled her to engage in the public struggle for African freedom as an extension of her devout Christian faith. Commenting on the "natural Rights" of Negroes in her 1774 letter to the Indian activist Samson Occom, Wheatley envisions the African struggle against American slavery as a "type" of the Old Testament struggle of Israel "for their Freedom from Egyptian Slavery." Like Jupiter Hammon in America, and like such writers of the black transatlantic as Olaudah Equiano and Ottobah

Cugoano, Wheatley represents the contemporary struggle of Africans against their "Modern Egyptian" masters as part of a global providential movement toward liberation and deliverance: "In every human Breast," she writes, "God has implanted a Principle, which we call Love of Freedom; it is impatient of Oppression, and pants for Deliverance, and by the Leave of our Modern Egyptians I will assert, that the same Principle lives in us. God grant Deliverance in his own way and Time, and get him honor upon all those whose Avarice impels them to countenance and help forward the Calamities of their Fellow Creatures" (11 February 1774, *PPW*, 204). Here as in her biblically inspired poem, "Goliath of Gath," Wheatley identifies her own anger against slavery with the voice and wrath of God, predicting—like Jefferson a decade later—the "scenes of slaughter" and "seas of blood" that would come if Americans did not stop visiting the calamity of slavery on "their Fellow Creatures."

Within a month after the publication of her *Poems* in London in September 1773 and at the urging of her English supporters, Phillis Wheatley was freed by John Wheatley. "Since my return to America my Master, has at the desire of my friends in England given me my freedom," she wrote to Colonel David Wooster on 18 October 1773. Solicitous about the sales of her book in America, she further observed: "I am now upon my own footing and whatever I get by this is entirely mine, & it is the Chief I have to depend upon" (*PPW*, 197). Both literally and figuratively, Wheatley's poems—like those of her forebear, Terence—became a means of writing herself into freedom. Through them she would continue to write for her own survival and the freedom of her race in poems that imagine the end of slavery as Christian redemption, African liberation, and Revolutionary change of world.

On 26 October 1775, Phillis Wheatley sent a poem titled "To His Excellency General Washington" to Washington himself. Inspired by "the goddess" Freedom and impelled by the "wild uproar" of Freedom's warriors, the poem represents a subtle attempt to enlist Washington, who had been appointed commander in chief of the Continental Army, as a freedom fighter for real as well as metaphoric slaves. "We demand," the poet writes:

The grace and glory of thy martial band.
Fam'd for thy valour, for thy virtues more,
Hear every tongue thy guardian aid implore! (*PPW*, 167)

Like the addresses to Washington written by other Revolutionary poets, including Joel Barlow and Philip Freneau, the poem suggests the potential power of writing at a time when poets as well as politicians were engaged in the process of creating a new American order. Speaking not as a republican wife or mother but as a patriot of liberty, Wheatley's address to Washington enlarges the definitions of the public sphere, civic virtue, republicanism, and the Revolution to include women, Africans, and slaves. As in Wheatley's verse epistles to other figures of political power, including King George III, the Earl of Dartmouth, and the lieutenant governor of Massachusetts, Andrew Oliver, her poem also suggests an openness and fluidity in black and white relations during the Revolutionary years that would begin to close and rigidify once the war was over and slaves were written into the political Constitution as three-fifths human.[28]

In 1784, only a year after the close of the war, Phillis Wheatley died and was buried in an unmarked grave. During this same time period, Thomas Jefferson set very distinct limits on the Revolutionary rhetorics of freedom, equality, and "self-evident" truth, when in *Notes on the State of Virginia* he advanced it "as a suspicion only, that blacks, whether originally a distinct race, or made distinct by time and circumstances, are inferior to the whites in the endowments both of body and mind" (143). The potential danger of Wheatley's *Poems* as cultural proof refuting Jefferson's "suspicion" of racial inequality is suggested by the fact that in advancing his argument, he singles out her work along with the *Letters* (1782) of the black British writer Ignatius Sancho for particular criticism. Jefferson not only dismisses Wheatley's work from serious literary consideration; he also, perhaps intentionally, transmutes her name from "wheat" to "what": "Religion indeed has produced a Phyllis Whately [*sic*]; but it could not produce a poet. The compositions published under her name are below the dignity of criticism. The heroes of the Dunciad are to her, as Hercules to the author of that poem" (*NV*, 140). At a time when the "loose and dangerous" notions of liberty, equality, representation, and consent were threatening to subvert traditional orders of white masculine authority, Jefferson's comment represents one of the first attempts of the founding fathers to counter the Revolutionary discourse of equality and natural rights with the post-Revolutionary discourse of racial and sexual difference.

"Loose and Dangerous" Women

Jefferson's attempt to draw the line between religion and poetry, female and male, black "composition" and white art, in his comment on Phillis Wheatley does not dispose of the fact that during the Revolutionary years one of the most accomplished, popular, and internationally known books of American poetry had been written by an African woman slave.[29] As a mixed figure, who crosses the either/or categories of her culture and challenges the major analytical categories—such as republican *wife* and *mother*—that later historians have used to describe her culture, Wheatley suggests what was perhaps the most radical transformation brought by the American Revolution: the widespread crossing of boundaries between private and public, domestic and political, feminine and masculine, servant and master, black and white, culture and polity, religion and revolution.

One of the immediate effects of the Revolutionary struggle was to politicize the domestic space of the home and those functions traditionally associated with women. During the Revolution, the act of spinning assumed a highly charged political valence as women throughout the colonies organized to spin cloth in the name of liberty, self-sovereignty, and republican virtue. The support of women was essential to the struggle against Britain. From the first, the Sons as well as the Daughters of Liberty were enjoined to practice a politics of nonimportation and nonconsumption. A Revolutionary broadside circulated in Boston in January 1770 urged men and women to boycott the British goods of a local importer: "It is desired that the Sons and Daughters of LIBERTY, would not buy any one thing of him, for in so doing they will bring Disgrace upon *themselves,* and their *Posterity,* for *ever* and *ever,* AMEN."[30] In the same month, three-hundred Boston women signed a pledge agreeing to support the boycott of tea.

Local papers carried verse by women asking female patriots to enlist in the Revolutionary struggle. In "The Female Patriots, Address'd to the Daughters of Liberty in America, 1768," which was composed by the Philadelphia Quaker Milcah Martha Moore and published anonymously in the *Pennsylvania Gazette,* the poet's Revolutionary call for women to "point out their duty to men" by boycotting British products slips into a critique of male authority and the masculine systems of power in which women have "no Voice":

If the Sons (so degenerate) the Blessing despise,
Let the Daughters of Liberty, nobly arise,
And tho' we've no Voice, but a negative here,
The use of the Taxables, let us forbear.[31]

On 25 October 1774 in Edenton, North Carolina, fifty-one female patriots signed a declaration pledging "to do everything as far as lies in our power" to support the public policy of nonimportation. The specter of women trespassing upon the traditionally male terrain of politics was unsettling enough to be satirized in the British press. In the widely circulated political cartoon, "A Society of Patriotic Ladies" (1775), hierarchies of sex, class, race, and blood dissolve as the ladies, pen in hand, take political command and move from private to public sphere: "A female at the table with a gavel is evidently a man," noted one contemporary commentator.[32] A black woman servant, bearing pen and ink—and a resemblance to the portrait of Wheatley that appeared in her *Poems*—mingles freely with the female "politicians," while a feminized man makes sexual advances, a neglected child misbehaves, and a dog urinates under the table (Figure 9). The cartoon aptly illustrates the fear of a more general collapse of boundaries—between home and politics, female and male, servant and master, black and white, beast and baby—that accompanied anxieties about the potentially radical effects of the American Revolution on hitherto colonial and colonized women.

At the center of these anxieties was the specter of the writing woman. As the women patriots of Edenton suggest, the increased access to literacy and print in the mid to late eighteenth century in America enabled large numbers of women to turn to the pen as a form of personal and political empowerment. "A sister's hand may wrest a female pen, / From the bold outrage of imperious men," wrote Mercy Otis Warren in "To Mrs. Montague."[33] During the Revolutionary and post-Revolutionary years, women's writing and women's voices proliferated in a multiplicity of private and public genres and forms, from Abigail Adams's letters and Phillis Wheatley's *Poems* to Mercy Otis Warren's plays, Judith Sargent Murray's essays, Esther Reed's broadside, "The Sentiments of an American Woman," Belinda's petition on behalf of slave women, and the many works published anonymously by women. Some women, like the Philadelphia poet Hannah Griffitts, circulated their writing in letters and manuscript.[34] In journals, diaries, letters, broadsides, petitions, pamphlets, poems, essays, plays, fiction, and histories written during and after the war, women began to articulate concepts of female citizenship, republican virtue, civic participation, and political community that challenged the male-defined space of print, politics, and the public sphere.

The intermingling of traditionally masculine and feminine spheres continued throughout the war as politics moved into the home and women moved into politics. In 1776, Abigail Adams wrote to John that she, Mercy Otis Warren, and Hannah Winthrop had become members of "a Committee of Ladies" appointed to question local Tory women (*AFC*, 1:391). Large numbers of less privileged women became camp followers, joining their husbands or male relatives on the war front and sometimes engaging in combat alongside them. Others, including "Molly Pitcher," Margaret ("Dirty Kate") Corbin, Sally St. Clair, and Lydia Barrington Darragh, actively entered the war effort—and later the popular imagination—as soldiers, couriers, and spies.[35]

In 1781, Deborah Sampson Gannett dressed as a man and enlisted as a soldier in the Continental Army. She fought in the battles at White Plains, Tarrytown, and Yorktown, where she was wounded but refused to

A SOCIETY of PATRIOTIC LADIES.

Figure 9. "A Society of Patriotic Ladies, at Edenton in North Carolina," 1775. This widely circulated British cartoon links the scene of women writing in support of the American policy of nonimportation with a specter of total collapse signified by mixture and crossing at every level. Courtesy the Library of Congress, Prints and Photographs Division, LC-USZ62–12711.

make much of her injuries for fear of exposing her sex. "The whole history of the American Revolution," wrote the Congressional Committee on Revolutionary Pensions, "furnishes no other similar example of female heroism, fidelity, and courage." "[I]ndeed," her husband, Benjamin Gannett, "was honored much by being the husband of such a wife."[36]

The war also gave rise to the first national organization of women. The movement was launched in Philadelphia in 1780 when Esther Reed, the wife of the president of Pennsylvania, circulated a broadside titled "The Sentiments of an American Woman," in which she called on women to organize locally and throughout the colonies in an effort to raise money for the Continental Army. Invoking past models of female patriotism, including Joan of Arc, she subtly protested the exclusion of women under the current "Constitution." "Our ambition is kindled by the fame of those heroines of antiquity, who have rendered their sex illustrious, and have proved to the universe, that, if the weakness of our Constitution, if opinion and manners did not forbid us to march to glory by the same path as the Men, we should at least equal and sometimes surpass them in our love for the public good." Having raised $300,000 in Pennsylvania alone, Reed wanted to give "the Presents of the American Women" directly to the soldiers in hard specie.[37] Here she came into conflict with George Washington. In a symbolically nuanced gesture that anticipates postwar efforts to contain revolutionary female energies within traditional bounds, Washington insisted that the women use the money to buy linen and make shirts for the boys.[38]

The potential danger associated with the crossing of sexual boundaries during the Revolution is suggested by the woodcut of a female soldier that began to appear on broadsides several years before the war. Carrying a rifle and musket and wearing a dress and a tricornered hat, the woman is ambiguously depicted as a cross-dressed figure on the margins of traditional male and female spheres. She is surrounded by a blank space and visually grounded not in the domestic but in the political sphere as the hemline of her dress merges with the image a fortress bearing a flag. In 1779, this same woodcut appeared in a broadside titled "A New Touch on the Times. . . . By a Daughter of Liberty, Living in Marblehead." Troubled by the effects of "this bloody war" on women, the Daughter of Liberty prays for a return of peace and order (Figure 10).

As Linda Kerber, Mary Beth Norton, and other scholars of the period have shown, the American Revolution fostered certain measurable changes in white women's lives, including an increased emphasis on the affectionate rather than the authoritarian family and a rise in the moral authority and stature of women within both the household and the

Figure 10. "A New Touch on the Times, well adapted to the distressing Situation of every Sea-port Town. By a Daughter of Liberty, living in Marblehead." Broadside, 1779. The potential danger associated with the crossing of gender bounds during the Revolution is suggested by this cross-dressed figure on the margins of traditional male and female spheres. Courtesy Collection of the New-York Historical Society.

Figure 11. *Liberty Displaying the Arts and Sciences.* Oil on canvas by Samuel Jennings, 1792. This first pictorial representation of African Americans in the new republic represents them freely enjoying "the boundless blessings" of liberty, knowledge, and commerce in public space. Courtesy the Library Company of Philadelphia.

republic.[39] The republican emphasis on knowledge as the foundation of independence, virtue, and liberty also brought improvements in female education in the postwar period. In the literary and artistic production of the time, America herself was represented as a Goddess of Liberty spreading art and learning to the world—an image that is linked with "an aversion to Slavery" and the "boundless blessings" of black emancipation in *Liberty Displaying the Arts and Sciences*, which was painted for the Philadelphia Library Company by Samuel Jennings in 1792 (Figure 11).[40] Given the fact that it would take over a half-century and the Civil War to end slavery in the United States, and yet another century for African Americans to gain the legal right of equal access to education and public space, it is significant that this first pictorial representation of African Americans in the new republic displays them freely enjoying the "blessings" of liberty, knowledge, and commerce in the public sphere. What the painting suggests is that in Philadelphia at least, where the state constitution was also the most democratic of the time, larger notions of human freedom, education, and a "mixed" republic of blacks and whites, women and men, circulated in the cultural imaginary, than were written into the political Constitution of the time.

In the post-Revolutionary period, education for black and lower-class women was largely informal, and advances in middle-class white women's education became a double-edged enterprise. While there was widespread insistence on the necessity of educating women, there was also a growing fear that learning would unsettle their blood and turn them into free-loving men. Even the most liberal spokespersons for female education, such as Murray and Rush, advocated women's education as a means of improving a woman's essential role as wife and mother of the future sons of the republic.[41]

In 1794, Rush wrote: "The excess of the passion for liberty, inflamed by the successful issue of the war, produced in many people, opinions and conduct which could not be removed by reason nor be restrained by government." This "constituted a species of insanity, which I shall take the liberty of distinguishing by the name of *Anarchia*."[42] The American Revolution had produced in many women "opinions and conduct" that could not and would not be restrained by government. Rhetorically and iconographically, the Revolution was female, represented over and over again as a bold and self-sovereign Daughter of Liberty revolting against a cruel father or a monstrous mother. In the post-Revolutionary period, particularly during the years of the constitutional founding, the American retreat from the excess of revolution both at home and abroad corresponded with a widespread attempt to manage and control the potentially anarchic female energies released by the American Revolution.

Whereas during the Revolutionary period the sentimental heroine of Samuel Richardson's *Clarissa* was popularized as a figure of America herself revolting against the tyranny of a cruel patriarch, in the literature of the post-Revolutionary period there is a concerted effort to restore the rebellious Daughter of Liberty to the order of family and father. "Democracy is Lovelace, and the people are Clarissa," John Adams wrote, in a comment that associates the American masses with the sexual excess and vulnerability of the female body and the seductions of democracy with the sentimental love plot.[43] The dread of a liberated and self-seeking female subject unleashed by the American Revolution is suggested in a 1790 article by "Philanthropus," who feared that equality could be "taken in too extensive a sense, and might tend to destroy those degrees of subordination which nature seems to point out," such as the natural subordination of women to men. "However flattering the path of glory and ambition may be, a woman will have more commendation in being the mother of heroes than in setting up, Amazon-like, for a heroine herself."[44]

As part of the process of constituting the American republic both politically and culturally, the literature of the early national period turned to an obsessive focus on the construction of sexual difference, the definition of male and female spheres, and the reconstitution of female nature and desire under the sign of the father. The manly woman and the sexualized woman—often figured in the high-blooded volatility of the coquette (or little *cock*)—are the female villains of post-Revolutionary writing. As women who cross over, who refuse to observe the strict bounds between male and female, who are not interested in motherhood, home, or family, who attempt to set up, "Amazon-like," as heroines for themselves, they are either killed off or restored to their natural place as heroines in the father's script.

The essential plot of post-Revolutionary literature, enacted over and over again in the plays, stories, and novels of the early American republic, is the return of the wayward daughter to family order and the law of the father. In Royall Tyler's popular play, *The Contrast* (1787), for example, the sexual and self-determining energies of the coquettes, Letitia and Charlotte *Manly*, are negatively contrasted with the virtuous and dutiful daughter Maria, who refuses to disobey her father even though he wants her to marry a self-interested fortune hunter of questionable morals.[45] In "The Panther Captivity" (1787), one of the most popular stories of the post-Revolutionary period, a daughter revolts against her father's will and flees in 1776 with her lover into the wilderness, where she engages in a series of symbolically nuanced "revolutionary" actions. After escaping from a band of Indians, murdering and decapitating a "man of gigantic figure" who threatens to violate and subdue her, and living self-sufficiently in a cave for nine years, she is restored "to her father's house" by two white hunters in the concluding passages of the narrative.[46]

Charles Brockden Brown, the putative "father of American fiction," enacts a similar drama of restoration in his first novel, *Wieland* (1798). As a descendant of Richardson's Clarissa, Brown's heroine Clara is a figure of female virtue—and the American republic itself—besieged by the seemingly insatiable phantoms of her own body and mind. Driven to near insanity by the energy of her sexual passion and her imagination, Clara is ultimately restored by a return to the "ancient land" of England, where she marries her sometime companion Harry Pleyel. Since the story takes place before the Revolution at the time of the French and Indian Wars, her restoration to the ancient land and law of the fathers might be read as a renunciation, an attempt to undo fictively

THE HERO WHO DEFENDED THE MOTHERS   WILL PROTECT THE DAUGHTERS

Engraved By T.Kelly

Washington's reception on the Bridge at Trenton in 1789 on his way to be Inaugurated 1st Pres. of the U.S.

Designed Expressly for the Columbian Magazine By J.L.Morton

Figure 12. *Washington's Reception on the Bridge at Trenton.* By J. L. Morton after Thomas Kelly, 1789. The Revolutionary Daughters are reconstituted under the "conquering Arms" of the "Father of the Country." Courtesy the Library of Congress, Prints and Photographs Division, LC-USZ62–1629.

the radical—and female—excess of the American Revolution even before it begins.

The story of the Revolutionary daughter's return to the order of the fathers is scripted visually in the famous painting of *Washington's Reception on the Bridge at Trenton* (1789), where "Virgins fair and Matrons grave" are reconstituted under the "conquering Arms" of the "Father of the Country" (Figure 12).[47] The father, family, master, and state that had been divested of authority by Tom Paine's *Common Sense* had to be reinvested with power under the terms of the new Constitution. In fact, some of the troubling female energies released by the war appear to be absorbed and contained by the iconography of Washington as the benevolent ruler and gentle mother/man that emerges in the 1790s and receives its fullest articulation in Parson Weems's *Life and Memorable Actions of George Washington* (1800).

Within the repressive atmosphere of post-Revolutionary America, women continued to write and aspire, but, like Phillis Wheatley in the

1770s, they learned to speak with a double tongue, manipulating the language of republicanism in a manner that challenged while it appeared to enforce traditional female bounds. In the frontispiece of the first volume of *The Lady's Magazine* (1792), "The Genius of the Ladies Magazine" presents a petition for the Rights of Woman to American Liberty; and passages from Mary Wollstonecraft's *Vindication of the Rights of Woman* (1792) are excerpted within it (Figure 13). But while the frontispiece and the contents of the magazine challenge the cultural trivialization of women by bearing Wollstonecraft's revolutionary appeal to women's rights and minds, the potentially radical nature of their female enterprise is masked by the more prescriptive rhetoric of the preface, in which the ladies avow their intent to "inspire the Female Mind with a love of religion, of patience, prudence, and fortitude—In short, whatever tends to form the ACCOMPLISHED WOMAN, the COMPLETE ECONOMIST, and the greatest of all treasures—a GOOD WIFE."[48]

Similarly, in Hannah Foster's *Coquette; or The History of Eliza Wharton* (1797), the "volatile" heroine begins in Revolutionary pursuit of liberty, independence, and pleasure outside marriage, home, and family: "It is *pleasure;* pleasure, my dear Lucy, on leaving my paternal roof!" Eliza writes to her friend Lucy Freeman at the outset of the novel.[49] But the story ends tragically with her death in childbirth, alone and repentant in a roadside inn. As the tale of a fallen woman, *The Coquette,* like Susanna Rowson's *Charlotte Temple* (1791) and other sentimental novels of the time, appears to endorse woman's proper role as virtuous republican wife and mother. And yet, as Cathy Davidson and other feminist critics have argued, the social and emotional *affect* of the sentimental plot was frequently at odds with its conservative moral message.[50] While *The Coquette* enacts on the overt level the strict limitations placed on women's lives in the early American republic, it also embeds a more radical critique of women's lack of rights, power, representation, and voice within the social, political, and legal structures of the time.

As Eliza's sexually inflected use of the Revolutionary language of liberty and the pursuit of happiness in *The Coquette* suggests, the Revolution gave women a politically volatile grammar that could be, in Bakhtin's terms, "hybridized" and accented in support of multiple and at times contradictory futures for women. In a poem written early in the Revolutionary years titled "Impromptu, on Reading an Essay on Education. By a Lady" (1773), one anonymous woman warned:

If they our free-born minds would not enslave,
No other Boon of Heaven they need crave;
But while our Minds in Fetters are enchain'd;

FRONTISPIECE.

Publish'd at Philad.ª *Dec.ʳ 1ˢᵗ 1792.*

Figure 13. "The Genius of the Ladies Magazine, accompanied by the Genius of Emulation, who carries in her hand a laurel crown, approaches Liberty, and Kneeling, presents her with a copy of the Rights of Woman." Frontispiece, *The Lady's Magazine and Repository of Entertaining Knowledge*, 1792. Courtesy the Library Company of Philadelphia.

On it rely your Hearts will e'er be pain'd.[51]

By the end of the war, in a pamphlet titled *Women Invited to War, or A Friendly Address to the Honourable Women of the United States. By A Daughter of America* (1787), the historian Hannah Adams would invoke the Revolutionary language of "life and liberty" to turn women away from the political struggle toward the fundamentally religious and moral struggle they must lead against the Devil.

Other women continued to accent the language of revolution in favor of expanded social and political rights for women. "I expect to see our young women forming a new era in female history," Murray wrote in *The Gleaner,* a series of essays originally published in the *Massachusetts Magazine* (1792–94), in which she deftly deployed the language of equality and natural rights in support of sexual equality, improvements in women's education, and an expanded role for women in the political and cultural creation of the new republic. Priscilla Mason also invoked the Revolutionary language of rights, freedom, and voice when, in 1793, she used the occasion of a public address to the Young Ladies Academy of Philadelphia to call for women's "right of being heard on more public occasions" and for "their equal participation" in traditionally male "honor and office." "The Church, the Bar, the Senate are shut against us. Who shut them?" she asked. "*Man;* despotic man, first made us incapable of duty, and then forbid us the exercise. Let us by suitable education, qualify ourselves for these high departments—they will open before us." In an equally revolutionary and more comic gesture, the anonymous author of "Lines, Written by a Lady, who was questioned respecting her inclination not to marry" (1794) resists the institution of marriage in language that challenges the sexually normative constitution of republican national space and the naturalness of a social order grounded in male and female pairs: "Round freedom's fair standard I've rallied and paid / A Vow of allegiance to die an old maid."[52]

Although historians have tended to emphasize changes in voting rights and marriage laws as a measure of what women gained or lost during the Revolution, this emphasis does not fully measure the revolutionary transformation in women's access to the public sphere, public voice, and non-state forms of political activity during the war years and after. Like the concepts of the republican wife and mother, the notion that there was an increasing separation between male and female spheres in the early national period and later is somewhat misleading. The public space of the American republic was in fact full of women's voices, women's writings, and writings about women in the post-Revolutionary years. Along with the political governance of the new nation, the culture endlessly debated the constitution of "the sex": her body, her sexuality, her skin color, her class, her difference, her blood. Far from being separate from the cultural and political formation of the American republic, women were crucial to the new definitions of self, society, polity, and world that emerged during the Revolutionary years and after.

"What do We Mean by the Revolution?" John Adams asked in a letter to Thomas Jefferson written in 1815. "The war? That was no part of the Revolution. It was only an Effect and Consequence of it. The Revolution was in the Minds of the People, and this was effected, from 1760 to 1775, in the course of fifteen Years before a drop of blood was drawn at Lexington."[53] While Adams recognized that the real American Revolution took place in the "Minds of the People," he saw the Revolution as something that ended with the break from England. This reading of the American Revolution appeared to be confirmed by the 1787 Constitution, which reined in the more radical and egalitarian possibilities of the Revolution by representing slaves in what Madison called "the mixed character of persons and of property" and women as nonexistent under the supreme law of the land.[54]

For Abigail Adams, Phillis Wheatley, and others who participated in the Revolutionary struggle, the American Revolution was multiple and ongoing rather than single and closed. "If we were to count our years by the revolutions we have witnessed, we might number them in the antediluvians," Abigail Adams wrote to Mercy Otis Warren in 1807. "So rapid have been the changes, that the mind, though fleet in progress, has been outstripped by them."[55] What the American Revolution gave to women finally was not real legal or political rights, but the language, the knowledge, the desire, and the forms to foment further rebellion. In fact, the politicization of the domestic and the domestication of the political that were fostered by the war gave women the political and ethical ground from which to launch their future assaults on the constituted orders of male authority in family, society, and state. Abigail Adams was right: John Adams was wrong. The Revolution was not over.

Chapter 4

The Poetics of Whiteness

Poe and the Racial Imaginary

I am not a spook like those who haunted Edgar Allan Poe.
—*Ralph Ellison*, Invisible Man

In his now classic study *Charles Baudelaire: A Lyric Poet in the Era of High Capitalism*, Walter Benjamin observes: "In *l'art pour l'art* the poet for the first time faces language the way the buyer faces the commodity on the open market. He has lost his familiarity with the process of its production to a particularly high degree."[1] In this chapter, I want to look at the concept of the aesthetic itself as a mixed and contingent production within rather than outside the domain of historical struggle. Focusing on the poetry and poetics of Edgar Allan Poe, I want to connect what Poe called the "poem written solely for the poem's sake" (*ER*, 76) and the emergence of aestheticism more generally with the social, political, and specifically racial struggles of his time and ours. I want to suggest the relation between the emergence of the aesthetic as a distinct mode of organizing and isolating the subjective experience of beauty in art and the simultaneous emergence among scientists and philosophers of notions of national and racial difference and purity grounded in an Enlightenment metaphysics of whiteness. Rather than begin with the theories of national and racial difference that frame Immanuel Kant's *Observations on the Feeling of the Beautiful and the Sublime* (1764), I would like to begin closer to home with Thomas Jefferson's *Notes on the State of Virginia* (1787).

Skin Aesthetics

Written while the American Revolution was still being fought, *Notes on the State of Virginia* was central to the early national formation of American culture and society: it is one of the first works to define an American sublime; it is the locus classicus of the myth of the virtuous American republic; it defends the American continent and its Native inhabitants against the degenerative theories of Count Buffon; it advances it "as a suspicion only" that blacks "are inferior to the whites in the endowments both of body and mind" (*NV,* 143); it argues that to preserve the "dignity and beauty" of "human nature," blacks must be colonized elsewhere, "beyond the reach of mixture" (*NV,* 143); and, under the pressure of the contradiction between the Revolutionary rhetoric of American liberty and the historical reality of black enslavement, it is spooked, over and over again, by the fear of black insurrection and the specter of the "extirpation" of the white "masters" (*NV,* 163).

Jefferson's racial hierarchies and his social fears translate into and shape his judgment of beauty and art. His phobia about the black body, "that eternal monotony, which reigns in the countenances, that immoveable veil of black which covers all the emotions of the other race," leads him to assert skin color, the difference of white from black, as "the foundation of a greater or less share of beauty in the two races." Even blacks prefer the "superior beauty" of whites "as uniformly" as "the Oran-ootan" prefers "black women over those of his own species" (*NV,* 138). This erotically charged skin aesthetics becomes the basis for a series of artistic judgments in which black painting, sculpture, music, and writing are excluded, along with the passions and the body, from the realm of true beauty and true art.

In Jefferson's skin aesthetics beauty and the imagination are, like his ideal American republic, by definition white. And yet, whiteness needs blackness to establish its own cultural precedence. To solicit our admiration for white poetry and white art, Jefferson must simultaneously cast out from the realm of the aesthetic a black body capable of no more than animal creation. "Among the blacks is misery enough," he writes, "but no poetry. Love is the peculiar oestrum of the poet. Their love is ardent, but it kindles the senses only, not the imagination. Religion indeed has produced a Phyllis Whately [*sic*]; but it could not produce a poet" (*NV,* 140). Here, as in Kant's *Observations on the Feeling of the Beautiful and the Sublime* and other eighteenth-century writings on aestheticism, the social subordination of blacks to whites develops in tandem with the cultural valorization of aesthetic beauty. Jefferson's aesthetic hierarchies are driven by the social logic of slavery: If "Phyllis Whately" was in fact Phillis Wheatley the Revolutionary poet, if her poetry was worthy of comparison with the poetry of Alexander Pope, if blacks were as capable of imaginative creation as whites, then the political justification of black enslavement and the "enlightened" social ground of the white

American republic would begin to erode, as it subsequently did, under the pressure of its own contradictions.

What is racially marked in Jeffersonian aesthetics becomes less so in the nineteenth century. Gesturing toward "a wild weird clime that lieth, sublime, / Out of SPACE—out of TIME," the poetic theory and practice of Edgar Allan Poe would appear to be completely removed from the devastating cruelty of black enslavement and the sordid reality of whips, rape, blood, violence, and the torture of black bodies. But Poe was raised in the South and spent his formative years there. He was brought up in a slaveholding family in Richmond: "You suffer me to be subjected to the whims & caprice, not only of your white family, but the complete authority of the blacks," Poe complained to his foster father John Allan in 1827.[2] In at least one instance, Poe appears to have sold a slave, "a negro man named Edwin aged twenty one years . . . to serve until he shall arrive at the age of thirty years no longer."[3] As in Jefferson's writings, the presence and labor of blacks in the social landscape, a simultaneous identification with and revulsion against the figure of the slave, the specter of slave insurrection, fear of a reversal of the master-slave relation, and an apocalyptic vision of the domination of blacks appear to energize and propel Poe's aestheticization of whiteness, his attempt to create forms of white beauty, white art, white writing, and white culture against and beyond time, history, the body, the black, the other.

Despite, or perhaps because of, Poe's Southern roots, the mainstream of American criticism has tended to treat him as an exotic alien, a strange and otherworldly purveyor of pure poetry, fractured psyches, and un-American gloom. To Vernon Parrington, in *Main Currents in American Thought* (1927), Poe was an "aesthete and a craftsman" who "lies quite outside the main current of American thought."[4] The primarily linguistic emphasis of modernist and postmodernist critics, from T. S. Eliot and Paul Valéry to John Irwin and Jacques Lacan, has also tended to locate Poe's writings outside time and history. This ahistorical and un-American face of Edgar Allan Poe has been vigorously challenged in recent years, most notably by Toni Morrison's extended meditation on what she calls in *Playing in the Dark* "a real or fabricated Africanist presence" in white American writing. Commenting on the "shrouded human figure" whose skin "was of the perfect whiteness of snow" at the end of Poe's *Narrative of Arthur Gordon Pym* (1838), Morrison asserts uncategorically: "No early American writer is more important to the concept of American Africanism than Poe."[5]

But while Morrison and others have offered a useful corrective to the erasure of race in past approaches to Poe, there is a tendency among recent critics to reduce Poe to his proslavery sentiments and American literature to American Africanism. "It was this Africanism," writes Morrison, "deployed as rawness and savagery, that provided the staging ground and arena for the elaboration of the quintessential American identity."[6] This exclusive focus on the shaping presence of "American Africanism" in the constitution of American national identity seems much too simple. For one thing, there were other races, cultures, and nationalities that vied for geopolitical space and presence in writing and naming America. Moreover, blackness and Africanism cannot be separated from a whole complex of personal and cultural phobias and fetishes around the body, nature, women, race, blood, the Orient, and the democratic masses that haunt and spook the American imaginary. To reverse the hierarchical relation of white to black by claiming black precedence risks reinstating the exclusions of the white literary tradition; it also isolates blackness and Africanism from the complicated network of religious, cultural, historical, economic, and ultimately transnational relations in which it was involved. Morrison's focus on the shaping presence of Africanism in creating a distinctively American literature keeps both "American" and "African American" neatly contained within a nationalist and exceptionalist frame and thus tends to erase the cross-currents of international exchange, economic as well as cultural, imperial as well as textual, in which the figure of Edgar Allan Poe and the writing of the United States have played a commanding role.

While there has been renewed interest in the historical and racial contexts of Poe's work, critics have also tended to focus almost exclusively on Poe's prose rather than his poetry. Thus, for example, in his important work on Poe and the masses, Terry Whalen turns to Poe's tales as a "privileged" site of his social and economic analysis.[7] Given the constitutive role that Poe's notions of supernal Beauty, art for art's sake, pure poetry, and poetic craft have played, both nationally and internationally, in the emergence of nineteenth-century aestheticism, New Critical formalism, postmodern texuality, and the ongoing struggle to claim or reclaim the social being of language and literature, it is important that we not repeat Poe's own ahistorical gestures in seeking to grant poetry a special status outside history and beyond the reach of cultural analysis.

Tamerlane, the Orient, and American Indian Policy

The ways in which Poe's work intersects with a complex network of international relations is particularly evident in his first two volumes of poems, *Tamerlane and Other Poems* (1827) and *Al Aaraaf, Tamerlane, and Minor Poems* (1829). In these volumes the shaping presence is not Africanism but Orientalism—particularly the geopolitical space, race, and religious beliefs of the Near East and Islam. Published during the years when Andrew Jackson came to power bearing a public rhetoric (if not reality) of democracy and the common man and a nationalist vision of westward expansion and progress, Poe's early volumes of poetry, which were printed and circulated in limited editions, suggest his aristocratic refusal, as gentleman and poet, to write for the masses or the market. Both volumes assert the integrity of private, subjective, and ultimately poetic desire against the debased imperatives of democracy and the marketplace. In the preface to *Tamerlane and Other Poems,* Poe writes that in his title-poem "he has endeavoured to expose the folly of even *risking* the best feelings of the heart at the shrine of Ambition."[8] Traditionally, "Tamerlane," like much of Poe's poetry, has been interpreted as personal lyric inscription: "Poe took little from historic and dramatic sources," writes Thomas Mabbott. "[H]is poem is largely a personal allegory, based on his unhappy love for his Richmond sweetheart, Sarah Elmira Royster" (*CW,* 1:24). But while Poe appropriates the fourteenth-century Mohammedan ruler for the expression of his own "agony of desire" as both lover and poet, "Tamerlane" cannot be separated from the broader politics, at once national and global, of imperial conquest.

Like "Al Aaraaf" and other Poe poems and tales, "Tamerlane" participates in and is shaped by the Orientalism of Byron's *Giaour,* Thomas Moore's *Lala Rookh,* and Chateaubriand's *Itinéraire de Paris à Jérusalem, et de Jérusalem à Paris,* all of which were themselves engaged in what Edward Said calls the "Orientalist" struggle of Britain and France to extend their empires and dominion to the Near and Far East in the nineteenth century.[9] Although the United States had not yet emerged as a power in the Near East, it is simply not true to say, as Said does, that the United States did not emerge as a major power in the struggle for empire until after World War II. From the time of the First Continental Congress in the Revolutionary period to the Monroe Doctrine, the Indian removal policy, the Mexican War, and the politics of manifest destiny in the nineteenth century, the United States struggled to extend its territories and its empire in North and South America, the Caribbean, and the Pacific.[10] Moreover, the imaginary figures of the Islamic Orient, the Arabs, and the Ottomans have been constitutive of American national and republican self-definition from the period of the founding to the present.

Like James Fenimore Cooper's *Last of the Mohicans* (1826), which prophesies the doom of the Indian at the same time that it celebrates the eventual triumph of American empire over the British, the French, and the Spanish in North America, Poe's *Tamerlane* offers an illuminating cultural instance of the ways even the most seemingly *otherworldly* American writing participated in the broader politics of imperial struggle not only in the nineteenth century but in ways that continue to shape American global relations today. Written at a time when Poe had enlisted in the U.S. Army, "Tamerlane" is on the most fundamental level a poem about the lust for empire. "I was ambitious," Tamerlane asserts: "A cottager, I mark'd a throne / Of half the world as all my own" (*CW*, 1:57). In a note to the 1827 version of the poem, Poe further observes: "The conquests of Tamerlane far exceeded those of Zinghis Khan. He boasted to have two thirds of the world at his command" (*CW*, 1:37). Although the narrative sets Tamerlane's desire for woman, love, and beauty against his "unearthly pride" and ambition for fame, conquest, and "the crush / Of empires" (*CW*, 1:55) in a manner that suggests Poe's own historical resistance to the Jacksonian rhetoric of Western conquest and imperial advance, as in other writings by Poe, the poem also participates in the structures of knowledge, the Orientalist relation of West to East, white to other, that would frame Jackson's Indian removal policy in the 1830s and, more broadly, that had framed and would continue to frame the Western strife for empire in the Middle East, Asia, Africa, and elsewhere.[11]

As a signifier of the Orient, Tamerlane is a split figure, an embodiment at once of white desire and white fear. Tamerlane is, on the one hand, a "kingly" figure whose love for a woman is represented as a version of white pastoral, a utopian scene of purity, beauty, and light. Within this "holy grove," Tamerlane remembers:

I wandered of the idol, Love,
Who daily scents his snowy wings
With incense of burnt offerings
From the most unpolluted things,
Whose pleasant bowers are yet so riven
Above with trellic'd rays from Heaven
No mote may shun—no tiniest fly—
The light'ning of his eagle eye— (*CW*, 1: 61)

On the other hand, as an embodiment of the passionate excess of the desert—"where the grand— / The wild—the terrible conspire / With their own breath to fan his fire" (*CW*, 1: 58)—Tamerlane is also ruled by Eblis, the Mohammedan prince of evil spirits and darkness, who creeps into the "unpolluted" bower of love in the form of Ambition:

I do believe that Eblis hath
A snare in every human path—
. . . .
[Else how] was it that Ambition crept,
   Unseen, amid the revels there,
Till growing bold, he laughed and leapt
   In the tangles of Love's very hair? (*CW*, 1:60–61)

Taken over by Ambition, Tamerlane becomes, in this concluding passage of the poem, the Oriental as fiery figure of passion and excess who pollutes and destroys the "holy grove" of "snowy" whiteness signified by woman, beauty, and love. As a topos of pure woman, pure beauty, and pure love, Poe's "holy grove" suggests the ways his aestheticization of whiteness becomes bound up with a deep cultural fear of mixture with and pollution by the racial other. In the concluding image of Eblis tangled in the "very hair" of pure love, Orientalism intersects with Africanism and a whole complex of white cultural fears about mixture with and violation by the dark other, whether black, red, or Mohammedan.

In Poe's early poems, the Orientalist story of "Tamerlane" is dispersed and refigured in a symbolic dialectics of East versus West. In "Sonnet—To Science," which serves as an introduction to "Al Aaraaf" in *Al Aaraaf, Tamerlane, and Minor Poems,* the Orient becomes the emblem of an exotic otherworld of the imagination that is opposed to the Western world of time, change, and history, signified by the "peering eyes" and "dull realities"of reason and science. As in "Romance," in which the "idle" and dreamy world of romance, "lyre and rhyme," signified by the "painted paroquet," is set against the "eternal Condor years" and "tumult" of the present, in "Sonnet—To Science" the poet rejects Western history and progress in favor of a timeless and Orientalized world of mythological creatures and "jewelled skies" where he can pursue "[t]he summer dream beneath the tamarind tree" (*CW,* 1:91).

In "Al Aaraaf," the Orient serves as both figure and locus of poetry itself. Poe explains his use of the title "Al Aaraaf," which is drawn from the Koran, the sacred text of Islam: "With the Arabians there is a medium between Heaven and Hell, where men suffer no punishment, but yet do not attain that tranquil and even happiness which they suppose to be characteristic of heavenly enjoyment" (*CW,* 1:111–12). According to George Sale, the English translator of the Koran, the term *al Araf* derives from "the verb, *arafa,* which means to *distinguish* between things, or to *part* them."[12] Poe was not so much interested in the Koran or the religious beliefs of the Arabs as he was in "the Arabians" as figures of romantic *apartness* and otherworldliness. Located in a distant star, beyond the reach of earthly "dross" and the passions of the body, Al Aaraaf represents the otherworldly space of beauty and pure poetry, a place of purely aesthetic experience where flowers speak "in odors" and language is closer to "silence" than to our "world of words" (*CW,* 1:102, 104). As Poe writes of the spirit world of "Al Aaraaf" in the opening of the poem:

O! nothing earthly save the ray
(Thrown back from flowers) of Beauty's eye,
. . . .
O! nothing earthly save the thrill

Of melody in woodland rill—
. . . .
Oh, nothing of the dross of ours—
Yet all the beauty—all the flowers
That list our Love, and deck our bowers—
Adorn yon, world afar, afar—
The wandering star. (*CW*, 1:99–100)

Within the Orientalist frame of "Al Aaraaf," Poe conducts what is, in effect, his most radical experiment in pure aestheticism, his attempt to invent a language of pure musicality, rhythm, spirit, and sound. He also anticipates in figurative and poetic form the "Idea of Beauty" and the idea of poetry as a realm of purely aesthetic experience apart from both bodily passion and intellectual knowledge that he would begin to articulate in his prose introduction to *Poems by Edgar A. Poe* (1831). In "Al Aaraaf" as in his 1831 poem "Israfel," it is finally because Poe's "Arabians" lack bodies and historical being that they can be consigned to the realm of pure aestheticism.

A few months earlier, in an address to Congress on 6 December 1830, Jackson announced the near completion of the Indian removal policy, which was initiated by Jefferson, supported by James Monroe and John Adams, and passed by Congress in 1830:

It gives me pleasure to announce to Congress that the benevolent policy of the Government . . . in relation to *the removal of the Indians beyond the white settlements* is approaching to a happy consummation. . . . To follow to the tomb the last of his race and to tread on the graves of extinct nations excites melancholy reflections. But true philanthropy reconciles the mind to these vicissitudes as it does to *the extinction of one generation to make room for another*. . . . What good man would prefer a country covered with forest and ranged by a few thousand savages to our extensive Republic, studded with cities, towns, and prosperous farms?[13]

For all Poe's efforts to locate poetry and "the Arabians" in a world elsewhere, they are part of a social formation that includes U.S. Indian policy, the literary and pictorial convention of the dying Indian from Cooper's *Last of the Mohicans* to Tompkins H. Matteson's painting *The Last of the Race* (1847), and a more global imperial movement that requires that the wandering tribes of the East die off in order to, as Jackson says, "make room for" the advance of "white" civilization. Whether it is a site of pure love, pure passion, or pure poetry, the Orient has no contemporary reality in Poe's early poems: it is not so much a place as it is a space for the imaginative figuration of white fear and white desire. As in Cooper's *Last of the Mohicans* and Jackson's "melancholy" reflection on the Indian as "the last of his race," Poe's Orientals are figures of the past and myth with no historical presence or agency in the ongoing struggles of the present and the future.

Poe's Spooks

"I am not a spook like those who haunted Edgar Allan Poe," says the protagonist in the opening of Ralph Ellison's *Invisible Man*. Drawing on Ellison's pun on the double meaning of "spook" as the ghostly specters that haunt Poe's writings and the vernacular meaning of spook as a black person, in this section I want to examine the ways Orientalism intersects with Africanism and a whole series of social subordinations—of black to white, female to male, nature to spirit, body to mind, democratic mob to genteel aristocrat—in the formation of Poe's poetics of whiteness. More specifically, I want to argue that Poe's poetics of whiteness is, in effect, shaped and spooked by the historical presence of enslaved and laboring black bodies in the social landscape of America. Whereas Poe's Arabs existed as distant and bodiless figures of the past and myth, blacks had an immediate corporeal presence not only in the plantation economy of the South but also in the periodic acts of violent resistance, the ongoing fear of slave insurrection, and the state of public and private crisis, in the North as well as in the South, provoked by the institution of slavery in America.[14] Like Poe's *Mob*, "a giant in stature—insolent, rapacious, filthy" and "a foreigner, by the by" ("Mellonta Tauta," *CW*, 3:1300), blacks were a part of the democratic and specifically racial history against which his poetics of whiteness was formed.[15]

Poems by Edgar A. Poe, which was sold by subscription to West Point cadets and dedicated "To the U.S. Corps of Cadets," is introduced by a "Letter to Mr. —— ——" in which Poe seeks for the first time in prose to articulate his theory of poetry as a realm of purely imaginative activity: "A poem," he asserts, "is opposed to a work of science by having, for its *immediate* object, pleasure, not truth; to romance, by having for its object an *indefinite* instead of a *definite* pleasure, being a poem only insofar as this object is attained" (*ER*, 11). Written at a time when Poe was being disinherited from his expectations as a Southern gentleman by his foster father, John Allan, Poe's "Letter," which is dated "West Point, 1831," seeks to defend poetry and the poet as part of a cultural elite—a kind of aristocracy of the mind—against both the masses and his own diminished status as the son of actors. Against "the world's good opinion," as it is represented by the masses and the market, Poe sets what he calls "the Andes of the mind," a hierarchy of critical judgment and good taste that rises "ascendingly" from the fools on the bottom to "a few gifted individuals" and "the master spirit," the poet, who stands at the top (*ER*, 5).

The dialectical relation between the "master spirit" of the poet and the body of the dark other in Poe's poetics is suggested by the oppositional structure of his "Letter." As in Poe's poetic dreamlands, poetry is defined against all that is corporeal, animal, dark, earthly: "Think of all that is airy and fairy-like," Poe writes, "and then of all that is hideous and unwieldy; think of his huge bulk, the Elephant! and then—and then think of the Tempest—the Midsummer Night's Dream—Prospero—Oberon—and Titania!" (*ER*, 11). In Poe's Shakespearean definition of the purely imaginative space of poetry, the aesthetic becomes a line that marks the boundary between light and dark, Prospero and Caliban, civilization and its others. And yet, in the very process of marking this boundary, Poe simultaneously produces the fantasies of mixture and seepage, doubling and impurity, penetration and crossing which are the obsessive subject of his work.

While *Poems* is still framed by an Orientalist structure, with "Romance" at the beginning, "Al Aaraaf" and "Tamerlane" at the end, and a new poem, "Israfel," added, in this volume Poe begins to accentuate three motifs that would become increasingly central to his poetry and poetics: the idealized figure of woman as emblem of pure beauty, pure love, and pure poetry in "To Helen"; fantasies of female violation by figures of darkness and dissolution in "Irenë" (later "The Sleeper") and "A Paean" (later "Lenore"); and the specter of dark apocalypse in "The Doomed City" (later "The City of Sin" and "The City in the Sea"). I want to suggest that the increasing emphasis on these racially inflected motifs in Poe's 1831 *Poems*—which was published the same year that William Lloyd Garrison began publishing *The Liberator,* a weekly newspaper dedicated to the immediate abolition of slavery and universal enfranchisement of blacks—represents, at least in part, a response to the growing state of crisis provoked by the "hideous" presence of enslaved and potentially unruly black bodies within the virtuous and putatively white body of the American republic. During this "new post-1830 era in pro-slavery ideology," writes Drew Gilpin Faust, "the slavery controversy not only became a matter of survival for the southern way of life; it served for Americans generally as a means of reassessing the profoundest assumptions on which their world was built."[16]

In "To Helen," Poe presents the ideal woman who is at the center of his aesthetics of whiteness. Associated with artifice, stasis, light, soul, distance, and "statue-like" perfection, Helen is not a flesh-and-blood woman but a dead woman—light, bright, white, and dead:

Helen, thy beauty is to me
  Like those Nicéan barks of yore,
That gently, o'er a perfumed sea,
  The weary, way-worn, wanderer bore
  To his own native shore.

On desperate seas long wont to roam,
  Thy hyacinth hair, thy classic face,

Thy Naiad airs have brought me home
  To the glory that was Greece,
  And the grandeur that was Rome.

Lo! in yon brilliant window-niche
  How statue-like I see thee stand,
The agate lamp within thy hand!
  Ah, Psyche, from the regions which
  Are Holy-Land! (*CW,* 1:165–66)

With its varied metrics, intricate patterns of rhyme and alliteration, and
its exquisite use of language, phrase, and image, "To Helen" is, in the
words of Mabbott, "often regarded as the finest of Poe's lyrics" (*CW,*
1:163). But what gets written out of critical assessments of the poem is
that Helen, as a metonymic figure of ideal woman, beauty, and art, is
also a representative of the Western ideal of whiteness signified by the
classical culture of Greece and Rome. This meaning is more evident in
the 1831 version of the poem, in which the poet is brought home

To the beauty of *fair* Greece
And the grandeur of old Rome. (*CW,* 1:166; emphasis added)

Although critics continue to speculate about which woman inspired
Poe's poem, Helen lacks any particular historical embodiment. With her
"hyacinth hair," "classic face," and "Naiad airs," she is a representative
of all women as white woman. As a perfect emblem of the Western ideal
of white beauty, white value, and white art, Helen is the prototype of
the impossibly pure, fair-haired, and blue-eyed maidens who begin to
proliferate in Poe's poems and tales of the 1830s and 1840s.

In a specifically American context, "To Helen" marks an increasing
fetishization of whiteness and purity—of woman, of beauty, of culture,
of skin color, of blood—that comes in response to the growing historical
fear of mixture, violation, and encroaching darkness. For Poe, as for the
proslavery apologists, the ideal of white womanhood—of what W. J. Cash
has called "the South's Palladium . . . Athena gleaming whitely in the
clouds"—breeds fantasies of defilement, mixture, and reversal that
undermine the distinctions of sex, race, and class he seeks to enforce.[17]
What is socially forbidden and excluded returns as an obsessive set of
imaginative representations—the ghosts, spooks, and black phantasms
that haunt Poe's work.

Whereas Helen is located in a "Holy-Land" beyond the reach of
bodily mixture and mortality, in "The Sleeper" (originally "Irenë"), the
"lady bright," as a figure of "All beauty," is exposed to the ghostly
hauntings of darkness and night:

Oh, lady bright! can it be right—
This window open to the night?
The wanton airs, from the tree-top,
Laughingly through the lattice drop—
The bodiless airs, a wizard rout,
Flit through thy chamber in and out,
And wave the curtain canopy
So fitfully—so fearfully—
Above the closed and fringéd lid
'Neath which thy slumb'ring soul lies hid,
That o'er the floor and down the wall,
Like ghosts the shadows rise and fall!
Oh, lady dear, hast thou no fear? (*CW,* 1:187)

Like the threat of violation by worms ("Soft may the worms about her creep!") and the "Triumphant" figure of the "black /And wingéd pannels" of the family vault "fluttering back" to engulf the female corpse at the end of the poem (*CW,* 1:188), the "wanton airs" and "wizard rout" that "Flit through thy chamber in and out" are associated with both bodily dissolution and a vaguely implied fear of sexual or social takeover by ghostly "shadows" of blackness and night. Along with the terrorization of women and the specter of bodily dissolution, the fear of mixture, penetration, violation, and domination by harrowing figures of blackness and death is at the very sources of the mechanics of horror in Poe's work and, not surprisingly, at the symbolic center of the American cultural imaginary in the mid-nineteenth century.[18]

In "Lenore" (originally "A Paean"), the poet needs to kill off the "fair and debonair" heroine with "her yellow hair" in order to save woman, beauty, and the ideal of whiteness from the "fiends" of "damnéd Earth." The aristocratic lover, Guy de Vere, sings the death of his young bride as a "flight" away from earth into a "golden" world of "high estate," without history, without bodies, without blacks:

"Avaunt!—avaunt! to friends from fiends the indignant ghost is riven—
From Hell unto a high estate within the utmost Heaven—
From moan and groan to a golden throne beside the King of Heaven:—
Let *no* bell toll, then, lest her soul, amid its hallowed mirth
Should catch the note as it doth float up from the damnéd Earth!" (*CW,* 1:337)

Poe's fantasy of a spirit world beyond the reach of color or mixture is underscored in the 1831 version of the poem in which the heroine's soul is lifted to the "untainted mirth" of angels in heaven. More explicitly than other dead-woman poems, "Lenore" suggests the relation between aesthetics and social desire in Poe's work: between the poet's desire for a pure white space of beauty and pleasure, signified by the death of woman, and the aristocratic desire for an alternative social order, signified by the "high estate" and "untainted mirth" of "utmost Heaven."

Like other Southern writers, Poe associated the ideal of fair woman-hood with the social ideals—and health—of Southern culture. "The glory of the Ancient Dominion is in a fainting—is in a dying condition," he wrote in 1835, in a comment that suggests the relation between the dying women of his poems and the failing plantation economy of the South. Virginia had become "a type for 'the things that' *have been*."[19] Although critics have tended to read Poe's lyrics as forms of merely personal or perverse psychology, the tone of mournfulness in his poetry and its thematics of disintegration might also be read as a melancholic response to the loss of a whole way of Southern life, grounded in what Poe called "the laws of *gradation*," under the pressure of democratic and specifically Northern industrial transformation. This elegiac tone is particularly evident in "The Colloquy of Monos and Una" (1841), in which the poets as "master-minds" set themselves against Enlightenment reason, science, knowledge, and "the progress of civilization": "these men, the poets, pondered piningly, yet not unwisely upon the ancient days . . . holy, august, and blissful days, when blue rivers ran undammed, between hills unhewn, into far forest solitudes, primaeval, odorous, and unexplored. . . . Meantime *huge smoking cities arose, innumerable.* Green leaves shrank before the hot breath of furnaces. *The fair face of Nature was deformed as with the ravages of some loathsome disease*" (*CW*, 2:609–10; emphasis added). Whereas in the poem "The Valley of Unrest" (originally "The Valley Nis") the poet's mournfulness about "the ancient days" is associated more generally with an "unquiet" landscape of "restlessness" and "perennial tears"—"Nothing there is motionless" (*CW*, 1:195–96)—in "The City in the Sea" (originally "The Doomed City"), as in "The Colloquy of Monos and Una," this melancholia is associated more specifically with the city, "the ravages" of the "fair face of Nature," and a hellish vision of modern apocalypse.

Drawn originally from a passage in an early version of "Al Aaraaf" describing the fallen city of Gomorrah, the landscape of death in "The City in the Sea" is represented in Orientalist images of "shrines and palaces and towers" and "Babylon-like walls":

Lo! Death has reared himself a throne
In a strange city lying alone
Far down within the dim West,
Where the good and the bad and the worst and the best
Have gone to their eternal rest.
There shrines and palaces and towers
(Time-eaten towers that tremble not!)
Resemble nothing that is ours.

Around, by lifting winds forgot,
Resignedly beneath the sky
The melancholy waters lie. (*CW*, 1:201)

Critics have usually identified the city with the legendary ruined cities of
the Dead Sea, but Poe's reference to "a strange city" in "the dim West"
also suggests the spiritual destiny of America as "a city upon a hill" and
Enlightenment notions of the advance of civilization westward, which
Poe associated with the rise of industry, the city, republican government,
"omni-prevalent Democracy," and the emancipation of slaves (*CW*,
2:610). Although the city lacks specific historical reference, here, as in
"The Masque of the Red Death" and other Poe writings, the association
of figures of blackness ("the long night-time of that town") with the
vision of apocalyptic doom that closes the poem ("Down, down, that
town shall settle hence. / Hell, rising from a thousand thrones") registers a widespread—and still prevalent—cultural fear of the fall of the
West that will come as a result of some sort of catastrophic uprising of
the dark other, associated with blackness, the satanic, the Orient, the
city, blood, and death.[20] In 1845, Poe underscored the prophetic dimension of his poem when he published it under the title "A City in the Sea:
A Prophecy." Unlike the apocalyptic warnings that proliferated in other
mid-century works, including most notably "the wrath of Almighty God"
that closes Harriet Beecher Stowe's *Uncle Tom's Cabin* in 1852, Poe's
prophecy is grounded not in fear of punishment *for* the contradiction of
slavery in the American republic but fear that the logic of the American
republic—founded on "the queerest idea conceivable . . . that all men
are born free and equal" ("Mellonta Tauta," *CW*, 3:1299)—will lead to
the emancipation of slaves or, even worse, as Jefferson had predicted, to
the extirpation of the white masters.

Nat Turner, Slave Insurrection, and Pure Poetry

Only a few months after Poe published "The Doomed City" in his 1831
Poems, his fear of some sort of apocalyptic uprising of blacks assumed
palpable bodily form when in August 1831 Nat Turner led the bloodiest
slave insurrection in U.S. history in Southampton County, Virginia.
"Whilst not one note of preparation was heard to warn the devoted
inhabitants of woe and death," wrote Thomas R. Gray of Turner's revolt,
"a gloomy fanatic was revolving in the recesses of his own dark, bewil-
dered, and overwrought mind, schemes of indiscriminate massacre to
the whites—schemes too fearfully executed as far as his fiendish band
proceeded in their desolating march."[21] The insurrection, which
resulted in the death of sixty whites, the torture and execution of scores

of innocent blacks, and widespread hysteria about the possibility of further uprisings, led to a tightening of slave laws and an increasingly vigorous defense of the institution and culture of slavery throughout the South. Emancipation would lead to the South's "relapse into darkness, thick and full of horrors," wrote the proslavery apologist Thomas Dew in his influential defense of the institution of slavery following the debates about the future of slavery in the Virginia legislature in 1831–1832.[22]

It was into this heightened atmosphere of panic about the possibility of bloody slave insurrection and hysteria about the security and survival of the institutions and culture of the Old South that Poe entered when he returned to Richmond, where he would serve as editor of the *Southern Literary Messenger* between 1835 and 1837.[23] In a much-disputed review of two proslavery books, *Slavery in the United States* by James Kirke Paulding and *The South Vindicated from the Treason and Fanaticism of the Northern Abolitionists* by William Drayton, which appeared in the *Southern Literary Messenger* under Poe's editorship in April 1836, the reviewer asserts the relation between the logic of progressive history, as signified by the French Revolution and the rights of man, and the specter of black emancipation, violent or otherwise.[24] Commenting on the irreligious fanaticism of the French Revolution, he warns: "[I]t should be remembered now, that in that war against property, the first object of attack was property in slaves; that in that war on behalf of the alleged right of man to be discharged from all control of law, the first triumph achieved was in the emancipation of slaves." Alluding to the violent slave insurrection in San Domingo (Haiti), where blacks rose up, killed their white masters, and, in the name of liberty and individual rights, set up an independent black republic in 1804, the reviewer calls attention to the "awful" significance of the San Domingo revolution for the South: "The recent events in the West Indies, and the parallel movement here, give awful importance to these thoughts in our minds." The South is haunted by "despair," "apprehensions," foreboding "superstitions," and "vague and undefined fears" in response to "recent events," which appear to include the revolt of slaves in San Domingo, the "triumph" of Haiti against the French empire in 1804, Nat Turner's insurrection in 1831, the emancipation of slaves in the British West Indies in 1834, the rise of the abolition movement in the 1830s in the United States, and the attack on "Domestic Slavery," which is "the basis of all our institutions" (*SLM*, 269). Whether this review was written by Poe, as some believe, or by his friend Beverly Tucker, as a defense of "all our institutions" and "all our rights" written from the collective point of view of the South—and presumably reflecting the views of the *Southern Literary Messenger* and its editor—the review shares Poe's own grim vision of democratic history as a triumph of blacks, blood, and dark apocalypse.

Haunted by similarly "vague and undefined fears" in response to "recent events in the West Indies, and the parallel movement here," Poe's poetry and tales of the 1830s and 1840s continue to be spooked by the terrifying logic of progressive history, the fear of black emancipation, the specter of blood violence, the ongoing attack on the institution of slavery, an apocalyptic vision of the triumph of "blackness," and a flight away from history into fantasies of whiteness and purity: pure white woman, pure white beauty, pure white art, pure white poetics. *The Narrative of Arthur Gordon Pym* (1838) makes explicit the phobia about the dark other, the fear of black insurrection, and the flight into an otherworldly space of pure whiteness that remain just beneath the surface in several of Poe's poems. Influenced by the specter of blood violence in both San Domingo and the American South, the "massacre" of whites by the natives of the all-black island of Tsalal leads Pym to assert: "In truth, from everything I could see of these wretches, they appeared to be the most wicked, hypocritical, vindictive, blood thirsty, and altogether fiendish race of men on the face of the globe."[25] Referred to interchangeably as savages, barbarians, desperadoes, and "warriors of the black skin" (*IV*, 186), the natives of Tsalal suggest the ways anti-black feeling intersects with a more generalized fear of the racial other—Indian, Mexican, African, or other—in the American cultural imaginary.[26] Here as elsewhere in Poe's poems and tales, the narrative underscores the ways the terror of what Pym calls "the blackness of darkness" (*IV*, 175) drives the imaginative leap toward an other world of pure whiteness: Faced with the prospect of "brute rage," "inevitable butchery," and "overwhelming destruction" in the concluding passages of the story, the protagonists rush into the milky white embrace of a "shrouded human figure": "And the hue of the skin of the figure was of the perfect whiteness of the snow" (*IV*, 206). But while the ending appears to promise entrance into a utopian world of "perfect whiteness," as the multiple and conflicted readings of *Pym's* conclusion suggest, the precise nature of this "shrouded human figure" is at best ambiguous: Is it biblical apocalypse or metaphysical sign, utopian dream or perfect terror, pure race or pure hoax? It might be the "White Goddess," or mother, but it might also be the ghost of the all-black Nu-Nu returned from the dead.[27]

As in *The Narrative of Arthur Gordon Pym*, Poe's seemingly stable taxonomies of black and white would continue to be spooked by fantasies of mixture, seepage, revenge, and reversal. In "The Haunted Palace," which was initially published in April 1839 and incorporated a few months later into Poe's story "The Fall of the House of Usher," the poet's dream of "perfect whiteness" is corroded by the "encrimsoned" spectacle of invasion and dark apocalypse that closes the poem. Associated with "the monarch Thought's dominion," the palace is, in its unsullied form, an emblem of white mind: it is fair, yellow, golden, pallid, luminous, wise, harmonious, beautiful, and, in the original version of the poem, "Snow-white" (*CW*, 1:315, 317). The poem enacts the compulsive dream-turned-bad of mid-nineteenth-century American fantasy—the fall of white mind to the dark and "hideous throng":

But evil things, in robes of sorrow,
　　Assailed the monarch's high estate.
· · · · · · · · · · · · · · · · · ·
And travellers, now, within that valley,
　　Through the encrimsoned windows see
Vast forms that move fantastically
　　To a discordant melody,
While, like a ghastly rapid river,
　　Through the pale door
A hideous throng rush out forever
　　And laugh—but smile no more. (*CW*, 1:316–17)

By the palace, Poe wrote Rufus Griswold in 1841, he meant "to imply a mind haunted by phantoms—a disordered brain" (*LP*, 2:161). Whether "The Haunted Palace" is an allegory of the individual mind or the mind of the world, the "phantoms" that haunt it conjoin a terror of the dark other and the democratic mob with the specter of insurrection and blood violence and a more generalized fear of madness, dissolution, and the fall of Western civilization. In fact, the connection between Poe's "Haunted Palace" and the threat posed by the "hideous throng" of Negroes and lower classes in the American city was made explicitly by one of Poe's contemporaries, Henry B. Hirst, who parodied Poe in "The Ruined Tavern," a poem about a brawl in a Philadelphia tavern frequented by "tough Negroes," which includes the lines: "Never negro shook a shinbone / In a dance-house half so fair."[28]

Against this apocalyptic vision of the blackness and blood of progressive history—a vision that gets powerfully enacted in the story of the collapse of "the last of the ancient race of the Ushers" into "a black and lurid tarn" in "The Fall of the House of Usher" (*CW*, 2:404, 398)—Poe seeks to define poetry as a separate and purer realm, grounded in an ethos of social subordination, of men over women, imagination over body, and white over black. The "sentiment of Poesy" is, he wrote in an 1836 review, linked with the sentiment of reverence and the hierarchical "relations of human society—the relations of father and child, of master and slave, of the ruler and the ruled" (*ER*, 510). In other words, the "sense of the beautiful, of the sublime, and of the mystical" is "akin" to the slave's reverence for the white master: to aspire to Beauty is to aspire to God and thus affirm the "primal" subordination of slave to master (*ER*, 510). As in later modernist manifestos, including Ezra Pound's *Patria Mia* (1912) and the Southern Agrarians' *I'll Take My Stand* (1930), in Poe's "Colloquy of Monos and Una" (1841), aesthetic judgment and the poet's craft become forms of social salvation: "taste alone could have led us gently back to Beauty, to Nature, and to Life" and thus "purify" the "Art-scarred surface of the Earth" from the ravages of Enlightenment "knowledge," "progress," "universal equality," and "omni-prevalent Democracy" (*CW*, 2:610, 611–12).[29]

In his essays and reviews of the 1830s and 1840s, Poe is on a kind of rescue mission to save both poetry and criticism from the "daily puerilities" of public opinion and the popular press (*ER*, 506), as well as from the black facts and blood violence of American history. The social and specifically racial shaping of Poe's aesthetics is particularly evident in his reviews of Longfellow and other abolitionist poets of New England. As Kenneth Hovey has argued, "Poe attacked Longfellow and the poets of the Northeast unsparingly for their double error of didacticism and progressivism." "Fearing the advancing truth of what he called 'fanatic[ism] for the sake of fanaticism,' he advocated a beauty no truth could invade, the 'poem written solely for the poem's sake.'"[30]

In an 1845 review of Longfellow's *Poems on Slavery* (1842), Poe cites the following lines from "The Warning" as an instance of "absolute truth":

There is a poor, blind Sampson in this land,
    Shorn of his strength and bound in bonds of steel,
Who may, in some grim revel, raise his hand,
    And shake the pillars of the common weal,
Till the vast temple of our Liberties,
A shapeless mass of wreck and rubbish lies. (*ER*, 764)

Poe blames Northern abolitionist poets for the "grim" prospect of blood violence against the white masters: "One thing is certain:—if this prophecy be *not* fulfilled, it will be through no lack of incendiary doggrel on the part of Professor LONGFELLOW and his friends" (*ER*, 764).[31] At a time when there was an increasing emphasis on the social power of the word, especially the black word, in bringing an end to the historical contradiction of slavery in the American republic, Poe seeks to strip poetry of its moral imperative, its "truth" claims, and its historical power by establishing "the radical and chasmal difference between the truthful and the poetical modes of inculcation" (*ER*, 684–85). And yet, for all of Poe's emphasis on the formalist and protomodernist values of "pure beauty" and unity of poetic effect—as opposed to "instruction" or "truth"—as the sole legitimate province of poetry (*ER*, 690–91), his aestheticism cannot be separated from his political judgment that Longfellow, like James Russell Lowell, is part of a Boston "junto . . . of abolitionists, transcendentalists and fanatics" whose writings are "intended for the especial use of those negrophilic old ladies of the north" (*ER*, 760, 762). It is, he writes, "very comfortable" for the professor "to sit at ease in his library chair, and write verses instructing the southerners how to give up their all with good grace, and abusing them if they will not" (*ER*, 762–63). Poe's attack on the didacticism of Longfellow, Lowell, and others was not only a defense of pure poetry and the sanctity of art: it was also a defense of whiteness, slavery, and a whole way of Southern life against the increasing threat of Northern, and particularly black, defilement.

The Croak of the Raven and the Poetic Principle

"The croak of the raven is conveniently supposed to be purely lyric," wrote Hervey Allen in 1927 of the contemporary lack of concern with "what Mr. Poe had to say of democracy, science, and unimaginative literature."[32] While recent critics have turned with renewed attention to the historical and specifically Southern contexts of Poe's writing, there is still a tendency to pass over Poe's poems as sources of "purely lyric" expression. And yet, as I have been trying to suggest, whether they are read as forms of aesthetic resistance or as perverse symbolic enactments that ooze darkness and death over the American dream of progress, freedom, and light, Poe's poems are deeply embedded in the sociohistorical traumas of his time. This is particularly true of Poe's most popular poem, "The Raven," a poem that, in the words of Arthur Hobson Quinn, "made an impression probably not surpassed by any single piece of American poetry."[33] What does it mean in the context of the heightening social, sexual, and racial struggles of the United States in the 1840s for a dead white woman to come back as an "ominous" and ambiguously sexed black bird? Although critics have tended to follow Poe in interpreting the raven as an emblem "of *Mournful and Never-ending Remembrance*" ("The Philosophy of Composition," *ER*, 25), I want to suggest that the "ghastly" figure of the black bird "perched" upon "the pallid bust of Pallas" also evokes the fear of racial mixture and the sexual violation of the white woman by the black man that was at the center of antebellum debates about the future of the darker races in white America.[34]

In the July-August 1845 issue of the *Democratic Review,* which had published Poe's essay "The Power of Words" only a month before, John O'Sullivan declared that it was the "manifest destiny" of Anglo-Saxon

America "to overspread the continent allotted by Providence for the free development of our yearly multiplying millions." Critical of those who opposed the annexation of Texas because it would lead to the increase and perpetuation of the institution of slavery in America, O'Sullivan argued that, on the contrary, the "Spanish-Indian-American populations of Mexico, Central America and South America" would provide a kind of national sewage system to "slough off" emancipated Negroes in order to leave the United States free and pure to realize its white Anglo-Saxon destiny: "Themselves already of *mixed and confused blood*," writes O'Sullivan, "and free from the 'prejudices' which among us so insuperably *forbid the social amalgamation which can alone elevate the Negro race out of a virtually servile degradation* even though legally free, the regions occupied by those populations must strongly attract the black race in that direction; and as soon as the destined hour of emancipation shall arrive, will relieve the question of one of its worst difficulties, if not absolutely the greatest."[35] In O'Sullivan's formulation, the United States will, in effect, expel the degraded and "servile" bodies of "the black race" in order to "relieve" the country of the prospect of "social amalgamation."

Although "The Raven" was published before O'Sullivan's article, I want to suggest that the figure of Poe's "grim, ungainly, ghastly, gaunt, and ominous" black bird registers symbolically and more pessimistically some of the same national anxiety about "mixed and confused blood" that O'Sullivan expresses in his famous declaration of America's white manifest destiny. Moreover, I want to argue that in "The Raven," as elsewhere in Poe's writings, the dead white woman and the ominous black presence are foundational to Poe's poetics, his attempt to achieve "that intense and pure elevation of the *soul*" that he associates with "Beauty" as "the sole legitimate province of the poem" (*ER*, 16). In fact, the poem's dramatic contrasts of black and white are productive of its scene of terror and the melancholy tone of sadness, which is Beauty's "highest manifestation" (*ER*, 17).

While "The Raven" is not explicitly about race, like Poe's use of the "ourang-outang" in "The Murders in the Rue Morgue" to commit "*excessively outré*" acts of violence against two white women, his idea of using "a *non-*reasoning [black] creature capable of speech" in writing "a poem that should suit at once the popular and the critical taste" (*ER*, 18, 15) evokes popular notions of blacks as parrots incapable of reason: its story of a dead white woman coming back in the form of an "ominous" black bird of prey who penetrates the heart and overtakes the mind and soul of the white speaker registers the simultaneous fear of and fascination with penetration, mixture, inversion, and reversal that emerges alongside (and as part of) an increasingly aggressive nationalist insistence on sexual, social, and racial difference, white superiority, and Anglo-Saxon destiny. Perhaps better than other antebellum American writers, Poe reveals the linked processes of demonization, mixture, and reversal in the national imaginary.[36] In "The Raven," as in other Poe poems and tales, the expelled other of American national destiny—the dark, the corporeal, the sexual, the female, the animal, the mortal—returns as an obsessive set of fantasies about subversion, amalgamation, and dark apocalypse.[37]

Like O'Sullivan's essay on manifest destiny, "The Raven" is all about boundaries—and the horror of their dissolution. Associated with the name Helen and its derivatives, Ellen, Elenore, Lenore, which mean, in Poe's terms, "light" and "bright" (*CW*, 1:331), Lenore is another of those "rare and radiant" maidens whose death enables both poetry and beauty. As Poe famously wrote in his scientific analysis of "The Raven" in "The Philosophy of Composition" (1846): "the death, then, of a beautiful woman is, unquestionably, the most poetical topic in the world" (*ER*, 19). In the poem, however, the "lost Lenore," like Ligeia and Madeline Usher, refuses to stay dead. Although her radiant whiteness is at first set against the darkness of time, history, and the colors of the body, in the course of the poem she is confused with—and indeed replaced by—the darkly foreboding and sexually ambiguous black bird of prey. Expecting to find Lenore at his bedroom window, the protagonist opens the shutter to find, "with many a flirt and flutter," an uppity black bird in human drag who collapses the boundaries between animal and human, black and white, female and male, body and spirit, real and supernatural, dead and undead:

In there stepped a stately Raven of the saintly days of yore;
Not the least obeisance made he; not a minute stopped or stayed he;
But, with mien of lord or lady, perched above my chamber door—
Perched upon a bust of Pallas just above my chamber door—
    Perched, and sat, and nothing more. (*CW*, 1:366)

While the raven's hypnotic croak—"Nevermore," "Nevermore," "Nevermore"—appears to have a "purely lyric" reference to the death of the "sainted maiden" and the futility of joining her in another world, the "ebony" bird's physical location on "a bust of Pallas" suggests a broader reference to the negation of whiteness: not only the death of white beauty and white art but the death of white mind and an entire regime of classical and Enlightenment order, reason, and knowledge associated with Pallas Athena. Although Poe does not say so in "The Philosophy of Composition," the black bird's physical presence in the bedroom "perched" on the "bust of Pallas," a locale that is marked by the bereaved lover's obsessive repetition—"upon the sculptured bust," "on the placid bust," "on the pallid bust of Pallas"—also evokes the specter of sexual violation, racial mixture, and a reversal of the master-slave relation.[38]

At issue is not only the prospect of black domination but, as in *The Narrative of Arthur Gordon Pym* and "Instinct vs Reason—A Black Cat," the question of black intelligence. "Startled" by the apparent prescience and wisdom of the bird's "aptly spoken" reply, the speaker assumes that he is merely parroting the words of "some unhappy master":

"Doubtless," said I, "what it utters is its only stock and store
Caught from some unhappy master whom unmerciful Disaster
Followed fast and followed faster till his songs one burden bore—." (*CW*, 1:367)

The speaker's words link the "croak" of the raven with the master-slave relation and an entire Western philosophical defense of white mastery. "There scarcely ever was a civilized nation of any other complexion than white," wrote David Hume in 1748 in defense of the superiority of white—and especially English—civilization. "In JAMAICA, indeed," he writes, "they talk of one negroe as a man of parts and learning; but 'tis likely he is admired for very slender accomplishments, *like a parrot, who speaks a few words plainly.*"[39] Edgar Allan Poe, or at least the sorrowful white scholar of "The Raven," would "doubtless" agree.

If "The Raven" aspires toward "that pleasure which is at once the most intense, the most elevating, and the most pure" through "the contemplation of the beautiful" (*ER*, 16), it is, paradoxically, a pleasure and a beauty that are achieved through the death of the female body and the cultural terror of the black body. This bodily terror is perhaps most startlingly figured in the fluid interpenetration of light and dark in the concluding passage of the poem:

And the Raven, never flitting, still is sitting, *still* is sitting
On the pallid bust of Pallas just above my chamber door;
And his eyes have all the seeming of a demon's that is dreaming,
And the lamp-light o'er him streaming throws his shadow on the floor;
And my soul from out that shadow that lies floating on the floor
   Shall be lifted—nevermore! (*CW*, 1:369)

More than a "purely lyric" expression of "*Mournful and Never-ending remembrance,*" the demonic and shadowy figure of the black bird sitting "[o]n the pallid bust of Pallas" also projects some of the culture's deepest fears about the sexual violation of the white woman (or man) by the dark other, a possible reversal of the master-slave (or male-female) relation, and the apocalyptic specter of the end of Western wisdom and civilization in unreason, madness, and the bodily domination of black over white (Figure 14).[40]

In "The Poetic Principle," which was delivered as a lecture on several occasions in 1848 and 1849, Poe gives more explicit critical formulation to the racially inflected poetics of whiteness that frames his poems.[41] Against "the heresy of *The Didactic,*" the notion that the object of poetry is truth or the inculcation of a moral, Poe asserts the absolute value of the "poem *per se*—this poem which is a poem and nothing more—this poem written solely for the poem's sake" (*ER,* 76). Recapitulating in slightly revised form many of the same notions of poetic purity that Poe had originally set forth in his 1842 review of Longfellow's *Ballads and Other Poems,* this foundational text in the history of modern aestheticism represents, at least in part, an historical response to the moral imperative and abolitionist politics of New England poetry.[42]

But while "The Poetic Principle" is shaped by national and race-centered debates about "true Beauty" and true Americanism, it also participates in and makes a distinctive contribution to broader philosophical and political contests about the meaning of the aesthetic. Against the Emersonian definition of the poem as "a meter-making argument"[43] and the abolitionist emphasis on literature as a form of moral action, Poe follows Kant's *Critique of Judgment* (1790) in seeking to distinguish among the good, the true, and the beautiful.[44] Focusing on the aesthetic *affect* rather than the aesthetic object, Poe argues that "a work of art" is to be judged "by the impression it makes, by the effect it produces" in creating "that pleasurable elevation or excitement, *of the soul,* which we recognize as the Poetic Sentiment, and which is so easily distinguished from Truth, which is the satisfaction of the Reason, or from Passion, which is the excitement of the heart" (*ER,* 72, 78). He reiterates the notion of a tripartite division of the mind that he had originally set forth in his 1842 review of Longfellow: "Dividing the world of mind into its three most immediately obvious distinctions, we have the Pure Intellect, Taste, and the Moral Sense. I place Taste in the middle, because it is just this position, which, in the mind, it occupies. . . . Just as the Intellect concerns itself with Truth, so Taste informs us of the Beautiful while the Moral Sense is regardful of Duty" (*ER,* 76). Drawing on eighteenth-century constructions of the individual mind and subject and the effort to discover what Burke had called "the logic of Taste,"[45] Poe's attempt to carve out a separate space of pure pleasure and pure beauty might be read as a radical affirmation of human being and spirit in the face of the theoretical abstractions of Enlightenment rationalism, the dehumanizing technologies of modern science, and the increasingly mechanistic and alienating effects of the industrial marketplace. "An immortal instinct, deep within the spirit of man, is thus, plainly, a sense of the

Figure 14. Illustration by Gustave Doré from *The Raven* by Edgar Allan Poe, 1884. The shadowy figure of the black bird sitting "[o]n the pallid bust of Pallas" projects some of Euro-American culture's deepest fears about the end of Western wisdom and civilization in the bodily domination of black over white. Courtesy McCormick Library of Special Collections, Northwestern University.

Beautiful," Poe writes. "It is at once a consequence and an indication of his perennial existence. It is the desire of the moth for the star. It is no mere appreciation of the Beauty before us—but a wild effort to reach the Beauty above" (ER, 77). Whereas in the work of Alexander Baumgarten and other early philosophers of the aesthetic, the *aesthetic* was meant to designate perception *through* the body and the senses in opposition to abstract reason and immaterial thought, in Poe, as in Kant, the aesthetic represents an effort to climb out of the body in order to attain what Poe calls "but brief and indeterminate glimpses" of the beauty beyond.[46]

And yet, for all of Poe's effort to lay claim to a separate space of pure beauty, pure art, and pure pleasure beyond empirical knowledge and the passions of the body, the subject he seeks to affirm and the pure space of beauty toward which he aspires continue to be shaped by the racial codes, hierarchies, and values of Western (and specifically Anglo-American) culture. Poe's emphasis on what he calls "radical and chasmal differences between the truthful and the poetical modes of inculcation" (ER, 76), his desire to distinguish and differentiate the aesthetic as a separate realm of activity, participates in, even as it seeks to surmount, an emergent scientific discourse of racial difference, purity, and distinction that grounds both modern "white" subjectivity and Western aestheticism. Thus, for example, in Kant's *Observations on the Feeling of the Beautiful and the Sublime* (1764), his attempt to distinguish Beauty as a purely subjective and disinterested realm of aesthetic activity is grounded in his assertion of fundamental national and racial difference. In a section of *Observations* titled "Of National Characteristics, so far as They Depend upon the Distinct Feeling of the Beautiful and the Sublime," Kant writes that there is a "fundamental difference" between the black and white "races of man, and it appears to be as great in regard to mental capacities as in color." The aesthetic is, in effect, color coded in Kant's cultural taxonomy: blacks are not only different from and inferior to whites; they are also incapable of experiencing or producing beauty. "The Negroes of Africa have by nature no feeling that rises above the trifling," Kant writes in support of Hume's observation that "not a single [Negro] was ever found who presented anything great in art or science or any other praise-worthy quality."[47]

Poe's "Poetic Principle" is similarly grounded in the bodily presumption of white over black. In the passages he cites from Percy Bysshe Shelley, Thomas Moore, Thomas Hood, Lord Byron, Alfred Tennyson, and Edward Coote Pinckney to exemplify his aesthetic theory, beauty and poetry are associated with whiteness, purity, love, and fair womanhood; blackness is associated with "muddy impurity," corporeality, pain, horror, and the "stain" of mortality. And yet, as in "The Raven," in which the whiteness of the marble bust of Pallas necessitates the blackness of the raven and the desire for beauty is intensified by the physical presence and social horror of blackness, in Poe's aesthetic theory, as in Kant's, beauty paradoxically incorporates blackness as part of its own self-definition and subjective "effect."

In its most utopian form, Poe's theory of "Supernal Beauty" represents an attempt to unite a fractured nation and an increasingly atomized world on the common ground of culture. But while Poe seeks in "The Poetic Principle" to establish a kind of science of aesthetic value as a means of bridging the apparent division between the poet-critic, the popular press, and what he calls "the mass of mankind' (*ER*, 80–81), his desire to locate pure beauty "Anywhere, anywhere / Out of the world!" (*ER*, 89) is also linked with his lifelong ambition to establish an aristocracy of taste and intellect that will decide—against the debased judgment of the masses and the moral pieties of the New England literary establishment—what counts as true art. This is particularly evident in Poe's ongoing dream of founding his own magazine. In 1848 Poe wrote to Helen Whitman requesting her aid in financing the *Stylus*: "Would it not be 'glorious'," he asked, "to establish, in America, the sole unquestionable aristocracy—that of intellect—to secure its supremacy—to lead & to control it?" (*LP*, 2:410). Here, as elsewhere in Poe's writing, culture becomes the ground at once of "unquestionable aristocracy" and social control. For Poe, no less than for Jefferson, this cultural aristocracy and its ideals of pure beauty cannot finally be separated from the question of race and the ongoing historical struggle over the color of American skin. Emerging out of the broader taxonomies of the Western Enlightenment, the aesthetic is itself an historically marked signifier that would continue to play a key role in national and international efforts to fix the boundary not only between races and nations but also between civilized and uncivilized, culture and its others.

Poe in Blackface

In his review of Poe scholarship in *Eight American Authors*, Jay Hubbell observes: "Poe was the one black sheep in the American literary flock, and very black indeed he seemed when placed beside the great New Englanders."[48] Associated with the South, the city, the masses, excess, dissolution, and the terror of blackness, Poe may have been written out of the American tradition precisely because he so nearly touched the trauma of race and the crisis of national identity at the center of nineteenth-century American culture. From Rufus Griswold's representation of Poe as a figure of "morbid excess" with "a face shrouded in gloom," to Whitman's evocation of Poe as "a dim man" with "an incorrigible propensity toward nocturnal themes, a demoniac undertone behind every page," to Henry James's observation that "an enthusiasm for Poe is the mark of a decidedly primitive stage of reflection," critical responses to Poe have had at their center debates about American national identity conducted in a racially inflected language of black and white, demon and angel, primitive and civilized.[49] If Poe's aesthetic theory was driven, as I have tried to suggest, by an imaginative flight away from the historical presence of blacks in the social landscape of America, it is ironic that following his death he himself became the dark other, the demon, the "one black sheep in the American literary flock," who needed to be expelled from the social body in order to make way for the New England-centered moral and spiritual imperatives of American national destiny as they came to be embodied by what F. O. Matthiessen calls the "American Renaissance."[50]

It was not until Poe went to France where he was in some sense cleansed of his blackness and his history that he could reenter American literature in the cold war period in the name of art for art's sake, aesthetic formalism, otherworldly metaphysics, and *la poésie pure*. Although Edmund Wilson had invoked the French response to Poe as early as 1926 in calling on Americans to focus on "Poe's absolute artistic importance" rather than "his bad reputation as a citizen,"[51] it was the "French face" of Poe in T. S. Eliot's *From Poe to Valéry* (1948) and Allen Tate's "Angelic Imagination: Poe as God" (1953) that prepared the way for his emergence in the post-World War II period as an icon of modernist and New Critical method and sensibility.[52] Whereas Tate urged a philosophical rather than a merely personal or psychological approach to Poe as the anticipator of "our great subject, the disintegration of personality," Eliot emphasized the importance of Poe's theory of the "poem written solely for the poem's sake" for an aesthetic tradition that focuses with "increasing consciousness of language" on "what we may call *la poésie pure*."[53] Looking at Poe "through the eyes of Baudelaire, Mallarmé and most of all Valéry," Eliot underscores Poe's lack of relation to his time: "There can be few authors of such eminence who have drawn so little from their own roots, who have been so isolated from any surroundings." Although Eliot concedes that the language of Poe's poetry is not pure, he argues that Poe represents the origin of the French symbolist theory of *la poésie pure* in the sense that "the subject is little, the treatment is everything."[54] This evacuation of the subject and history from the terrain of writing—an evacuation that anticipates the linguistic and nonreferential emphasis of poststructuralist criticism—is commonly regarded as the defining characteristic of symbolist theory and practice from Poe to Valéry.

And yet, if we return for a moment to the three seminal essays that

Baudelaire wrote on Poe between 1852 and 1857, what is striking is the extent to which they are embedded in Baudelaire's own historical and racially marked attack on "democracy, progress and *civilization*."[55] "Nature produces only monsters, and the whole question is to understand the word *savages*," he wrote in response to the "rising tide of democracy," "modern philosophy," and "misguided equalitarians" (*NN*, 128, 124, 125, 126). Baudelaire was, in fact, one of the first to draw attention to the relation between Poe's pursuit of "pure beauty" and "pure poetry" and the racial turmoil of "a country in which slavery exists" and "chained Negroes" are burned (*NN*, 135, 132). "Aristocrat by nature even more than by birth," Poe was "the Virginian, the Southerner," the "true poet . . . who does not wish to be elbowed by the crowd and who runs to the far east when the fireworks go off in the west" (*NN*, 125). To Baudelaire, Poe was himself the exotic other of the West—the orientalized "Arab" and "savage" who bodied forth "the primordial perversity of man" (*NN*, 126) at the same time that he wrote poetry that was "carefully wrought, pure, correct, and as brilliant as a crystal jewel."[56]

The word *pure* figures at the center of a similarly marked racial aesthetics of black and white, primitive and civilized, "bawling" mass and pure signifier in Mallarmé's famous sonnet, "Le Tombeau d'Edgar Poe," which was written to commemorate the dedication of Poe's tomb in Baltimore in 1876. Against the detestable "hydra" of his age and time, Poe is evoked as a purifying "angel" who cleanses language and poetry of its darkness and its history in order to give "a purer meaning to the words of the tribe" ("un sens plus pure aux mots de la tribu"). Fallen from some "obscure disaster" and surrounded by darkness, Poe's tomb will stand, Mallarmé suggests, as a barrier against the "black flights of Blasphemy" ("noirs vols du Blasphème") that will be scattered about it in years to come.[57]

The racially inflected response to Poe in the work of Baudelaire and Mallarmé, who both contributed to the development of a symbolist aesthetics of the "poem itself" and a language purified of the "words of the tribe" during the very years when France emerged as a major imperial power, suggests the more transnational histories, racial as well as textual, in which Poe's aesthetics of purity has played a role. In the history of Poe criticism, however, as in T. S. Eliot's *From Poe to Valéry*, the French response to Poe has served as a kind of aesthetic purifier, cleansing Poe's face of the marks of race and history in order to save him for the transcendence of art. This tradition, and its various permutations among decadents, modernists, postmodernists, and proponents of art for art's sake, has continued to be one of the main traditions of Poe criticism. Whether the approach is archival or theoretical, aesthetic or psychoanalytic, formalist or poststructuralist, until recently, critics have tended to focus on the primarily textual, linguistic, and psychological meanings of Poe's art. By seeking to locate Poe's poetic theory and practice within rather than outside history, I have attempted to suggest the ways that even calls for a purely aesthetic appreciation of Poe cannot finally be separated from the racial and imperial struggles of the past and present. T. S. Eliot and Paul Valéry, notwithstanding, there is no such thing as a pure poem.

Chapter 5

Whitman and the Homosexual Republic

Within there runs his blood . . . . the same old blood . . the same red running blood;
There swells and jets his heart . . . . There all passions and desires . . all reachings and aspirations.

—Whitman, Leaves of Grass *1855*

Affection shall solve every one of the problems of freedom . . .
The dependence of Liberty shall be lovers,
The continuance of Equality shall be comrades.

—Whitman, Leaves of Grass *1860*

In a letter dated 13 March 1946, Malcolm Cowley wrote to Kenneth Burke: "I'm working on Whitman, that old cocksucker. Very strange amalgam he made between cocksucking and democracy."[1] The letter itself seems strange coming from Malcolm Cowley, who in his famous 1959 introduction to the Viking edition of the 1855 *Leaves of Grass* became a key figure in the critical construction of Whitman as an essentially spiritual poet who had been miraculously transformed from hack journalist to prophetic poet by a "mystical experience."[2] The difference between Cowley's private and public comments is characteristic of a critical tradition that has insisted on silencing, spiritualizing, heterosexualizing, or marginalizing Whitman's sexual feeling for men.[3]

Recent works on Whitman by gay critics and others have sought to name the sexual love of men that earlier critics insisted on silencing, but while these approaches have emphasized the centrality of Whitman's sexuality and homosexuality to his work, they have also tended to maintain a distinction between Whitman the private poet and Whitman the public poet, Whitman the homosexual poet and Whitman the poet of democracy, which unduly privatizes and totalizes Whitman's sexual love of men.[4] It is this distinction between private and public, homosexuality and democracy, that I would like to complicate and challenge in this chapter by exploring what Cowley aptly called the "[v]ery strange amalgam" between "cocksucking *and* democracy" in Whitman's work.

I would like to begin by describing a brief public service announcement produced by the Philadelphia Lesbian and Gay Task Force in 1990 as a means of reflecting on the uses to which Whitman may and may not be put in contemporary American culture. A young man sits at the Delaware River's edge, with the Walt Whitman Bridge in the background, and says: "Hey, I just found out Walt Whitman was gay . . . you know the guy they named the bridge after. I wish I had known that when I was in high school. Back then, I got hassled all the time by the other kids, 'cause I'm gay—and the teachers—they didn't say anything. Why didn't they tell me Walt Whitman was gay?"

All six television stations in the Philadelphia market refused to air this public service announcement, arguing that it was too "controversial" and that it "advocated a particular lifestyle." When two of the stations called the Walt Whitman Cultural Arts Center in Camden, New Jersey, the director said that to tell the world that Whitman was gay "would really be detrimental to the Center. A lot of our programming is geared to teens. Kids don't need a lot to scare them off."[5] At issue in this controversy was not the question of whether or not Whitman was gay: there seemed to be widespread if covert agreement that he was. At issue was the idea that Whitman's gayness must not be aired publicly and the belief that such public airing would be detrimental to the American public and "scare" young kids. What the controversy suggests, finally, is the extent to which Whitman as the poet of the people, the poet of democracy, and the American poet has also become an American public property whose image is bound up with the maintenance of American public health and American national policy. It is not only the academic and critical establishment but those in positions of social and cultural power and, I would add, the national government itself that are heavily invested in keeping Whitman's sexuality, specifically his sexual love for men, out of any discussion of his role as the poet of democracy and *the* American poet.[6] The fantasy seems to be, at least in part, that if we can control Whitman's sexuality, we can somehow control the sexuality of the nation.

This struggle over an appropriate public representation of America's poet continues in the controversy surrounding the Whitman exhibit mounted by the Walt Whitman State Historical Site in Huntington, Long Island, where Whitman was born. On 31 May 1997 the Whitman Birthplace Museum opened a new Visitors Interpretive Center and a major exhibit on Walt Whitman that chooses not to represent—in effect to silence and erase—the sexual love of men at the center of Whitman's life and work.[7] The underlying romantic story of Whitman's life, we are led to believe in a panel titled "To Celebrate the Need of Comrades: Whitman's Life of Love," is the story of his relationship with Anne Gilchrist, an English admirer who came to Philadelphia in 1876 with the mistaken intention of marrying Whitman. To get this story, the museum's designers must literally cut, crop, and alter a painting titled *The Tea Party* in order to invent for public consumption a portrait of Whitman having tea *alone* with Anne Gilchrist. The original picture, which was painted by Gilchrist's son, Herbert Gilchrist, in 1882, shows Whitman looking ill at ease and absorbed in smelling a flower as Anne Gilchrist and her daughter look elsewhere (Figure 15). In the Birthplace exhibit, the daughter is neatly cut and cropped out of the picture so as to present Whitman and Gilchrist as a heterosexual couple. This picture of Gilchrist and Whitman (minus the daughter) dominates the panel on Whitman's "Life of Love" in a manner that heterosexualizes the simultaneously homoerotic and democratic meanings of comradeship and love in Whitman's life and work. What the exhibit does not tell us is that the primary relationship in this picture is not between Anne Gilchrist and Whitman but between Whitman and Herbert Gilchrist, who had also sketched a pen and ink drawing of Whitman sunbathing in the nude at Timber Creek in 1878 (Figure 16).

"Strange Amalgam"

As the title of this chapter suggests, I want to try to read against the either/or oppositions that have structured past scholarly and public representations of Whitman: either Whitman the private poet or Whitman the public poet, Whitman the poet of gay men or Whitman the democratic poet, Whitman the homosexual or Whitman the poet of the American republic. I want to argue that Whitman's sexual love of men cannot be separated from his work and vision as the poet of American democracy. In fact, it is this fluid mixture and crossing of homosexual and democratic voices in Whitman's writings that may constitute their most sexually radical and politically provocative gesture. Whitman's male lovers refuse to remain cordoned off in the privacy of the bedroom or the closet: they lay claim to public space, political voice, and representation.

Thus, I want to suggest that we take Whitman seriously when, in the preface to an edition of *Leaves of Grass* published on the occasion of the centennial of the American Revolution in 1876, he says of the "ever new-interchange of adhesiveness, so fitly emblematic of America" that "the special meaning of the 'Calamus' cluster of 'Leaves of Grass' (and *more or less running through the book*, and cropping out in 'Drum-Taps,') mainly resides in its *political significance*." "It is," Whitman goes on to say, "by a fervent, accepted development of comradeship, the beautiful and sane

Figure 15. *The Tea Party*. A painting of Walt Whitman and Anne Gilchrist by
Herbert Gilchrist, 1882. In the exhibit on Whitman that opened at the Whitman
Birthplace Museum in 1997, this painting of Whitman and Gilchrist, with
Gilchrist's daughter neatly cropped out of the picture, dominates the panel on
Whitman's "Life of Love" in a manner that erases and silences the sexual love
of men at the center of Whitman's life and work. Courtesy Annenberg Rare
Book and Manuscript Library, University of Pennsylvania.

affection of man for man, latent in all the young fellows, north and
south, east and west—it is by this, I say, and by what goes directly and
indirectly along with it, that the United States of the future, (I cannot
too often repeat,) are to be most effectually welded together, interca-
lated, anneal'd into a living union" (*PW*, 2:471; emphasis added).

Figure 16. Whitman sunbathing in the nude at Timber Creek in 1878. Original pen and ink drawing by Herbert Gilchrist. Courtesy Henry W. and Albert A. Berg Collection of English and American Literature, The New York Public Library, Astor, Lenox and Tilden Foundations.

In arguing for the political significance of adhesiveness as a fervent passion among and between men in the "Calamus" poems, *Drum-Taps*, and throughout *Leaves of Grass*, I do not mean to return to older interpretations of Whitman's love poems to men as allegories of American democracy. Rather, I want to argue that Whitman's sexual love of men was central to the democratic vision and experimental poetics of *Leaves of Grass* and to Whitman's hopes for welding the American republic into a "living union," especially in the post-Civil War period. In making this argument, I want to explore the ways the language of democracy intersects with material transformations in labor, industry, and social relations in the nineteenth century in the United States to construct homosexuality as a type and a pathology.[8] But in exploring the emergence of homosexuality as a modern type and sensibility in nineteenth-century America, and in Whitman's work in particular, I want to try to avoid the tendency among critics—despite their distinction between what Jeffrey Weeks calls "homosexual behavior, which is universal, and a homosexual identity, which is historically specific"—to construct both homosexual behavior and homosexual identity as transhistorical and monolithic categories.[9] I want to insist, that is, on the fact that the word and the category *homosexual* did not exist when Whitman began writing.

As he himself put it in *An American Primer.* "The lack of any words . . . is as historical as the existence of words. As for me, I feel a hundred realities, clearly determined in me, that words are not yet formed to represent."[10] The words Whitman did use to articulate and name his erotic feeling for men were the words of democracy—of comradeship, brotherhood, equality, blood kinship, social union, and the glories of the laborer and the common people. But Whitman also used other languages. And thus, against those who tend to treat homosexuality as an a priori or universal given in Whitman's work, I want to argue the fluidity of Whitman's expression of same-sex love among men as the language of democracy intersects with other languages, including the languages of temperance, sexual reform, artisan republicanism, antislavery, phrenology, marital love, familial and specifically father-son relationships, and spirituality, in Whitman's attempt to express "a hundred realities, clearly determined in me, that words are not yet formed to represent."[11]

In the past, critics have tended to discuss the arc of Whitman's poetic development as if he emerged miraculously as a "homosexual poet" in the 1860 *Leaves of Grass* and then disappeared or sublimated his homosexual desire just as miraculously during the Civil War and post-Civil War period. As Charley Shively and Michael Moon have pointed out, however, Whitman's desire to name his erotic attraction to men is already evident in his early story "The Child's Champion" (1841, later titled "The Child and the Profligate") and in his temperance novel *Franklin Evans; or the Inebriate,* 1842), both published by *The New World,* a popular and widely circulated workingman's newspaper.[12] But while these stories name a kind of sexual cruising among men in the city, to which youths newly arrived from the country are particularly drawn, they also locate physical relations among men under the sign of intemperance as a threat to the virtuous republican body and body politic that the stories appear to advocate. While the "profligate" in "The Child's Champion" is transformed into a provider by his erotic attraction to the child, and while he sleeps that night with the young boy folded in his arms, the narrator suggests that this is not a totally "unsullied affection": "Fair were those two creatures in their unconscious beauty—glorious, but yet how differently glorious! One of them was innocent and sinless of all wrong: the other—O to that other, what evil had not been present, either in action or to his desires!" (*EPF,* 76).

Similarly, while *Franklin Evans* seems driven by a narrative urge to kill off women and heterosexual marriage in the interest of affirming the primacy of social and erotic bonding among men, these relationships are associated with enslavement to "The Snake Tempter," drink, and thus forms of "dissipation," "strange infatuation," and bodily compulsion at odds with the temperance and virtue necessary for a healthy republican body politic. When Franklin Evans is transformed from ine-briate into advocate of temperance, the change is figured in the political language of republican regeneration and manifest destiny: "Now man is free! He walks upon the earth, worthy the name of one whose prototype is God! We hear the mighty victory chorus sounding loud and long. Regenerated! Regenerated! . . . Victory! Victory! The Last Slave of Appetite is free, and the people are regenerated!"[13]

Sometime in the 1840s this apparent antinomy between unhealthy but pleasurable sexuality among men and a healthy republican body politic begins to break down in Whitman's work as he begins to articulate a position different from but often expressed in the same language as such popular male purity and antimasturbation tracts as Sylvester Graham's *Lecture to Young Men on Chastity* (1834) and Orson Fowler's *Amativeness: Or Evils and Remedies of Excessive and Perverted Sexuality* (1844). In these sexual purity tracts, masturbation and sexual play, especially among young men, are presented as destructive to the physical and moral health of a productive, reproductive, and ultimately heterosexual American republic grounded in marriage and the family.

In a notebook dated 1847, in which Whitman begins working toward the experimental language and form of *Leaves of Grass,* he insists on locating the soul and vision in the body and matter. He presents masturbation, which doubled in the nineteenth century as a code for sexuality between men, as a source at once of sexual ecstasy, mystical vision, and poetic utterance:

I do not wonder that one feeling now does so much for me,
He is free of all the rest,—and swiftly begets offspring of them, better than the
    dams
A touch now reads me a library of knowledge in an instant.
It smells for me the fragrance of wine and lemon-blows.
It tastes for me ripe strawberries and melons,—
It talks for me with a tongue of its own,
It finds an ear wherever it rests or taps.[14]

Just as in "Song of Myself," in which the pleasures of touching either oneself or "what is hardly different from myself" and the orgasmic spilling of male seed give rise to the regenerative vision of "Landscapes projected masculine full-sized and golden" (*LG* 1855, 53, 54), so in this early notebook entry Whitman reverses the nonreproductive figurations of masturbation and same-sex touching in the male purity tracts. He associates the sexual pleasure of "He" who "is free of all the rest" and "better than the dams" with the "offspring" of vision, poetic voice, and a gloriously reproductive image of nature, nation, and world.

This figuration of the body, sexuality, and love between men as the site of ecstasy, vision, and poetic utterance becomes even more emphatic in the first edition of *Leaves of Grass*. In his long opening poem, later titled "Song of Myself," the poet describes the "sexual experience" that is at the origin of his democratic voice and vision:

I believe in you my soul . . . . the other I am must not abase itself to you,
And you must not be abased to the other.

Loafe with me on the grass . . . . loose the stop from your throat,
Not words, not music or rhyme I want . . . . not custom or lecture, not even the best,
Only the lull I like, the hum of your valved voice.

I mind how we lay in June, such a transparent summer morning;
You settled your head athwart my hips and gently turned over upon me,
And parted the shirt from my bosom-bone, and plunged your tongue to my barestript heart,
And reached till you felt my beard, and reached till you held my feet. (*LG* 1855, 28–29)

"Isn't this cocksucking plain and simple" Charley Shively asks, arguing that in this passage "Whitman demonstrates part of his Americanness by placing cocksucking at the center of *Leaves of Grass*."[15] But before we completely literalize this passage as a direct transcription of cocksucking between men, it is important to recognize that the "I" and "you" are unspecified and ungendered in the passage and that the passage has also been read as the transcription of what James E. Miller calls an "inverted mystical experience."[16]

Rather than posing cocksucking and mysticism as antithetical readings, however, or arguing that Whitman seeks consciously to disguise his homosexuality through the language of the soul, I want to suggest that this passage is representative of the ways the languages of sexuality and spirituality, same-sex love and love between men and women, private and public, intermix and flow into each other in Whitman's work. It is unclear finally whether Whitman is describing sexuality in the language of spiritual ecstasy or a mystical experience in the language of sexual ecstasy, for he seems to be doing both at once. What is clear is that the democratic knowledge the poet receives of an entire universe bathed in an erotic force that links men, women, God, and the natural world in a vision of mystic unity is associated with sexual and bodily ecstasy, an ecstasy that includes but is not limited to the pleasures of cocksucking among men. In other words, here we have precisely Malcolm Cowley's strange amalgam "between cocksucking and democracy" in Whitman's work. Giving tongue is associated at once with sexuality, including sexuality between men, democracy, spiritual vision, and poetic utterance.

Homoeroticism and Political Crisis

This amalgam between men loving men and democracy would become even more marked in Whitman's work as the actual political union—on which Whitman had staked his identity and faith as a democratic poet—began to dissolve. What Whitman found in the loving affection of man for man was a means of resolving the democratic paradox of liberty and social union and the political crisis of the nation on the level of the body, sex, and homoerotic love.

In past and recent readings of Whitman's life and work, biographers and critics have argued that at some time in the late 1850s Whitman had a love affair that caused him to turn away from his public role as the poet of democracy toward the privacy of homoerotic love. To disguise the real "homosexual" content of his "Calamus" poems in the 1860 edition of *Leaves of Grass,* it is argued, Whitman interspersed more public poems of democracy, such as "For You O Democracy," with more private and personal poems of homosexual love. Joseph Cady argues that Whitman's attempt to invent a "new order based on his private experience as a homosexual" was only partially successful because in the "least satisfying" strain of "Calamus," Whitman does not sustain his separation and conflict but seeks to "translate" his experience into the language of common culture.[17]

This notion of a neat division between the more revolutionary impulses of the private poet of homosexual love and the more conventional impulses of the public poet of democracy is not borne out by a close reading of the "Live Oak, with Moss" sequence, the original sheaf of twelve love poems of "manly love" out of which the "Calamus" poems emerged. In this sequence, it is precisely in and through rather than against the more conventional languages of republican affection, democratic comradeship, phrenological adhesiveness, and brotherly love that the poet articulates his feelings for men.[18] "I dreamed in a dream of a city where all men were like brothers," Whitman wrote in the poem that would later become "Calamus" 34:

O I saw them tenderly love each other—I often saw them, in numbers, walking hand in hand;
I dreamed that was the city of robust friends—Nothing was greater there than manly love—it led the rest,
It was seen every hour in the actions of the men of that city, and in all their looks and words.[19]

What this poem suggests is that in its most visionary embodiment, the dream of democracy will give rise to a city, and ultimately an American republic, in which men loving men can live and love and touch openly—a dream city, I might add, that we are still very far from achieving despite the fact that the first lines of "Calamus" 34 ("I dreamed in a dream, I saw a city invincible") are now inscribed on the Camden city hall in New Jersey.

Although the "Live Oak, with Moss" sequence and the "Calamus" sequence bear the traces of a rather appealing crisis of representation in which Whitman's poet-lover realizes that he does not speak for everybody, there is no distinct separation between the poet of democracy and the poet of "manly love." Like other poems in the "Live Oak" sequence and in the "Calamus" sequence, "I Dream'd in a Dream" marks not so much a conflict between Whitman the democratic poet and Whitman the lover of men but a shift in Whitman's conceptualization of his role as democratic poet that locates his personal and sexual love for men at the very center of his vision, role, and faith as the poet of democracy. Thus, in the opening poem of "Calamus," "In Paths Untrodden," the poet avows his desire "To tell the secret of my nights and days, / To celebrate the need of comrades" (*LG* 1860, 342). While these lines might be read as a sign of the separation and conflict between private and public poet, they might also be read paratactically as an example of the ways Whitman's "secret" love of men is articulated together with, in the same language as, and as the very condition of his celebration of democratic comrades in the "Calamus" poems.

"Ah lover and perfect equal," Whitman writes in "Calamus" 41 ("Among the Multitude"), in words that suggest the relation among the spread of eighteenth-century rhetorics of equality and natural rights, the rise of democracy in the United States and elsewhere, and the production of "homosexuality" as a distinct category or character. It is no coincidence that the proliferation of the rhetoric (if not the reality) of democratic equality during the Age of Jackson corresponded with the emergence of the temperance movement, the male purity crusade, and an increasing cultural anxiety about drinking, masturbation, same-sex sexuality, and other forms of bodily excess and indulgence among and between men. As Whitman's early temperance tales and his poems suggest, democratic space is a fluid and potentially dangerous political space in which bodies and sexualities know no bounds. By equating democracy with the liberation of the body and sexuality, Whitman provoked among his unsympathetic readers what was (and perhaps still is) the deepest underlying fear of democracy in America: that in its purest form democracy would lead to a blurring of sexual bounds and thus the breakdown of a social and bourgeois economy based on the management of the body and sexuality and the polarization of male and female spheres.

"Singing the Phallus"

In past accounts of Whitman's poetic development, "Children of Adam" has been treated as an afterthought: a sequence of poems that Whitman added to the 1860 edition of *Leaves of Grass* in order to provide a legitimizing heterosexual context for the more radical personal love poems to men in the "Calamus" sequence.[20] But as expressions of sex and the body, the "Children of Adam" poems (originally titled "Enfans d'Adam") may indeed be the more sexually radical sequence that Emerson and the censors who banned *Leaves of Grass* in Boston in 1882 always believed it to be. A notebook entry suggests that Whitman initially conceptualized "Children of Adam" as a companion piece to his "Live Oak, with Moss" poems: "A string of Poems (short etc.), embodying the amative love of woman—the same as Live Oak Leaves do the passion of friendship for man."[21] Whatever Whitman's initial intentions, the "Children of Adam" poems do not read as a neatly "amative" or "heterosexual" counterpart to his poems of passion for men in the "Live Oak" sequence. (And here it is perhaps important to remember that the term *heterosexual* actually came later than the term *homosexual* in the construction of modern sexuality.) Though the "Children of Adam" poem "A Woman Waits for Me" (initially published in 1856 as "Poem of Procreation") consistently provoked nineteenth-century censorship for its representation of an athletic, sexually charged, and desiring female body, the poem is in fact atypical in its emphasis on the amative, and ultimately procreative and eugenically productive, love between men and women.

"Singing the phallus" and the "bedfellow's song," many of the "Children of Adam" poems are not about women or procreation or progeny at all but about amativeness as a burning, aching, "resistless," emphatically physical "yearning" for young men ("Enfans d'Adam" 2; later "From Pent-Up Aching Rivers"). Whereas in the "Calamus" poems physical love among men is represented in images of men touching, hugging, kissing, and sleeping together "under the same cover in the cool night" (*LG* 1860, 385), in the "Children of Adam" poems Whitman, in the figure of a "lusty," "tremulous," and insistently "phallic" Adam, names and bathes his songs in an active, orgiastic, and fleshy sexuality among men. "Give me now libidinous joys only!" the poet exclaims in "Enfans d'Adam" 8 ("Native Moments"), evoking scenes of nonreproductive sexual play and pleasure among men that recall similar scenes of "intemperance" in *Franklin Evans:*

I am for those who believe in loose delights—I share the midnight orgies of
    young men,
I dance with the dancers, and drink with the drinkers,
The echoes ring with our indecent calls,

I take for my love some prostitute—I pick out some low person for my dearest
    friend,
He shall be lawless, rude, illiterate—he shall be one condemned by others for
    deeds done;
I will play a part no longer—Why should I exile myself from my companions?
    (*LG* 1860, 311)

Even "Enfans d'Adam" 4 (later "A Woman Waits for Me") is as much a
celebration of a deliciously phallic male sexuality as it is a celebration of
sexual love between men and women. Associating the "woman" in the
poem with traditionally masculine activities, the language of the poem
slips ambiguously between celebrations of same-sex and opposite-sex
love. Moreover, in later revisions of the "Enfans d'Adam" poems, Whitman actually edited out several of the more explicit "heterosexual" references while retaining the emphasis on an insistently phallic and
physical male sexuality. Thus, Whitman's later deletion of the phrase "I
take for my love some prostitute" in the above passage from "Native
Moments" ends up underscoring the "libidinous joys" and "loose
delights" of an explicitly same-sex sexuality among and between men.[22]

Whereas in the 1860 *Leaves of Grass* the "Enfans d'Adam" poems are
immediately followed by "Poem of the Road" ("Song of the Open
Road"), "To the Sayers of Words" ("A Song of the Rolling Earth"), "A
Boston Ballad," and then the "Calamus" sequence, in the final edition
of *Leaves of Grass,* the "Calamus" poems immediately follow the "Children of Adam" poems. Rather than suggesting a neatly "heterosexual"
and "homosexual" pairing, however, this final arrangement further
accentuates the fluid relationship between the "lusty, phallic" and ultimately nonreproductive and nonmonogamous sexual play and pleasure
among men in the "Children of Adam" poems and the less insistently
phallic but nonetheless explicitly physical lover and democrat of the
"Calamus" poems. "Touch me, touch the palm of your hand to my body
as I pass, / Be not afraid of my body," says the naked Adamic speaker in
the final poem of the "Children of Adam" sequence, as he passes and
steps quite imperceptibly into the "paths untrodden" and more
emphatically (but not exclusively) male contexts of the "Calamus"
poems (*LG* 1860, 111).

Against popular nineteenth-century associations of masturbation and
excessive adhesiveness among men with solitude, impotence, and emas-
culation, Whitman extended and hybridized the social meanings of
adhesiveness—the phrenological term for friendship—to signify intense
and passionate love between men as a virile and politically productive
force for urban, national, and international community. He also
extended the meanings of *amativeness*—the phrenological term for procreative love between men and women—to include physical and procre-

ative love among men. Implicit in the sexual and social vision of "Children of Adam" is a New World garden and a new American republic ordered not by the traditional marital, procreative, familial, and monogamous bonds between men and women but by the sexually and socially productive and nonmonogamous bonds among men. While the "Children of Adam" appear to refer to *all* the children produced (presumably) by Adam and Eve, as the exclusive emphasis on Adam in the title suggests, these children are also the male children produced and "prepared for" by the "act divine" and "stalwart loins" of a phallic and virile Adam, whose sexual union with men bears the creative and procreative seeds of poetry, American polity, and the future of democracy worldwide.

In his important article " 'Here Is Adhesiveness': From Friendship to Homosexuality," Michael Lynch argues that when in the 1856 edition of *Leaves of Grass* Whitman wrote: "Here is adhesiveness, it is not previously fashioned—it is apropos" in reference to exclusively same-sex relationships among men, his words marked a major shift toward a definition of the homosexual and the heterosexual as distinct types. "Whitman's restriction of Adhesiveness to male-male relationships opened the way for an understanding of same-sex expression of a sexual instinct that was polar to an opposite-sex expression of it." Rather than representing the emergence of what Lynch calls "a distinct 'homosexual identity' and 'homosexual role,' "[23] I would argue that Whitman's "Calamus" and "Children of Adam" poems imply just the opposite. By conceptualizing and articulating his love for men in the language of democratic comradeship and by celebrating physical pleasure among men in the context of male and female amativeness and procreation, Whitman suggests the extent to which the bounds between private and public, male and female, heterosexual and homosexual, are still indistinct, permeable, and fluid in his work

The Homosexual War

In critical discussions of Whitman's life and work, it has become almost axiomatic to argue that Whitman's "homosexual" love crisis of the late 1850s was sublimated in the figure of the "wound-dresser" during the Civil War and ultimately silenced and suppressed in the "good gray" politics and poetics of the post-Civil War period.[24] Here, again, however, a close reading of Whitman's Civil War writings suggests that just the opposite may be the case: the rhetorics of desire and intimacy among men and the occasions and contexts for their expression in Whitman's work actually proliferated during the Civil War.[25] "How I love them! how I could hug them, with their brown faces, and their clothes and knapsacks cover'd with dust!" Whitman exclaims in the opening poem of *Drum-Taps,* "First O Songs for a Prelude," as the fire of his passion for men bursts forth along with and in the same language as the "torrents of men" and "the pent fire" of the Civil War ("Rise O Days from Your Fathomless Deeps").[26] Rather than sublimating his feeling for men, the historical role Whitman played in visiting thousands of soldiers in the Washington hospitals and the poetic role he played as the "wound-dresser" actually enabled a range of socially prohibited physical contact with and emotional exchanges among men. Soothing, touching, hugging, and kissing the sick and dying soldiers, the private poet merges with the public, female with male, "wound-dresser" with soldier, lover with democratic patriot, in Whitman's poems of the Civil War. "Many a soldier's loving arms about this neck have cross'd and rested, / Many a soldier's kiss dwells on these bearded lips," the poet wrote ("The Dresser," *DT,* 34).

The intensity of Whitman's passion for men, released and allowed by the "manly" context of war, is particularly evident in "Vigil Strange I Kept on the Field One Night," which along with "When I Heard at the Close of the Day" is perhaps Whitman's most fervent and lyrically moving expression of same-sex love. But having said this, it is also important to recognize the ways the languages of manly love, paternity, military comradeship, and maternal care intermix and mingle in the poem:

Vigil strange I kept on the field one night,
When you, my son and my comrade, dropt at my side that day,
One look I but gave, which your dear eyes return'd, with a look I shall never
    forget;
One touch of your hand to mine, O boy, reach'd up as you lay on the ground;
Then onward I sped in the battle, the even-contested battle;
Till late in the night reliev'd, to the place at last again I made my way;
Found you in death so cold, dear comrade—found your body, son of responding
    kisses, (never again on earth responding). (*DT,* 42)

As the poet carefully envelops his "dear comrade," his "son" and "soldier," and his "boy of responding kisses" in a blanket and buries him "where he fell," he, in effect, prepares the ground, which, as in "A March in the Ranks Hard-Prest, and the Road Unknown" and other Civil War poems, will enable him to carry on amid what he called the "malignancy," butchery, and surrounding darkness of the war.

The centrality of the Civil War in testing and affirming not only the American union but a range of physical and emotional bonds of affection and intimacy among men as the foundation of the future American republic is most explicitly expressed in "Over the Carnage Rose Prophetic a Voice."

Over the carnage rose prophetic a voice,
Be not dishearten'd—Affection shall solve the problems of Freedom yet;
Those who love each other shall become invincible—they shall yet make
    Columbia victorious. (*DT*, 50)

As in "I Dream'd in a Dream," the poet affirms the relation between "manly affection," physical touching among men across class and state bounds, and the dreams of democracy:

It shall be customary in the houses and street to see manly affection;
The most dauntless and rude shall touch face to face lightly;
The dependence of Liberty shall be lovers,
The continuance of Equality shall be comrades.

These shall tie you and band you stronger than hoops of iron;
I, extatic, O partners! O lands! With the love of lovers tie you. (*DT*, 50)

This poem, which, with the exception of the opening and closing lines, was transferred from the "Calamus" sequence into *Drum-Taps and Sequel* (1865), suggests the ongoing presence and sustenance of Whitman's homoerotic feeling for men during the Civil War and its aftermath. Rather than representing a retreat from the privacy of homoerotic love, in Whitman's writings of the post-Civil War period this love actually expands, even in the most public context of his famous wartime elegy for Abraham Lincoln, "When Lilacs Last in the Dooryard Bloom'd," where the poet mourns the death of Lincoln as "lustrous" comrade and lover.

The Civil War not only affirmed "manly affection" as the ground of a new democratic order; it also gave Whitman a more militant and combative language in which to affirm his commitment to the ongoing struggle for this order in the post-Civil War period. "I know my words are weapons, full of danger, full of death," the poet declares in "As I Lay with My Head in Your Lap, Camerado," urging his readers to join him in the democratic struggle:

For I confront peace, security, and all the settled laws, to unsettle them;
I am more resolute because all have denied me, than I could ever have been had
    all accepted me;
I heed not, and have never heeded, either experience, cautions, majorities, nor
    ridicule;
And the threat of what is call'd hell is little or nothing to me;
And the lure of what is call'd heaven is little or nothing to me;
. . . Dear camerado! I confess I have urged you onward with me, and still urge
    you, without the least idea what is our destination,
Or whether we shall be victorious, or utterly quell'd and defeated. (*DT*, 19)

Ironically, it was in the fields and hospitals of the Civil War that Whitman came closest to realizing his democratic and homosexual dream of a "new City of Friends." Included among the poems of demobilization, "As I Lay with My Head in Your Lap, Camerado" not only speaks a fluidly double language of homeroticism and democracy; it also registers uneasiness as the poet moves away from the true democracy of wartime comradeship toward the potentially oppressive structures of a peacetime—and heterosexual—economy. Addressing a "you" who is, as in "Calamus," both personal lover and democratic comrade, the poet expresses renewed dedication to a boundless democratic "destination" that will include and indeed be grounded in a new order of "manly affection" and love.

Whitman in Love

It is ironic that the iconography of the good gray poet came to dominate Whitman's public image and later critical treatments of his life and work during the very years when we have the most specific historical documentation of his intimate relationships with men.[27] "What did I get?" Whitman said of his service in the Washington hospitals during the Civil War. "Well—I got the boys, for one thing: the boys: thousands of them: they were, they are, they will be mine. . . . I got the boys: then I got Leaves of Grass: but for this I would never have had Leaves of Grass—the consummated book (the last confirming word): I got that: the boys, the Leaves: I got them."[28]

In addition to the extensive correspondence that Whitman carried on with the young men he met during the Civil War, Whitman's notebooks and his correspondence with Peter Doyle (Figure 17) and Harry Stafford (Figure 18) provide a particularly moving record of his emotional and loving attachments to young working-class men. "Dear Boy," Whitman wrote in 1868 to Peter Doyle, a streetcar driver and ex-Confederate soldier whom he met in Washington in 1865: "I think of you very often, dearest comrade, & with more calmness than when I was there—I find it first rate to think of you, Pete, & to know you are there, all right, & that I shall return, & we will be together again. I don't know what I should do if I had't you to think of & look forward to." "My darling," he wrote in 1869, "if you are not well when I come back I will get a good room or two in some quiet place. . . . and we will live together, & devote ourselves altogether to the job of curing you." "Good night, my darling son," he wrote in 1870, "here is a kiss for you, dear boy—on the paper here—a good long one—. . . I will imagine you with your arm around my neck saying Good night, Walt—& me—Good night, Pete."[29]

In a notebook entry that appears to refer to the "*enormous* PERTUR-

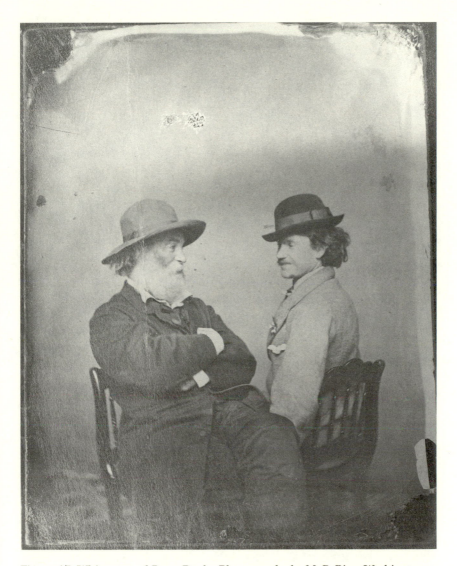

Figure 17. Whitman and Peter Doyle. Photography by M. P. Rice, Washington, D.C., c. 1869. "Dear Boy," Whitman wrote to Doyle from New York in 1868, "I think of you very often, dearest comrade, & with more calmness than when I was there." Courtesy the Library of Congress, Prints and Photographs Division, LC-USZ62–79930.

Walt Whitman & Harry Stafford
photo sent from U.S. in June 1924 by H.S.'s sister
Wildwood (or Kirkwood) N.J.

Figure 18. Whitman and Harry Stafford, who wears a ring that Whitman gave him on the little finger of his right hand. Photographer unknown; late 1870s. "Dear Hank," Whitman wrote Stafford in 1881, "I realize plainly that *if I had not known you . . . I should not be a living man to-day . . . you, my darling boy, are the central figure of them all—.*" Sheffield Archives, Carpenter Collection 8/76. Courtesy the Head of Leisure Services, Sheffield City Council, Sheffield, England.

BATION" of his "FEVERISH, FLUCTUATING" physical and emotional attachment to Peter Doyle, Whitman wrote:

Depress the adhesive nature
It is in excess—making life a torment
All this diseased, feverish disproportionate *adhesiveness*
Remember Fred Vaughan.[30] (*UPP*, 2:96–97)

In Whitman criticism, this entry is usually cited as an instance of the poet's attempt to suppress his sexual desire for men in order to transform himself into the safer and more publicly acceptable image of the good gray poet. But at no place in his notebooks does Whitman suggest that "adhesiveness" is itself "diseased." Rather, like the male purity tracts, what Whitman suggests is that it is "adhesiveness" in excess that makes "life a torment" and must be brought under control. "PURSUE HER NO MORE," Whitman wrote, coyly changing the object of his erotic desire from HIM to HER. But the change once again suggests the fluidity and convertibility of male and female identities and desires in Whitman's work. The poet's perception of his "adhesiveness" as "diseased" and "disproportionate" and "in excess" does not change even if the object of his excessive attachment has been written over as *HER* rather than *HIM*.

Although the intimacy between Whitman and Doyle appears to have subsided in the years following Whitman's paralytic stroke in 1873 and his move to Camden, New Jersey, to live with his brother George, by the mid-1870s he had entered into a passionate love relationship with Harry Stafford, a young man of eighteen to whom Whitman gave a ring as a sign of his deep affection. "My nephew & I when traveling always share the same room together & the same bed," Whitman wrote in 1876 to arrange for a room (and a bed) with Stafford on one of their trips to New York (*CORR*, 3:68). Their ardent and turbulent relationship lasted several years and had a major impact on Whitman's life. "Dear Hank," Whitman wrote Stafford in 1881, "I realize plainly that if I had not known you . . . I should not be a living man to-day—I think & remember deeply these things & they comfort me—& you, my darling boy, are the central figure of them all—" (*CORR*, 3:215).

In addition to leaving a written legacy of images of male-male desire that has functioned centrally in the constitution of modern homosexual identities and communities, Whitman also left a visual legacy of portraits, a small cache of "chum" photographs taken with his boyfriends: Peter Doyle in the 1860s (Figure 17), Harry Stafford in the 1870s (Figure 18), Bill Duckett in the 1880s (Figure 19), and Warren (Warrie) Fritzinger in the 1890s (Figure 20). Although these photographs were not

Figure 19. Whitman and Bill Duckett. Photographer unknown; tintype, ca. 1886. Sometime between 1886 and 1892 Duckett, who was Whitman's housemate in 1886 and companion in the late 1880s, posed as one of Thomas Eakins's nude models. Courtesy Rare Books Division, The New York Public Library, Astor, Lenox, and Tilden Foundations.

Figure 20. Whitman on the Camden wharf with Warren Fritzinger, who was
Whitman's nurse and companion during the last three years of his life.
Photograph by John Johnston, 1890. "I like [Warrie's] touch and he is strong, a
font of bodily power," Whitman told Horace Traubel in 1889; "he has that
wonderful indescribable combination—rarely found, precious when
found—which, with great manly strength, unites sweet delicacy, soft as a
woman's." Courtesy the Library of Congress, Prints and Photographs Division,
LC-USZ62–89910.

"published" until after Whitman's death in 1892 (and they are still little known or remarked upon by Whitman scholars), they were circulated among Whitman's friends and critics during his lifetime and used in the decade after his death both to canonize Whitman as the good gray poet, as in Richard Maurice Bucke's edition of Whitman's letters to Doyle in *Calamus* (1897), and, as in John Addington Symonds's *Walt Whitman: A Study* (1893) and Eduard Bertz's "Walt Whitman: Ein Charakterbild" (1905), to circulate Whitman's visual image as part of the cultural capital of a newly emerging international homosexual community.

As Ed Folsom argues powerfully in his essay "Whitman's Calamus Photographs," these revisionary portraits stage new identities and new versions of the family, marriage, and social relationships that blur the traditional roles of mother, father, husband, wife, brother, lover, friend.[31] Through their stunning visual enactments of the ways Whitman might be said to speak not so much *for* woman, bride, wife, and mother but *as* woman, bride, wife, and mother, these "family" and "marital" photographs further suggest the mixture and fluidity of gender identity and performance in Whitman's work. In fact, the photographs are all the more striking because they were taken during the last twenty-five years of Whitman's life, the very years when he is said to have sublimated his sexual passion for men in the more conventional roles of the "wound-dresser," the "good gray poet," and the patriotic nationalist. They were also taken at a time when greater public restraints were being placed on the popular and primarily working-class genre of male "chum" photographs.[32]

In support of the idea of the increasing split between private and public in Whitman's works in the postwar years, as Whitman the lover of men gives way to the iconography of the good gray poet, critics have emphasized the changes that Whitman made in his "Calamus" poems after he was fired by the Department of the Interior for moral turpitude in 1865.[33] But here again, a close study of the changes that Whitman made in future editions of *Leaves of Grass* reveals no clear pattern of suppressing or even toning down his love poems to men. In fact, Whitman's decision to delete three poems from "Calamus"—"Who Is Now Reading This?" "I Thought That Knowledge Alone Would Suffice," and "Hours Continuing Long"—suggests that he sought not to tone down or suppress his expression of "manly love" but to suppress the more anguished dimensions of his love for men and to blur the distinction between public poet and private lover he set forth in "I Thought That Knowledge Alone Would Suffice." Moreover, in "The Base of All Metaphysics," the one poem he added to the "Calamus" sequence in 1871, Whitman represents "The dear love of man for his comrade, the attraction of friend to friend" as the "base and finalè too for all metaphysics," underlying the philosophies of Plato, Socrates, and Christ, as well as the systems of German philosophy represented by Fichte, Schelling, and Hegel.[34]

Democratic Vistas

Whitman's representation of men loving men as the base of a new social order underlies the visionary democracy of *Democratic Vistas* (1871). In this major attempt to come to terms with the problems of democracy in America, Whitman concludes that "intense and loving comradeship, the personal and passionate attachment of man to man," represents "the most substantial hope and safety of the future of these States." "It is to the development, identification, and general prevalence of that fervid comradeship, (the adhesive love, at least rivaling amative love hitherto possessing imaginative literature, if not going beyond it)," Whitman explains in a footnote, "that I look for the counterbalance and offset of our materialistic and vulgar American democracy, and for the spiritualization thereof." Amid what he called the aggressive selfism, vulgar materialism, and widespread corruption of the Gilded Age, Whitman looked not to marriage or to the traditional family but to "the personal and passionate attachment of man to man" as the social base and future hope of the American republic. "I say democracy infers such loving comradeship as its most inevitable twin or counterpart, without which it will be incomplete, in vain, and incapable of perpetuating itself" (*PW*, 2:414–15).[35]

If what I have been arguing is correct, why did Whitman not just come out with it in his famous exchange with John Addington Symonds in 1890, when Symonds asked him outright if his "conception of Comradeship" included the possibility of "semi-sexual emotions & actions" between men? Whitman could have said, "Yes, John, *Leaves of Grass* is, indeed, about cocksucking and democracy. You found me out." Instead, he disavowed Symonds's "morbid inferences" about the "Calamus" poems as "undream'd," "unreck'd," and "damnable" and cautioned him about the necessity of construing "all parts & pages" of *Leaves of Grass* "by their own ensemble, spirit & atmosphere" (*CORR*, 5:72–73). Although Whitman's response is coy, it also seems right to me for all the reasons I have been trying to suggest. Whitman and Symonds were speaking two different though not entirely separable languages. Whereas Havelock Ellis and Symonds were central to the process of medicalizing and singling out the homosexual as abnormal and pathological, Whitman was talking about physical and emotional love between men as the basis for a new social and religious order.[36] Given his representation of male sexual love as the source of spiritual and poetic vision and the ground for a new democratic social order and given Ellis's and Symonds's medicalization of physical love between men as "sexual inversion" and "abnormal instinct," it makes sense that Whitman would disavow Symonds's attempt to medicalize and sexually categorize the "Calamus" poems as "morbid inferences" contrary to the "ensemble, spirit & atmosphere" of *Leaves of Grass* (*CORR,* 5:73).

Whitman's famous assertion, in this same letter to Symonds, that he had fathered six children is, to say the least, disingenuous. But it is not wholly at odds with the amative, reproductive, and familial languages and contexts in which he expressed the loving relationships among and between men. In fact, given the languages of paternal, maternal, and familial affection in which Whitman carried on his relationships and correspondence with Fred Vaughan, Peter Doyle, Harry Stafford, and some of the soldiers he met during the war, including Tom Sawyer and Lewis Brown, one might argue that Whitman was thinking of some of the "illegitimate sons" he adopted, fathered, and mothered over the course of his life.

In his attempt to give Whitman's conception of comradeship and his "Calamus" poems only one reading, Symonds in some sense anticipates the tendency among recent critics to treat Whitman's homosexuality as a single, transhistorical presence. Against those who read in Whitman's work an instance of what Symonds called "sexual inversion" or what Lynch has called "a distinct 'homosexual identity' or 'homosexual role,'"[37] I have been arguing that we read Whitman's expression of sexual, emotional, and social intimacy among men not as a monolithic homosexual presence but as the complex, multiply located, and historically embedded sexual, social, and discursive phenomenon that it was. To those who insist on dividing Whitman the private poet and Whitman the public poet, Whitman the lover of men and Whitman the poet of democracy, or in Cowley's apt phrase, "cocksucking and democracy," I have been trying to suggest that read within the context of what Whitman called the "ensemble, spirit & atmosphere" of his work, the homosexual poet and the American republic refuse any neat division; they intersect, flow into each other, and continually break bounds. "Who need be afraid of the merge?" Whitman asks in "Song of Myself." The answer to that question is still, in the new millennium, we all are.

Chapter 6

Emily Dickinson and Class

> *The Malay — took the Pearl —*
> *Not — I — the Earl —*
>
> —*Emily Dickinson*, Poems

> *Amalgams are abundant, but the lone student of the Mines adores Alloyless*
> *things —*
>
> —*Emily Dickinson*, Letters

As a feminist who crosses over, who works on both Walt Whitman and Emily Dickinson, I have been struck by a split in my critical voice and perspective in the writing that I have done on these two major nineteenth-century American poets. Whereas my work on Whitman has tended to be historical, contextual, and frequently critical of Whitman's politics, particularly his attitudes toward race and slavery, my work on Dickinson has tended to be biographical, psychosexual, and frequently celebratory of the affirming and specifically female dimensions of her life and work.[1] This split in my critical voice and practice corresponds with broader contests in the fields of literary, cultural, and gender studies about whether sex or class is the primary category of historical and cultural analysis.[2]

Nowhere is the controversy over the relative merits and limits and possible interdependence of class and gender as categories of historical and cultural analysis more evident than in feminist work on Emily Dickinson. From Rebecca Patterson's early emphasis on Dickinson's erotic relationships with women in *The Riddle of Emily Dickinson* (1951), to Adrienne Rich's important essay "Vesuvius at Home: The Power of Emily Dickinson" (1975), to the work of Sandra Gilbert, Joanne Feit Diehl, Barbara Mossberg, Vivian Pollak, and Wendy Martin, among others, feminist critics have overturned traditional representations of Dickinson as sentimental recluse, "Belle of Amherst," unrequited lover, or sublimated neurotic.[3] But through an almost exclusive focus on gender, psychosexuality, and patriarchy as the primary oppression, feminist critics have also tended paradoxically to take Dickinson out of history, reprivatizing her in the space of the home and the psyche, and subsuming the particularity and difference of her life and work into a repeat across time of the same familial romance: the story of the daughter's revolt against a demonized and transhistorical patriarch and her desire to return to a preoedipal and prehistorical mother.[4]

In this chapter, I would like to challenge the historical grounds of these polarizations by resituating Dickinson as fully and complexly as possible in relation to the social, political, and cultural struggles of her time. While it is certainly true to say that Dickinson was not an overtly political poet in the same sense that Whitman was, it is simply not true to say that she had no politics and no ideological investment in a particular order of power. Dickinson was, in fact, born into a more publicly active and politically engaged family than was Whitman: her grandfather Samuel Fowler Dickinson helped found Amherst Academy (1814) and later Amherst College (1821); her father, Edward Dickinson, and her brother, Austin, were actively involved in public projects and in the institutional ordering and administration of the church, college, and town of Amherst over many years. As William S. Tyler writes in his *History of Amherst College* (1873), Edward Dickinson "has been so long and so fully identified with the town, the first parish and the College, that the history of either of them cannot be written without writing the principal events of his life."[5] Following the panic of 1837, Edward Dickinson also served as a state representative in the Massachusetts General Court in 1838 and 1839 and later as a state senator in 1842 and 1843 and a member of the Governor's Council in 1845 and 1846. Between 1853 and 1855, at a time of intensified struggle over the issue of slavery, he served as a representative to Congress from the Tenth District of Massachusetts. Dickinson was a possible candidate for governor of Massachusetts in 1859 and a nominee for lieutenant governor in 1860 and 1861. Later, in 1873, only a year before his death, he was elected again to serve in the Massachusetts General Court.

As the multiple public and political engagements of her father suggest, Emily Dickinson lived in a political house. But politics is not only or always an involvement or concern with the governance of the state: politics is also the entire network of power relations ordering a society. If Dickinson was a more reclusive poet than Whitman, the metaphysical and linguistic space of her poems is traversed by her ideological assumptions and presumption as a member of New England's political—and Whig—elite. In this chapter, I want to seek to "de-naturalize" and make visible the historical and specifically class formation of Dickinson's life and work.[6]

House Politics

"In the family," Engels wrote, the man "is the bourgeois, the woman represents the proletariat."[7] Yet Dickinson's sister, Lavinia, described the economy of the Dickinson household in terms that suggest that Dickinson was not at all a proletarian in any modern or Marxist sense of the term: "As for Emily, she was not withdrawn or exclusive really. She was always watching for the rewarding person to come, but she was a very busy person herself. *She had to think*—she was the only one of us who had that to do. Father believed; and mother loved; and Austin had Amherst; and I had the family to keep track of."[8] While father "believed" and worked as a lawyer in the Amherst community, mother "loved," and Lavinia managed the house, Dickinson *thought*; meanwhile the Dickinson household, stable, and grounds were supported and maintained over many years by a number of Irish immigrant servants, including, at the time of Dickinson's death in 1886, six Irish workmen who carried her body across the fields to the family plot (*LD*, 3:959–60).[9]

As the privileged daughter of the town squire, Dickinson did not, like some of her middle-class New England sisters, have to enter the factory system that was then emerging locally. Nor did she, like some of the poorer women and children of Amherst, have to "put out" straw hats for David Mack's hat factory. Within the domestic economy of the Dickinson household, as in the larger political economy of nineteenth-century America, Dickinson was the "lady" and the intellectual whose leisure, freedom, and space "to think" were made possible by the manual labor and proletarianization of others.

If in relation to the larger social and industrial transformation of the United States in the nineteenth century the Dickinson household appears to represent the interests and economy of an emergent middle class, in the Amherst community it enjoyed the status and rank of an aristocratic and feudal estate. Amherst residents consistently referred to the Dickinson house as the "Homestead" and the "Mansion," terms that reveal a typically American slippage between farmhouse and manor, yeoman and aristocrat, an agrarian American order and an older English feudal order. Like his father Samuel Fowler Dickinson, Edward Dickinson was the local squire, which meant technically that he was a justice of the peace but which gave him the status of an English country gentleman and linked him with an older New England order of rule by a landed squirearchy of wealth and royal entitlement.[10] Edward Dickin-

son, wrote his niece Clara Newman Turner in 1894, "was a grand type
of a class now extinct—An Old-School-Gentleman-Whig!"[11]

Both within and outside the Dickinson family the sense of class consciousness and the potentially dangerous permeability of class boundaries was so strong that when, in 1856, Austin Dickinson married Sue
Gilbert, whose father was a local tavern owner, he was looked upon as
having married beneath his class. "The whole situation was another
illustration of the impossibility of a marriage between different grades
of society ever becoming a perfect fusion," wrote Mabel Loomis Todd,
who carried on a thirteen-year love relationship with Austin between
1882 and his death in 1895.[12] "Sue's father was a 'tavern keeper' of
decidedly convivial habits, and Austin's father was a dignified gentleman, a lawyer of the old school," Todd noted. "The two could hardly
have known of each other's existence, mentally, at least. In those early
days the democratic mixing of upper and lower classes was, to be sure,
much more easily accomplished than in these later and stricter days of
preserving family and training. And Sue always made a point of associating principally with daughters of the better class."[13] Todd's comments
suggest that the famous "War between the Houses" of Emily and Sue
was, in part, a class war, rooted in the socioeconomic differences
between Sue Gilbert as the orphaned, mobile, and socially aspiring
daughter of an Amherst tavern owner and Emily Dickinson as the privileged, homebound, and socially endowed daughter of the town squire.
Unlike Sue, Dickinson could exercise the class privilege of choosing to
stay at home and ultimately not to marry, to reproduce, or to circulate,
either herself or her poems.

The ways Dickinson's sense of identity and status became bound up
with the Dickinson property and her own fear of a "democratic mixing"
of classes are suggested by a dream she had when she was a student at
Mount Holyoke. In October 1847, she wrote to Austin: "Well, I dreamed
a dream & Lo!!! Father had failed & mother said that 'our rye field
which she & I planted, was mortgaged to Seth Nims.' I hope it is not true
but do write soon & tell me for you know 'I should expire with mortifi-
cation' to have our rye field mortgaged, to say nothing of it's falling into
the merciless hands of a loco!!!" (*LD*, 1:48–49). In addition to registering a more general Whig fear that the Democrats were censoring the
mails, Dickinson's dream registers her protest against the Jacksonian
democratization of the civil service and her personal anxiety that the
Dickinson property and class position were under siege by the leveling
spirit of Jacksonian democracy represented locally by the Locofoco postmaster Seth Nims.

In the same letter Dickinson half-humorously protested the expan-
sionist and nationalist Democratic policies of President Polk, policies

that had led to the Mexican War and that seemed to endanger Dickinson's own sense of identity, status, and place in rural New England. "Has the Mexican war terminated yet & how?" she asks her brother, imagining the possibility of invasion by Mexico or perhaps the U.S. government itself: "Do you know of any nation about to besiege South Hadley? If so, do inform me of it, for I would be glad of a chance to escape, if we are to be stormed" (*LD*, 1:49).

Dickinson's fear of downward mobility was not completely unfounded. Her childhood and adolescence had been marked by the panic of 1837 and a depression in the economy from which the country did not fully recover until the mid-1840s. During these years, the privileged socioeconomic status of the Dickinson family was not at all secure. Samuel Fowler built the Dickinson "Mansion" in 1813 at a time of rapid growth in manufacturing, agriculture, and the service industries in the Amherst community. After 1830 and particularly following the panic of 1837, however, as Amherst shifted from self-sufficiency to dependence on outside markets and control of manufacturing moved from independent household production to the factory, the town began to lose manufacturing strength and population both to the large-scale industrial development of eastern cities and to the expansion of settlement westward.[14]

In 1830, the year of Emily Dickinson's birth, her father had to buy half of the "Mansion" on Main Street, which had been mortgaged to creditors in 1825, in order to secure the house against the bankruptcy of her grandfather, who had lost the family fortune by overinvesting his time and money in public projects such as the founding of Amherst College.[15] In 1833, Samuel Fowler Dickinson departed for Ohio in financial ruin, and the entire Dickinson "Mansion" was sold to an outsider, General David Mack, Jr., who came to Amherst to set up a factory for the manufacture and sale of straw hats (Figure 21). While Edward Dickinson and his family continued as occupants of the former family house, they were forced to share it with the Mack family, from whom they rented the east half.

Left with half a house, an uncertain law practice, and his father's debt, Edward Dickinson experienced a sense of panic that he was losing status and ground to a new breed of entrepreneurs. "I must make money in some way," he wrote to his wife on 7 September 1835. "To be shut up forever 'under a bushel' while hundreds of mere Jacanapes are getting their tens of thousands & hundreds of thousands, is rather too much for my spirit—I must spread myself over more ground—half a house, & a rod square for a garden, won't answer my turn."[16] In 1840, at a time of ongoing economic depression, Edward Dickinson bought—with the help of his father-in-law and an advance on his wife's inheritance—a

Figure 21. Lithograph of Main Street, 1840, provides the earliest glimpse of
Dickinson Homestead (center background) with David Mack & Son Straw Works
in foreground. By permission of the Jones Library, Inc., Amherst, Massachusetts.

house on West Street, where the Dickinson family lived until 1855, when
they were able to repurchase the "Old Homestead" from Mack (Figure
22).[17]

As an "Old-School-Gentleman-Whig," Edward Dickinson embodied
the paradox of the Whig position at a time when an older New England
elite of landed wealth and social status was eroding under the pressure
of an ascendant capitalist economy of money and individual enterprise.
For all his aspiration to be an English country gentleman, his entitlement in the United States was neither natural nor hereditary but
grounded in his possession of a certain amount of land and, increasingly, large amounts of money. Edward Dickinson's fear of being "shut
up forever 'under a bushel' while hundreds of mere Jacanapes are getting their tens of thousands & hundreds of thousands" represents a
moment of socioeconomic crisis when the traditional New England ruling class realizes that it is about to be displaced not only by the so-called
self-made men of the Jacksonian era but by the entrepreneurial and progressive logic of Whig economic policy itself.

Arts of Resistance

During the 1850s, as the Whig Party dissolved under the pressure of the
slavery controversy and Edward Dickinson held to the conservative party

Figure 22. Bachelder lithograph, 1858, of "The Homestead," which Edward Dickinson repurchased in April 1855 from Samuel Mack. By permission of the Jones Library, Inc., Amherst, Massachusetts.

faith of Daniel Webster, even as many of his friends joined the newly formed Republican Party, Emily Dickinson sought to resist the forces of democratic, commercial, industrial, and national transformation by enclosing herself in ever smaller social units—first within Amherst, then within her house, and ultimately within her room and the space of her own mind. She not only set herself against the abolitionist, reformist, and democratizing energies of the times; she also set herself against the more public political engagement of her father. When he was serving as a representative in Congress between 1853 and 1855, Emily Dickinson resented the fact that he, like her grandfather, neglected the family for the public interest. "Caesar [Father] is such 'an honorable man,'" she wrote Austin, mimicking the republican rhetoric of personal sacrifice for the public good, "that we may all go to the Poor House, for all the American Congress will lift a finger to help us" (*LD*, 1:275).

Moreover, while her father was instrumental in bringing the Belchertown Railroad to Amherst in 1853, she looked upon the railroad as an intrusion from abroad that quickened the pace of life and thrust Amherst into the grip of outsiders and the "almighty dollar." "Our house is crowded daily with the members of this world," she wrote Austin; "the 'poor in this world's goods,' and the 'almighty dollar,' and 'what in the world are they after' continues to be unknown—But I hope they will pass away, as insects on vegetation, and let us reap together in golden harvest time—that is you and Susie and me and our dear sister Vinnie" (*LD*, 1:257).

Although Dickinson's acts of self-enclosure and her later refusal to "cross" what she called "my Father's ground" (*LD*, 2:460) were at least in part a means of protecting her artistic creation, they were also class acts, manifesting her desire to define herself against and distinguish herself from the potentially polluting incursions of the democratic multitude. Dickinson was driven by a "suppressed and ungratified desire for distinction," wrote her childhood friend Emily Fowler Ford. "She wore white, she shut herself away from her race as a mark of her separation from the mass of minds."[18] It was this same separation from the "common daily strife" of the masses that Ford emphasized in a poem to Dickinson published in the *Springfield Daily Republican* on 11 January 1891: "Nor will you touch a hand, or greet a face,— / For common daily strife to you is rude."[19] Although Ford may be merely angry because Dickinson had refused to see even her in 1882, her characterization corresponds with Dickinson's own representations of herself and others in her letters and in her poems.

As a student at Mount Holyoke in 1847, Dickinson wrote her friend Abiah Root: "When I left home, I did not think I should find a companion or a dear friend in *all the multitude*. I expected to find *rough & uncultivated manners*" (*LD*, 1:55; emphasis added). This sense of social difference and the urge to define herself against and apart from the "rough & uncultivated" multitude is a recurrent theme in Dickinson's poems:

The Soul selects her own Society —
Then — shuts the Door —
To her divine Majority —
Present no more —

Unmoved — she notes the Chariots — pausing —
At her low Gate —
Unmoved — an Emperor be kneeling
Upon her Mat —

I've known her — from an ample nation —
Choose One —
Then — close the Valves of her attention —
Like Stone — (*Fr* 409A)

Whether referring to an act of self-enclosure or enclosure within a specific class, what Dickinson describes in a monarchical language of emperors, chariots, and divine right is a rigidly stratified social order of rank, exclusion, and difference in which the "Door" of one's "own Society" is closed to all but a select few chosen from an "ample nation."

Similarly, in "*One life* of so much consequence!" and "The Soul's Superior instants," the poet sets herself omnipotently above and beyond the "thick" and "dense" multitude, identifying with a monarchical and privileged elite "*perceptible* — / Far down the dustiest Road!" (*Fr* 248). Even Dickinson's poems of romantic entrapment, including "Mute — thy coronation —," "I met a King this Afternoon!" "The *Sun — just touched* the Morning," "The Court is far away —," and "He put the Belt around my life —," are enacted as scenes of submission to superior men—dukes, masters, wheeling kings, and even God himself as "a distant — stately Lover —." In fact, in Dickinson's most anthologized poem, "Because I could not stop for Death —," Death himself comes courting as an aristocratic gentleman with horses and carriage to take the lady of "Gossamer" and "Tulle" for her "immortal" ride.

Like nineteenth-century Whig political rhetoric, the language of Dickinson's poems slips between the old and the new, between an aristocratic language of rank, royalty, and hereditary privilege and a Calvinist language of spiritual grace, personal sanctity, and divine election in which the aristocratic ideals of hierarchy and social subordination are displaced from the secular to the divine arena. Although Dickinson never converted to Calvinism, its terms continued to shape the language, imagery, and conceptual framework of her poems. For her, as for other conservative New England Whigs, the notion of a divinely elected spiritual aristocracy predestined to power and to rule served ultimately to support a hierarchical social order against the more public, egalitarian rhetorics of the time. In fact, until the nineteenth century, in New England at least, the Calvinist notion of an aristocracy of spirit had never existed apart from the fact of an economic elite who actually did rule politically, socially, and culturally.

Thus, in the poem "Mine — by the Right of the White Election!" Dickinson deploys a simultaneously aristocratic and Calvinist language of rank, royal entitlement, and divine right:

Mine — by the Right of the White Election!
Mine — by the Royal Seal!
Mine — by the sign of the Scarlet prison —
Bars — cannot conceal! (*Fr* 411)

Setting the speaker's own right to possession against the claims of some unnamed antagonist, the poem gives voice to the social and territorial as well as racial imperatives of New England's ruling class. Although the poet speaks the language of Revelation, here as in "A solemn thing — it was — I said — / A Woman — white — to be —" and other Dickinson poems, the language of the "Right" of "White Election" cannot finally be separated from nineteenth-century debates about the racial hegemony of the white race and the pure Anglo-Saxon blood of New Englanders in particular in the New World.

"Color — Caste — Denomination —"

Dickinson's elitism is evident in her lofty and at times strikingly unsympathetic response to some of the major social issues of her time. In a letter she wrote to Austin in 1851, she expressed a phobic and seemingly genocidal attitude toward foreigners and the masses. "Vinnie and I say masses for poor Irish boys souls," she wrote when Austin was having trouble disciplining his Irish students at Endicott School in Boston: "So far as *I* am concerned I should like to have you kill some—there are so many now, there is no room for the Americans" (*LD*, 1:113). Although uttered in jest, Dickinson's words reflect the increasingly virulent nativist and anti-foreign sentiments of the Northeast in response to the massive influx of Irish immigrants during the 1830s and 1840s, especially following the Great Famine in Ireland in 1845.[20] Like Daniel Webster, who believed that Englishmen had been chosen "for the great work of introducing English civilization, English law, and what is more than all, *Anglo-Saxon blood*, into the wilderness of North America" in order "to form the great republic of the world," Austin shared his sister's belief in the superiority of native New England class and blood.[21] Austin was "[a]ristocratic, contemptuous," remembered Millicent Todd Bingham, "the spare old Squire who despised the common herd."[22]

In her letters and poems, Dickinson assumes an aristocratic order of rank and difference as part of the natural order of things. Writing to her friends Josiah and Elizabeth Holland in November 1858, she referred to one of her father's workmen as a "serf" as she reflected on the democratic blurring of social bounds brought by death as the great leveler. "I buried my garden last week—our man, Dick, lost a little girl through the scarlet fever," Dickinson wrote, in a passage that disturbs not so much because she equated the loss of her garden with the loss of a workman's child, but because she placed her own loss an aristocratic and "purple" notch above the loss of the "serf's child": "Ah! dainty—dainty Death! Ah! democratic Death!" Dickinson exclaimed, "Grasping the proudest zinnia from my purple garden,—then deep to his bosom calling the serf's child!" "Say, is he everywhere? Where shall I hide my things?" (*LD*, 2:341), she asked, as her psychic and metaphysical fear of "democratic Death" begins to merge with a material and historical fear of losing the Dickinson property, goods, and name to the disruptive force of Jacksonian democracy represented by the "loco" postmaster Seth Nims.

This assumption of a natural social order of class and race informs several poems, including most notably "Color — Caste — Denomination —," which turns on the ironic contrast between a hierarchical and time-bound order of race and class difference, in which dark is subordinated to light, "Umber" to "Chrysalis of Blonde," and a "diviner" and timeless order in which these marks of social distinction will be erased by Death's "Democratic fingers":

Color — Caste — Denomination —
These — are Time's Affair —
Death's diviner Classifying
Does not know they are —

As in sleep — All Hue forgotten —
Tenets — put behind —
Death's large — Democratic fingers
Rub away the Brand —

If Circassian — He is careless —
If He put away
Chrysalis of Blonde — or Umber —
Equal Butterfly —

They emerge from His Obscuring —
What Death — knows so well —
Our minuter intuitions —
Deem unplausible. (*Fr* 836)

Although the poem, which was written after the Emancipation Proclamation toward the close of the Civil War, gestures toward a "large" and essentially utopian social order in which "All Hue" will be "forgotten," the speaker suggests that in time, at least, democracy is impossible. Any democratic "Obscuring" of the time-bound "Brand" of race and class difference, she concludes, "Our minuter intuitions — / Deem unplausible." What the poem suggests finally is that the speaker's "minuter intuitions" have led her to "deem" democracy "unplausible" and indeed rather horrifying not only within but beyond social time.

"The Malay — took the Pearl —" assumes a similarly unchangeable social order of racial and class difference and subordination:

The Malay — took the Pearl —
Not — I — the Earl —
I — feared the Sea — too much
Unsanctified — to touch —

Praying that I might be
Worthy — the Destiny —
The Swarthy fellow swam —
And bore my Jewel — Home —

Home to the Hut! (*Fr* 451)

The poem appears to use the language of racial and class difference to represent an essentially egalitarian spiritual order in which all—blacks as well as whites, "Swarthy" fellows as well as the "Earl"—have access to the "Jewel" of God's grace. Feminists have also read the poem as an articulation of a specifically female anxiety about "the primitivism of male dominance" and the fear of "homosexual conquest."[23] But these readings gloss over the fact that "The Malay" is a dark man of a lower social order and that the entire poem turns on the irony that "The Swarthy fellow," who is assumed to be less worthy, "took the Pearl," which the speaker as "the Earl" implicitly deserves. Indeed, the "Pearl" that the Malay "took" is not his at all; it is "my Jewel," belonging originally, it would seem, to the white and aristocratic speaker.

Read this way, the "Jewel" assumes a more specifically material and historical significance as a sign perhaps of social plenitude, possession, and the fulfillment of earthly desire. The poem—which was written at the time of the Civil War—appears to describe a historical situation in which others, specifically black others, are making gains, while the speaker, an aristocrat, is being "undone." In fact, the speaker's sense of deprivation and loss interestingly parallels Dickinson's father's sense that "mere Jacanapes" were "getting their tens of thousands & hundreds of thousands" while he was losing ground (*YH*, 1:30) and Emily Dickinson's own anxiety that the family might be losing ground amid large-scale social changes in ownership, wealth, and power.

Dickinson manifested little concern about the problems of slavery, industrialism, the urban poor, and the dispossession of the American Indians that sent other New England women out of the home to fight publicly against social injustice. When she did address the social problems of her time, in a poem such as "The Beggar Lad — dies early —," she seems removed from the subject: the "Beggar Lad" becomes a mere vehicle for a conventional spiritual allegory about the ultimate redress of God.[24] Defining herself against not only the lower orders but certain categories of middle-class women, including the Christian benevolent model of true womanhood represented by Mary Lyons at Mount Holyoke and such female proponents of Whig ideology as Catharine Beecher and Sarah Josepha Hale, Dickinson could be quite hard-hearted about the masses who were being dispossessed and impoverished by the same forces of socioeconomic transformation that threatened her own status in rural Amherst.[25]

In an 1850 letter to her friend Jane Humphrey, Dickinson mocked the benevolent notion of women as the feeders, caretakers, and reformers of the world represented by the local sewing society to which she refused to belong: "Sewing Society has commenced again—and held its first meeting last week—now all the poor will be helped—the cold warmed— the warm cooled—the hungry fed—the thirsty attended to—the ragged clothed—and this suffering—tumbled down world will be helped to it's feet again—which will be quite pleasant to all. I dont attend— notwithstanding my high approbation—which must puzzle the public exceedingly. I am already set down as one of those brands almost con- sumed—and my hardheartedness gets me many prayers" (LD, 1:84).

To Dickinson and her sister, the labor abuses, accidents, and increas- ing loss of life brought by industrial transformation became a form of sensational entertainment for the gleeful consumption of the leisure class: "Who writes those funny accidents, where railroads meet each other unexpectedly, and gentlemen in factories get their heads cut off quite informally?" Dickinson asked Samuel Bowles, the editor of the *Springfield Daily Republican,* which she read every night. "The author, too, relates them in such a sprightly way," Dickinson noted, "that they are quite attractive. Vinnie was disappointed to-night, that there were not more accidents—I read the news aloud, while Vinnie was sewing" (LD, 1:264).

"She's tearful — if she weep at all — / For blissful Causes," Dickinson later wrote in the poem "She's happy — with a new Content —," satiriz- ing the reformist energies of her New England sisters (Fr 587). Similarly, in the poem "What Soft — Cherubic Creatures — / These Gentle- women are —," Dickinson satirizes the pious and pure model of true womanhood associated with middle-class women who were, as Gerda Lerner observes, aspiring "to the status formerly reserved for upper-class women."[26] But while Dickinson mocked what she called the "Dimity Convictions" of the Angel in the House, she could also write such lines of pure domestic—and Whig—sentiment as "If I can stop one Heart from breaking / I shall not live in vain" (Fr 982). Moreover, by enclosing herself in the traditionally female space of the home, she ends by enforc- ing the sexual division of labor and the increasing division of public and private spheres that were at the base of the new bourgeois social order she seeks to resist and protest in her life and work.

Within the Dickinson household and in her poems, Dickinson was in some sense the spokesperson and representative of older ruling-class interests.[27] In setting herself against Whig commercial interests and her father's initiative in bringing the Belchertown Railroad to Amherst,

Dickinson identified herself with the "country party" tradition of the eighteenth century and the more specifically Federalist, anticommercial, and ruling-class heritage of John and Abigail Adams and later John Quincy Adams.[28] In fact, Dickinson's fears about the train's arrival in Amherst were borne out by its ultimately debilitating effects on the Amherst community. If it brought business, goods, and what Dickinson called the "almighty dollar" to Amherst, it also linked the town with large-scale and mechanized national and international markets, destroyed its nascent manufacturing economy, and eroded Amherst's population growth and status as an educational center by carrying young people out of the town to seek their fortunes in the east or the west.[29]

But while Dickinson contested Whig economic policies, she subscribed to an essentially Whig moral economy that fostered a personal and social regime of self-renunciation, hierarchy, and control, particularly control of a potentially unruly body. "I do not care for the body," Dickinson wrote Abiah Root in 1850, "the bold obtrusive body—Pray, marm, did you call *me*?" (*LD*, 1:103). Figuring the body as a servant of the lower class, Dickinson registers her experience of the body as the site of her oppression, the place where female nature, in particular the female capacity for reproduction, can be made to serve the needs of man and race. The body is also the site of her identification with and potential invasion by the "rough & uncultivated" desires she associated with the lower class.

Over and over in her poems, from "I dreaded that first Robin, so, / But He is mastered, now" to such erotic dream poems as "I started Early — Took my Dog —" and "In Winter in my Room" to more explicitly didactic poems such as "Renunciation — is a piercing Virtue —," Dickinson registers a fear of being overwhelmed by and a desire to retreat from the body, sexuality, and the specifically corporeal dimensions of experience. On a fundamental level, Dickinson's poems are about disciplining rather than unleashing sexual and social desire; they are about policing, mastering, and controlling the body within the regime of the mind, the soul, and the imagination. This dread of physical experience and the corresponding desire for social control are bound up not only with a fear of the body as the site of female colonization but with an essentially Whig distrust of the body of the democratic masses.

"How do most people live without any thoughts," Dickinson once asked, in a comment that suggests her own superior sense that "most people" lived on the level of the body "without any thoughts" (*LD*, 2:474). Within the political order of Dickinson's verse, the multitude and the democratic masses are consistently demonized. In "The Popular Heart is a Cannon first —" and "The Ditch is dear to the Drunken Man," the masses are associated with intemperance, criminality, and an explosive violence without past or future. The poem "I'm Nobody! Who are you?" appears to parody the politics of title and place:

How dreary — to be — Somebody!
How public — like a Frog —
To tell your name — the livelong June —
To an admiring Bog! (*Fr* 260)

From a gender point of view, the poet's lack of settled identity as "Nobody" represents a form of liberation from the structures of social authority that define and limit a woman's life. But this seemingly democratic "Nobody" masks an aristocrat who refuses to be defined in and through the demonized body of the democratic multitude—figured here as "an admiring Bog."

Like de Tocqueville in *Democracy in America,* Dickinson was critical of the dull conformity of democratic and majority rule. "'George Washington was the Father of his Country,'—'George Who?' That sums all Politics to me," she wrote toward the close of her life (*LD*, 3:849). Her words register her protest against the process of democratization and national political integration that led, in the post-Civil War period, to the enfranchisement of ignorant masses who did not even know the fundamentals about American heritage. "'George Who?'" she asks, mimicking the "Politics" of democracy and the political illiteracy of newly empowered and possibly newly arrived immigrant masses who do not recognize the name of George Washington. If Dickinson's poems bear traces of the individualistic and anti-authoritarian political rhetoric of her times, that rhetoric is translated not into a dream of democracy but into a royalist dream of rule by hereditary and divine right. Thus, in the poem "I'm ceded — I've stopped being Their's —," the speaker "cedes" herself to a higher form of being in the politically charged language of secession, but the secession she imagines is not in favor of a sovereign republican self or state. Rather, "With Will to choose, or to reject," she cedes herself to and secedes into an essentially monarchical order in which she will be "Queen."

Culture and Aristocracy

Read within the context of nineteenth-century American democratic culture, Dickinson's poetry becomes particularly—and politically—illuminating, for it articulates a residual aristocratic social ideal that had been suppressed in the more public political rhetoric of the Whig party. Whereas Douglass, Thoreau, Whitman, and Melville, and many of the women writers of her age, including Stowe, Fuller, Child, and Jacobs, embraced the democratic language of republican ideology even as they turned that language to a critique of the actual practice of American government, Dickinson returned to a pre-Revolutionary and aristocratic language of rank, titles, and divine right to assert the sovereignty of her self as absolute monarch. She not only sets herself against what F. O. Matthiessen calls "the possibilities of democracy" invoked by other writers of her age.[30] At a time when a woman, Victoria, was the queen of England, Dickinson's royalist language also bears witness to the political irony that it is under an aristocratic order of hereditary and divine right rather than under a democratic order of contract and inalienable rights that a woman was entitled to political power and to rule.

In *The Decline of American Gentility*, Stow Persons argues that "the destruction of gentry leadership and the emergence of a mass society in which powers were dispersed to a degree hitherto unknown constituted perhaps the greatest social transformation in American history."[31] Considered within their social moment, at a time when the older rhythms of gentry and rural life were being disrupted by rapid transformations in the socioeconomic landscape of nineteenth-century America, even Dickinson poems that seem most resistant to a historical, and specifically class, reading begin to assume a more than merely personal resonance. The strongly elegiac tone of Dickinson's verse and her constant return to the subjects of time, change, loss, mortality, and death represent a response not only to the death of this or that person but to change itself as the overwhelming social and economic fact of nineteenth-century American life, even in rural Amherst.

In Dickinson's poems, the garden as a site of social abundance is continually threatened by the leveling forces of time, change, and democratic death. In the poem "A loss of something ever felt I —" the poet articulates her sense of loss in explicitly social terms. "As one bemoaning a Dominion / Itself the only Prince cast out —"she experiences her bereavement as the loss of an entire way of social being associated with an aristocratic and essentially monarchical past. Exiled and "cast out" of her princely heritage, she longs for a restoration of her lost rank and estate, signified in the poem by her "Delinquent Palaces" (*Fr* 1072). Even in poems of seemingly "pure" imagination, such as "There is a morn by men unseen —" or "I taste a liquor never brewed —," the poet expresses her desire to retreat from social time into some "remoter green" of ease and stability protected from the motions of historical change. Thus, in the poem "Dare you see a Soul at the 'White Heat'?" the "finer Forge" within becomes a way of securing the speaker against the fact that real forges and real blacksmiths were being dispossessed as the country came increasingly under the control of money, markets, and what Dickinson called "the Mighty Merchant" (*Fr* 401C).

As if in response to the increasing valuation placed on money and material possessions as opposed to ascribed status in the new market-place economy, Dickinson's poems return almost obsessively to the problem of money—or rather, the poet's lack of it. During the depression of 1856–57, the *Hampshire and Franklin Express* commented on the plan to bring a good lecturer to Amherst every few weeks: "A half dozen of our young men, determined upon varying the monotony of the hard times by something that should remind us that we have minds and tastes too as well as pockets, formed themselves into a club, pledging each other for a first class lecture here as often as once a fortnight" (*YH*, 1:350). The cultural note suggests an underlying strategy of Dickinson's work. Whereas Edward Dickinson sought to secure his social position through the acquisition of more money and more land, Dickinson sought to secure the declining status of both her gender and her class through the accumulation of cultural and spiritual capital, what she called "My soul's *entire income* —" (*Fr* 248). Over and over again, Dickinson's poems assert the ultimate and real value of an interior, imaginative, and spiritual economy against the instability of the new market economy of wages, prices, contracts, merchants, securities, stocks, and sudden reversals. "Reverse cannot befall / That fine Prosperity / Whose Sources are interior —," the poet says, setting an inner "Prosperity" against the "Adversity" and "Misfortune" of an international market dependent on the happenings "In far — Bolivian Ground —" (*Fr* 565B). Similarly, in the poem "Some — Work for Immortality — / The Chiefer part, for Time —" the immediate compensation of the market-place, "The Bullion of Today —," is set against the cultural and spiritual "Work" of the poet as "the Currency / Of immortality": "One's — Money — One's — the Mine —," she says (*Fr* 536).

In a lithograph of Amherst dated 1886, two hat factories and a train appear in the foreground and the Homestead and the Evergreens (the house of Austin and Sue next door) appear in the background in a pictorial representation that sets rural past against industrial future, figuring how an older order of landed wealth, rank, and privilege was giving way to a new economic order of industry, entrepreneurs, and money as the ultimate measure of distinction and value (Figure 23). Read within the context of the declining status of her social class, Dickinson's poems might be said to represent that historical moment when the values of an old aristocracy of established rank and power were being translated from the public and political to the literary and aesthetic realm, forming a new kind of cultural aristocracy. For Dickinson, as for the club of young men who determined to bring "first-class" lecturers to Amherst during the depression of 1856–57, "mind and taste" became a means of compensating for the real losses of the "pocket" as a new cultural elite sought to perpetuate the values of stability, order, and degree

Figure 23. Lithograph of Amherst, 1886, with hat factories and train in foreground and the Dickinson Homestead and Evergreens just behind the factories. By permission of the Jones Library, Inc., Amherst, Massachusetts.

against the debased imperatives of the commercial marketplace and the democratic masses.

Dickinson's refusal to publish was marked by a similar aristocratic resistance to the twin forces of democratization and commercialization. In 1843, a reviewer for the prestigious, Whig-oriented *North American Review* expressed anxiety about the increasing commercialization and democratization of literature as the written word and authorship itself became subject to the laws of a marketplace economy. "Literature begins to assume the aspect and undergo the mutations of trade," he noted. "The author's profession is becoming as mechanical as that of the printer and the bookseller, being created by the same causes and subject to the same laws. The nature of the supply seems likely to be as strictly proportioned to the demand, as in any other commercial operation."[32]

In "Myself was formed — a Carpenter —," Dickinson registers a similar anxiety about the literary marketplace. At a time when the traditional artisan economy of craft and handwork was being reduced to wage labor, Dickinson imagines herself as an artisan whose craft is under siege by the marketplace values of speed, cost, and efficiency.

Myself was formed — a Carpenter —
An unpretending time
My Plane — and I, together wrought
Before a Builder came —

To measure our attainments —
Had we the Art of Boards
Sufficiently developed — He'd hire us
At Halves — (*Fr* 475)

Representing herself as a Christ-like figure, Dickinson responds "Against the Man" that she is engaged in another, more immortal kind of work: "We — Temples build — I said —."

Dickinson offered a similar response "Against the Man" in refusing to let her "Mind" be published and put to "use" by the male publishing world. In 1862 she wrote to Thomas Higginson: "Two Editors of Journals came to my Father's House, this winter—and asked me for my Mind—and when I asked them 'Why' they said I was penurious—and they, would *use it for the World*—" (*LD*, 2:404–5; emphasis added).[33] The terms of Dickinson's refusal to publish are inscribed in "Publication — is the Auction," a poem in which the rhetoric of antislavery protest intersects with the language of wage slavery as a new form of human enslavement. Against the "Auction" block of commercial publication, the speaker pleads: "Reduce no Human Spirit / To Disgrace of Price —."

When in 1872 Dickinson was approached by a "Miss P" (perhaps Elizabeth Stuart Phelps, the editor of the *Women's Journal* and author of *The Gates Ajar* [1868], a popular novel that materialized heaven as a middle-class, female-centered household complete with pianos), she responded with an irony that verged on hostility. "Of Miss P—I know but this, dear," she wrote her cousin Louisa Norcross. "She wrote me in October, requesting me to aid the world by my chirrup more. Perhaps she stated it as my duty, I don't distinctly remember, and always burn such letters, so I cannot obtain it now. I replied declining. She did not write to me again—she might have been offended, or perhaps is extricating humanity from some hopeless ditch" (*LD*, 2:500).

Dickinson explicitly mocks and, in effect, "burns up" the middle-class notion of women's writing as an extension of women's domestic role—the missionary idea that it is her "duty" to "aid the world by my chirrup more." Her choice of *chirrup* underlines the trivialization of women's songs and puns on the literary domestic notion that it is the woman writer's role to "cheer up" the world rather than, in Dickinson's terms, to make it "see" complexly, oppositely, and at times somberly. She also takes a parting shot at women reformers, aimed perhaps at Miss P's involvement in temperance reform and the work of "extricating humanity from some hopeless ditch."

In her own writing Dickinson appears to have been more interested in being immortal than in being merely useful, helpful, dutiful, or moral. Adhering to an essentially aristocratic and Carlylean notion of literature as the production of mind and genius for eternity, she set herself against not only the new commercialization and democratization but also the sentimental women writers of her time who had gained money and fame in the American marketplace. At a time when the traditionally productive space of the home and traditional female housework were being devalued, Dickinson also appears to have been engaged in reclaiming the home and women as producers of valuable and enduring work. Sometime in the late 1850s she began arranging and sewing her poems into groupings that Mabel Loomis Todd called "fascicles." Among Dickinson's manuscripts, there are forty groupings that have been threaded and bound together and twenty-five other groupings that have not been sewn. Although Dickinson may have been preparing her poems for eventual publication, her attitude toward the literary marketplace makes it more likely that she was engaged in an alternative form of publication.

Folding, sewing, and binding four or five sheets of paper together in groupings of eighteen to twenty poems, Dickinson, in effect, converted traditional female needlework into a different kind of housework and her own form of productive economy. She appears to have been engaged in a kind of home or cottage industry, a precapitalist mode of manuscript production and circulation that avoided the commodity and use values of the commercial marketplace. Along with the manuscripts that she produced, threaded, and bound herself, Dickinson also engaged in a more exclusive aristocratic form of "publication" by enclosing and circulating her poems in letters to her friends. The irony, of course, is that while Dickinson contested the values of the capitalist marketplace in her life and work, by retreating from historical time and social representation toward writing as a subjective, transcendent, and aestheticized act, she, like other Romantic poets, ended by enforcing the separation of art and society and the corresponding feminization, trivialization, and marginalization of art in the new bourgeois aesthetics.

In *The Madwoman in the Attic,* Sandra Gilbert and Susan Gubar argue that upper-class women "were denied the economic, social, and psychological status ordinarily essential to creativity" and "denied the right, skill, and education to tell their own stories with confidence."[34] I have been suggesting that, on the contrary, it was precisely Dickinson's upper-class economic, social, and psychological status that enabled in fundamental ways her poetic creation and the seeming radicalism of her vision. If Dickinson challenged the masculine orders of authority in home and family, church and state, it was an assault launched from within the confines and class privilege of her "Father's House." If from the point of view of gender her refusal to marry, to publish, and to circulate might be read as a radical act, from the point of view of class that refusal was paradoxically grounded in the privilege of her status as the daughter of a conservative Whig squire. In fact, Dickinson's decision not to marry was underwritten by her father, whose reluctance to have his daughters leave his house may have been related to a desire to keep family and class position intact against the potentially corrosive—and democratizing—influences of the time. It was because Dickinson had the economic privilege to choose to stay at home that she could finally refuse to go to market. "Poverty — be justifying / For so foul a thing / Possibly," she wrote in "Publication — is the Auction," apparently oblivious to the fact that other writers, including her friend Helen Hunt Jackson, really did have to write and to publish for money and survival.

At about the same time Dickinson began writing her poems, the Seneca Falls Convention of 1848 was calling on women to organize for women's rights, women's suffrage, and real political power. Margaret Fuller enjoined women to redeem the lost political ideals of America and pay for what she called "Isabella's jewels" in *Woman in the Nineteenth Century* (1845). And other women writers, including most notably Harriet Beecher Stowe and Harriet Jacobs, celebrated the networks among black and white women as a powerful means of subverting and contesting the slave system. Although Dickinson's recognition of the oppression she shared with other women had the effect of politicizing that experience, the bonds of assistance and resistance she formed with her women friends lacked any larger political reference. She never conceived of taking her struggle into the public sphere of political action.

"If women have a role to play," says Julia Kristeva in "Oscillation between Power and Denial," "it is only in assuming a *negative* function: reject everything finite, definite, structured, loaded with meaning, in the existing state of society. Such an attitude places women on the side of the explosion of social codes: with revolutionary movements."[35] If Dickinson was on the side of revolution, for her, as for Kristeva, it was a revolution located not in the political and economic but the linguistic sphere. Like Kristeva and other French feminists, including Hélène Cixous and Luce Irigaray, Dickinson showed little concern with politically transforming the material conditions of women's lives. Her revolution was enacted on the level of language by fracturing "everything finite, definite, structured, loaded with meaning" and thus challenging a metaphysical order and an entire way of knowing and signifying grounded in the transcendent power of the Word as Logos and Father.

Insofar as language is the symbolic structure that constitutes the social order, Dickinson's disruption of language and syntax might, as Kristeva suggests in *Revolution in Poetic Language,* register or anticipate a revolutionary transformation in the political sphere. But while Dickinson's poetic assault on the patriarchal orders of language parallels the more public agitation for a change in women's social, economic, and legal status in the United States, it is unclear how her poetic revolution might become an agent of political change. As Catherine Clément notes in *The Newly Born Woman*, in a comment on the distinction between Cixous's notion that language can be a vehicle of historical transformation through the writing of female desire and a more classical Marxist notion of language and history as seemingly different realms of struggle: "There is imagination, desire, creation, production of writing . . . and then somewhere else, on another level of reality, there is class struggle, and within it, women's struggle. There are missing links in all that, which we should try to think in order to succeed in joining our two languages."[36]

The "missing links" between Dickinson's revolutionary poetics and the revolutionary struggles of blacks, women, and workers that marked her time suggest a potential problem and contradiction in the current theoretical—and feminist—emphasis on language as the site of political transformation. Dickinson's revolutionary poetic practice seems unconnected with any real transformation in woman's historical status as object and other in a system of production and exchange controlled by men. Like James Joyce, Antonin Artaud, and other celebrated modern poetic "revolutionaries," her radical poetics was conjoined with an essentially conservative and in some sense reactionary politics. If on the level of language Dickinson might be celebrated as a kind of literary terrorist—a "Loaded Gun" and dancing "Bomb"—who blew up the social and symbolic orders of patriarchal language, it is also important that we recognize that her poetic revolution was grounded in the privilege of her class position in a conservative Whig household whose elitist, antidemocratic values were at the very center of her work.

Chapter 7

Beyond the Boundaries
C.L.R. James to Herman Melville

I know of few more thrilling moments in literature for a modern reader, one of us, than when Melville says that the crew is composed of renegades from all over the world.

—C.L.R. James to Jay Leyda, 1953

[T]he national state, every single national state, had and still has a racial doctrine. This doctrine is that the national race, the national stock, the national blood, is superior to all other national races, national stocks and national bloods.

—C.L.R. James, Mariners, Renegades, and Castaways

The modern world is organizing itself scientifically at such speed that either it must be ruled in totalitarian fashion or by a new conception of democracy beyond anything we have known.

—C.L.R. James, American Civilization

"Settled by the people of all nations, all nations may claim her for their own," observes the narrator of Herman Melville's sea novel *Redburn: His First Voyage* (1849) as he reflects on the mixture of American bloods. "You can not spill a drop of American blood without spilling the blood of the whole world," he says. "Be he Englishman, Frenchman, German, Dane, or Scot; the European who scoffs at an American, calls his own brother *Raca,* and stands in danger of the judgment. We are not a narrow tribe of men. . . . No: our blood is as the flood of the Amazon, made up of a thousand noble currents all pouring into one. We are not a nation, so much as a world" (238–39). Resonant with the nineteenth-century political language of America as New World paradise and redeemer nation, Melville's rhetorical figure of America as "the blood of the whole world" evokes a double image of the country as both democratic and imperialist, collective and nationalist, utopian and terrifying.

On the one hand, the blood of the entire world—of all history—appears to flow "from the flood of the Amazon" into the single commanding figure of the American nation. America as the end of history; or as Redburn affirms: "We are the heirs of all time." On the other hand, the image of America as a world family of *blood kin* suggests the possibility of a democratic future of mass empowerment and world community as "the people" flow together across and beyond the narrow boundaries of the nation-state. *We are not a nation, so much as a world.*

It is as a figure of utopian possibility—of "America being in future years a society of liberty and freedom, composed of all the races of the earth" (91)—that C.L.R. James cites this passage from Melville as an epigraph to *Mariners, Renegades, and Castaways: The Story of Herman Melville and the World We Live In* (1953), the boundary-breaking study that James wrote while he was being incarcerated as an illegal alien on Ellis Island in 1952.[1] Here, as in "Notes on American Civilization" (1950), the longer study from which his book on Melville is drawn, James sees in American literature, politics, and culture a powerful instance of popular struggle and the creative role of the masses—particularly the masses of color—in advancing the cause of world civilization and what he calls "the universal republic of liberty and fraternity" (*M*, 92).

As a labor and anticolonial activist in Trinidad, where he was born in 1901, and later in Britain, where he moved in 1932, and in the United States, where he moved in 1938, C.L.R. James worked within and across a number of different genres and geographical spaces. As a sports critic he wrote reports on cricket for the *Manchester Guardian* and other English journals. His 1932 political biography, *The Life of Captain Cipriani: An Account of British Government in the West Indies,* makes one of the strongest cases of the time against British imperial rule in the West Indies. He produced a play, *Toussaint L'Ouverture,* in London in 1936, the same year he published his novel *Minty Alley.* He wrote several important histories, including *The Black Jacobins: Toussaint L'Ouverture and the San Domingo Revolution* (1938) and *Nkrumah and the Ghana Revolution* (1977). Between 1938 and 1952 he published labor and race journalism in the United States under the pseudonym J. R. Johnson. He collaborated on numerous works of Marxist criticism, including *The Invading Socialist Society* (with F. Forest and Rita Stone, 1947), *State Capitalism and World Revolution* (published anonymously as a collective statement of the Johnson-Forest Tendency, 1950), and *Facing Reality* (with Grace C. Lee and Pierre Chaulieu, 1958); and he wrote two books of political criticism, *Modern Politics* (1960) and *Party Politics in the West Indies* (1962). His privately published book *Mariners, Renegades, and Castaways* pioneers in the field of cultural studies; and his autobiography, *Beyond a Boundary*

(1963), daringly focuses on the cricket field as a site of both artistic creation and West Indian political resistance to British colonial rule.

And yet, unlike Aimé Césaire and Franz Fanon, Raymond Williams and Walter Benjamin, or other cultural and political critics with whom C.L.R. James might be suitably compared, James's name and his work have been mostly absent from critical and theoretical discussions of culture, society, labor, race, colonialism, class, nation, empire, capitalism, revolution, and the future of democracy worldwide. Like Martin Glaberman, Paul Buhle, and Anna Grimshaw, who have sought over the last few decades to keep James's work in circulation and like the work of more recent critics, including Nicole King, Anthony Bogues, and Aldon Nielsen,[2] I want to use the occasion of the emergence of a new global order, dominated by the political, economic, and cultural presence of the United States, to insert C.L.R. James into the critical and theoretical conversation; or perhaps I should say to reinsert James into these conversations, for James lived, worked, and wrote during the same years when several of the founding fathers of American literary studies, including most notably Perry Miller and F. O. Matthiessen, were seeking to constitute America as both a distinctively national culture and a major political power in the world.[3]

I want to focus in particular on James's rereading of Herman Melville's *Moby Dick* in *Mariners, Renegades, and Castaways* as an attempt to reclaim both imaginative writing and literary criticism as forms of social and revolutionary activity. Against the traditional reading of *Moby Dick* as a work that stands outside its time and more recent attempts to locate Melville's work fully within its national historical moment, I want to argue that James's reading of *Moby Dick* in the context of the world crisis of the post-World War II period provides an innovative and provoking model of literary criticism as a form of *revolutionary rearticulation* that highlights the profound significance for the twentieth century of labor, race, class, and colonial struggle, the possibilities of resistance and community, the dignity of the masses, the future of democracy, and the power of imaginative writing and culture to bring about what James calls "world revolution." By reading *Moby Dick* from a contemporary, West Indian, and class perspective, James not only suggests the ways classic—and not so classic—nineteenth-century American writers can be revived and rearticulated for the purposes of contemporary social, political, and cultural struggle; by bringing into new voice and visibility certain readings and narratives that have not been available—or legible—within the specifically national and nationalist frames of past and recent approaches to American literature, he also provides a compelling model for a comparative cultural and political practice that reads beyond the boundaries of the nation-state.

In short, James's *Mariners* represents a kind of critical road not taken, an alternative to the primarily aesthetic and nationalist modes chosen by critics from the left and the right during the cold war years and after. Like James's longer study of "American Civilization," *Mariners* suggests the ways understandings of American democracy from outside the borders of the United States intersect, impact, and resist endemic definitions and push the boundaries of the study of American civilization toward a more international perspective. It has taken us a half century to get to the point where James started in "Notes on American Civilization" in 1950, and, as recent calls for a more global, international, or postnational approach to American literary and cultural studies suggest, we are still not there.[4]

The Poetics of Crossing

Whereas literary critics and consensus historians of the 1940s and 1950s focused on the exceptional and distinctively American qualities of American literature and history, James came to the United States and viewed its literary and political tradition as a Caribbean *creole* who had roots in the cultures of Africa, Europe, and the West Indies. As an African British colonial, James had been educated in the masterworks of the West and politicized by what he called "the clash of race, caste, and class" on the cricket fields of Trinidad.[5] Like many of his generation, James left the colonies for Britain in 1932 in search of a literary career in the metropolis. In England he collaborated with the popular West Indian cricket player Learie Constantine on *Cricket and I* (1932), and he published a shorter version of his biography of Cipriani under the more explicitly political title *The Case for West-Indian Self-Government* in 1933. James's conversion to Marxism in 1934 after reading Trotsky's *History of the Russian Revolution* and Oswald Spengler's *Decline of the West* and his simultaneous involvement with the Independent Labor Party, International Trotskyism, the Pan-African Movement (with George Padmore and Marcus Garvey), and other forms of labor, race, and anticolonial activism led him to that border-crossing mix of Marxist theorization, multigeneric writing, popular culture criticism, political and aesthetic analysis, and active political engagement that would distinguish all of James's work in and on the Americas, Europe, and Africa.

By the time James left England for the United States in 1938, he had produced his play, *Toussaint L'Ouverture*, on the London stage with Paul Robeson, published *Minty Alley*, one of the first West Indian novels, and written three histories of revolution: *World Revolution 1917–36: The Rise and Fall of the Communist International* (1937), *The Black Jacobins* (1938), and *A History of Negro Revolt* (1938). Although *World Revolution* was the "un-American and subversive" book that appears to have caused James the most trouble with the American authorities under the terms of the Mc Carran Internal Security Act of 1950, if the Justice Department had actually read the book it might have challenged the certainty about Soviet Communist designs on the world that underwrote cold war containment policy and that frames the Internal Security Act, which begins by asserting: "There exists a world Communist movement . . . to establish a Communist totalitarian dictatorship in the countries throughout the world through the medium of a world-wide Communist organization."[6] By 1934, James had joined a small group of Trotsky's followers who worked within the Britain's Independent Labor Party. *World Revolution,* which was dedicated to this Marxist group, was not only an anti-Stalinist attack on the Communist Comintern for abandoning the international struggle of the workers in favor of Soviet national interests; it was also a subtle critique of Trotsky for his ongoing support of the Communist Party and the intellectual vanguard against the self-activity of the workers.

James's distinctive set of interests as a Marxist, a West Indian, an anti-imperialist, and a Pan-Africanist coalesce in *The Black Jacobins,* a dialectical study of the relation between the leadership and the African masses in the San Domingo revolution that rewrites by *creolizing* economic, political, and world history at the same time that it presents a model of successful African, proletarian, and anticolonial revolt against the forces of capitalism and imperialism in the present.[7] *The Black Jacobins* revises Western historiography and traditional accounts of slavery and colonialism by foregrounding the agency of New World African masses in bringing about the revolution in Haiti and by locating the West Indies, slavery, colonialism, and the African diaspora at the center rather than the margins of the history of capitalism, modernity, and world revolution.

Although James's embrace of the masses rather than the vanguard as the agents of revolutionary history would eventually lead to his break with Trotsky in the 1940s, he was initially sent to the United States by Trotsky to help bring African Americans into the Socialist Worker's Party, which was the American organization of the Trotskyist movement. James originally planned to stay in the United States for only six months, but his passport expired, he went underground, and over the next fifteen years he would emerge as a powerful albeit pseudonymous voice of the radical left through his writings for *Labor Action,* the Worker's Party newspaper that was distributed to factory workers, *International African Opinion,* the journal of the International African Service Bureau, and the *New International,* a more theoretical Trotskyist journal that, in the words of Paul Buhle, James turned into "the outstanding Left journal in the USA."[8]

Under the pseudonym "J. R. Johnson," James also collaborated with
Raya Dunayevskaya ("F. Forest"), Grace Lee [Boggs], Martin Glaberman, and others in seeking to formulate what Glaberman has called "an
independent democratic and revolutionary Marxist tendency" in
response to debates about the nature of the Soviet state that ensued following the Stalin-Hitler Pact of 1939.[9] Known as the Johnson-Forest Tendency, this group sought to return to Marxist roots and Hegelian
dialectics to develop an independent theory of state capitalism and the
self-activity of the masses against Trotsky's notion of Russia as a "degen-
erated worker's state" and his emphasis on the role of the party or vanguard in world revolution. As James's 1948 article "The Revolutionary
Answer to the Negro Problem in the USA" suggests, against the notion
of African Americans as subordinate to the goals of socialism and the
proletarian movement, James and his group supported the independent
role of blacks within the revolutionary movement. In fact, James predicted a future in which blacks would be at the very forefront of democratic and proletarian revolution: "Let us not forget that in the Negro
people, there sleep and are now awakening passions of a violence
exceeding, perhaps, as far as these things can be compared, anything
among the tremendous forces that capitalism has created," James wrote,
in words that anticipate not only the civil rights movement and later
independence movements in the West Indies and Africa, but also the
multiple forms of social action and movement—among minority cultures, women, antiwar opponents, gay people, and others—that came to
characterize the New Left.[10] During his years in the United States, James
collaborated with Raya Dunayevskaya and Grace Lee in setting forth the
theory of Russia as a form of state capitalism in the pamphlet *The Invading Socialist Society* (1947) and in the book *State Capitalism and World Revolution* (1950), which marked their break with the Trotskyist movement
and the Socialist Worker's Party.

Rethinking the Margins

James's collaboration with the Johnson-Forest group bore fruit in two
major pieces of writing: "Notes on Dialectics," which was circulated in
manuscript in 1948 and published as *Notes on Dialectics: Hegel, Marx,
Lenin* in 1980; and "Notes on American Civilization," which was circulated in manuscript in 1950 and published as *American Civilization* in
1993. Both documents seek to rethink the modern world through the
lens of revolutionary Marxism and Hegelian dialectics. Whereas "Notes
on Dialectics" is a more theoretical work addressed to members of the
Johnson-Forest Tendency in which James seeks to theorize both Western
laissez-faire capitalism and Soviet *state* capitalism as forms of the same

dialectical movement of capital in order "to call for" and "to teach" what James calls "*spontaneity*—the free creative activity of the proletariat"; "Notes on American Civilization" is a more popularly oriented work in which James seeks "to teach" the dialectical and revolutionary movement of history toward "the free creative activity" of the masses he "calls for" in "Notes on Dialectics" by reading American history, literature, and popular culture from a Marxist point of view.[11]

"Notes on American Civilization" marks James's turn toward an increasing interest in culture as a form of political struggle, a turn that anticipates James's study of Melville in *Mariners, Renegades, and Castaways* and his later groundbreaking reading of cricket, sports, and popular spectacle as forms of art, politics, and aesthetic resistance in *Beyond a Boundary*. Like *Mariners, Renegades, and Castaways,* "Notes on American Civilization" creolizes Marxism and America, politics and culture, theory and practice, by reading Marx through the history of the American revolutionary struggle and America through the dialectics of revolutionary Marxism. Through forms of politically strategic substitution reminiscent of the ways Phillis Wheatley, Walt Whitman, W.E.B. Du Bois and others have *resignified* the languages of revolution for their own radically alternative political purposes, James *rearticulates* and *hybridizes* the Revolutionary languages of equality, liberty, independence, and the pursuit of happiness to signify Marxist notions of freedom and individualism as the full realization of the *person* in free creative activity and happiness as the desire of the masses for *social being* and community.

In tracing the tensions between the revolutionary ideals of individualism and social union and the increasing oppressiveness of bourgeois capital, especially in the years following the Civil War, James focuses on the historical agency of the masses, especially the black masses, in the development of a fully democratic American culture. Like Du Bois in *Black Reconstruction* (1935), James emphasizes the role of free and enslaved blacks in pressing abolitionists to the acts of social and political resistance that culminated in the Civil War and a black- and democratically inspired Reconstruction that failed to realize its radically transformative ideal of a just and equitable American society. Against the specifically nationalist frames of cold war consensus historiography, which read Reconstruction as a period of political anarchy that was overcome by the reunion of North and South in what Gregory Jay calls "a racialized nationalism of blood purity," James links the Civil War with the insurrection of slaves in San Domingo, Marx's formation of the First International in 1864, the establishment of the Paris Commune in 1871, and the ongoing democratic and anticolonial uprisings of the post-World War II years.[12]

Whereas in the nineteenth century, the struggle between the democratic masses and capital was given voice and form in the writings of Melville, Whitman, and Twain, James argues, in the twentieth century the repressed desires of the workers for freedom, creativity, and association were expressed through the popular arts. As James writes in *American Civilization:* "The modern popular film, the modern newspaper (the *Daily News, not* the *Times*), the comic strip, the evolution of jazz, a popular periodical like *Life*, these mirror from year to year the deep social responses and evolution of the American people in relation to the fate which has overtaken the original concepts of freedom, free individuality, free association, etc." It was not in T. S. Eliot, Hemingway, Joyce, or even famous directors like John Ford or Réné Clair but in the "serious study" of Charlie Chaplin, Dick Tracy, Gasoline Alley, James Cagney, Rita Hayworth, and Humphrey Bogart, popular novels by Frank Yerby, and "men like David Selsnick, Cecil de Mille, and Henry Luce" that one found "the clearest ideological expression of the sentiments and deepest feelings of the American people and a great window into the future of America and the modern world"[13] Rather than separating aesthetics and mass culture in the manner of Adorno and the Frankfurt school or dropping a consideration of aesthetics in the affirmation of popular culture as a site of resistance in the manner of later cultural studies critics, in *American Civilization* as in the letters he wrote to Constance Webb and various literary and cultural critics in the cold war years, James seeks to get beyond more reductive Stalinist and 1930s notions of art as a direct expression of politics and the masses by formulating a *popular political aesthetics* that engages the simultaneously political and aesthetic dimensions of what he called "the popular arts."[14]

Critical Citizenship

James's plans to publish his study of American civilization were cut short when he was served a deportation notice by the Immigration and Naturalization Service (INS) in 1948 at a time of mounting national hysteria about the spread of "the world Communist movement" both at home and abroad. Like the war on terror following the attack on the World Trade Center on September 11, 2001, the domestic war against communism translated into a massive war not only against the infiltration of American society by "un-American" ideas but also against non-Western European "aliens," many of whom—like James—had resided and worked in the United States for years before being apprehended for passport violations. Under the cold war tactics of the State Department, McCarthyism, and the red scare, the domestic war against communism also became an attack on First Amendment rights of freedom of speech and all forms of difference—African Americans, Asian Americans,

Native Americans, Latino/a Americans, Eastern Europeans, Jews, Catholics, homosexuals, women—that did not fit within an increasingly normative and cleansed notion of pure blood American.

While James sought to make a legal case for American citizenship by working through the courts, his application was rejected in October 1950 under the terms of the McCarran Internal Security Act of September 1950, which legalized the arrest and deportation of aliens with radical ties on the grounds that they represented "a clear and present danger to the security of the United Sates and to the existence of free American institutions."[15] James sought to appeal his case, but on 10 June 1952 he was apprehended again for passport violations and taken to Ellis Island for deportation.

On Ellis Island, where James was "placed in a special room for political prisoners" with five Communists, the terms of his case appear to have changed (*M*, 126). What had begun as a plea for U. S. citizenship had turned into a defense of himself against charges of Communist subversion and his status as a racially undesirable alien under the terms of the Internal Security Act and the national origins principle of the McCarran-Walter Immigration and Nationality Act of 1952. Caught between the injustice of the Justice Department and the racism of the INS, James decided—in the very midst of the cold war witch hunt—to take his case for American citizenship directly to the American people by writing a study of Herman Melville that is drawn from his unpublished "Notes on American Civilization."

Like the subterranean, pseudonymous, anonymous, and manuscript forms in which James was forced to circulate his writings in the United States in the 1930s, 1940s, and 1950s, the circumstances surrounding the writing and publication of *Mariners* might themselves serve as the subject of a fascinating cultural materialist analysis of the history of the leftist book as cultural grotesque and the nationalist paranoia of the cold war era in which it was produced and repressed. Written and published privately while James was being detained—or, in his terms, "imprisoned" like a criminal—on Ellis Island as an undesirable alien, *Mariners* is presented to the American public as part of James's claim for American citizenship. The front cover of the book, in the racially marked colors of black, red, and yellow, cites the passage from Chapter 26 ("Knights and Squires") in *Moby Dick* that describes the workers of the world—the "meanest mariners, and renegades and castaways"—who make up the crew of the *Pequod* and to whom James's title refers. The back of the book bears a picture of James, which locates his "story" within the "protest" tradition of both the slave and the prison narrative, and a citation from the final chapter, "Natural but Necessary Conclusion" (Chapter 7), in which he describes his experience of being incarcerated on Ellis

Island by the Department of Immigration in 1952 as part of his "Story of Herman Melville and the World We Live In" (Figure 24): "I publish my *protest* with the book on Melville because, as I have shown, the book as written is a *part of my experience.* It is also a *claim before the American people,* the best claim I can put forward, that my desire *to be a citizen* is not a selfish nor a frivolous one" (back cover; emphasis added). There are many things one might say about the material presentation and publication history of *Mariners,* which James distributed himself and sent to members of the U.S. Congress. Given James's critical emphasis on melding the putatively distinct domains of life, art, and politics, it is ironic, for example, that the final chapter was excised from subsequent editions of *Mariners,* for it is in this chapter that James protests his brutalizing "experience" at the hands of the Department of Justice, presents Ellis Island as a miniature of America's own colonizing relation to "renegades and castaways from all parts of the world" (*M,* 150), and lays his "claim" for American citizenship "before the American people."[16]

In the context of what James calls the "national arrogance" of the Department of Immigration, the increased policing of the boundaries between "citizen" and "alien" legislated by the McCarran Internal Security Act and the McCarran-Walter Immigration and Nationality Act, and the Mc Carthy purges of the early 1950s, James's presentation of a book of literary criticism as part of his "claim" for U.S. citizenship makes visible the ways acts of writing, reading, and interpretation become intricately bound up with the maintenance of national borders, with who does and does not belong in American society. Like the repressive Alien and Sedition Acts of 1798, which prohibited immigrants with Republican politics from entering the country and all forms of utterance, writing, or publishing "against the government of the United States," the Internal Security Act contains specific provisions against "any written or printed matter" that is "subversive of the national security."[17] As James puts it: "the Department of Justice now assumes the right to say what a citizen or would-be citizen should study. Or if he does choose for himself, it warns in advance that it must approve the conclusions he should come to" (*M,* 190).

James knows that his appeal to remain in the United States is rejected by the Department of Justice not because his activities represent "a clear and present danger to the people of the United States" (*M,* 191) but because he has written several books on the subject of revolution. "This is my chief offense, that I have written books of the kind I have written," he says. "And I protest against it as a violation of the rights of every citizen of the United States" (*M,* 192). By appealing directly to "the rights of every citizen of the United States," James not only invokes the First Amendment right of "freedom of speech" guaranteed by the Constitu-

"I publish my protest with the book on Melville because, as I have shown, the book as written is a part of my experience. It is also a claim before the American people, the best claim I can put forward, that my desire to be a citizen is not a selfish nor a frivolous one."

C. L. R. James

from Chapter VII, p. 201

An Original book; not a reprint.

Figure 24. Back cover of *Mariners, Renegades, and Castaways: The Story of Herman Melville and the World We Live In* by C.L.R. James, 1953. James was forced to leave the United States in 1953 as part of an increasingly aggressive cold war immigration policy directed at writing and dissent by residents of color. Courtesy Robert A. Hill, literary executor, estate of C.L.R. James.

tion; he also seeks to return constitutional and juridical authority to its Revolutionary origin in the will of "the People."

Reading Over, Writing Back

In protest against the criminalization of both writing and dissent by the Department of Immigration on Ellis Island and the Department of Justice in American society, James writes a book of literary criticism in which he argues that, as Melville had foreseen in the figure of Ahab in *Moby Dick,* capitalism had spawned the "totalitarian madness" that would consume its own citizens—not only Melville and James but the Revolutionary founders themselves. "Should I have deplored the freeing of the slaves in San Domingo," James asks, "or marshalled arguments to show how the Bourbons and the landed aristocrats should have triumphed over the great revolution in France? Would I have been more welcome as a citizen? Unfortunately that would compel me also to denounce George Washington, Thomas Jefferson, and Benjamin Franklin" (*M*, 191). Like other Africans in the New World, including Phillis Wheatley, Frederick Douglass, and W.E.B. Du Bois, and like the civil rights movement that *Mariners* anticipates, James *reads over* the Revolutionary ideals of the founding so as to give them a more expansive and fully democratic significance in the ongoing struggles of the present.

At a time when Lionel Trilling, the New York intellectuals, and other cold war critics were seeking to reaffirm the distinctions that F. O. Matthiessen had made in *American Renaissance* (1941) between background and foreground, literature and history, aesthetics and politics, culture and the masses, James's reading of Melville insists on what he calls "the inseparability of great literature and of social life" (*M*, 149).[18] James not only reads Melville's work through the lens of world history; he also reads history through the metaphoric and narrative frame of *Moby Dick.* As the book cover and introduction to James's *Mariners* suggests, there is a fluid interchange among what James calls the history of "the last twenty years" (*M*, 2), his experience on Ellis Island, and his reading of *Moby Dick.* Melville's writings provide the imaginative frame through which James reads twentieth-century history, and James's experience of twentieth-century history deepens his understanding of Melville's writing. Thus, in James's view, Ellis Island is like the *Pequod,* "where American administrators and officials, and American security officers controlled the destinies of perhaps a thousand men, sailors, and 'isolatoes,' renegades and castaways from all parts of the world" (*M*, 150). "[M]y experiences there," James writes, "have not only shaped this book but are the most realistic commentary I could give on the validity of Melville's ideas today" (*M*, 150).

What James suggests, finally, is that twentieth-century history has made the writings of the antebellum period in the United States available to modern audiences in ways that they were not available to nineteenth-century readers. "It is only today when democracies and republics once more have to examine their foundations," writes James, "that the work of Poe, Hawthorne, Whitman, Garrison and Phillips, and Melville can be fully understood" (*M*, 148). Unlike Matthiessen, who cordons off the American Renaissance as an idyllic time that was destroyed by the factory, technology, and "the rising forces of exploitation" in the post-Civil War period,[19] James argues that the antebellum period "ushered in the world in which we live." The Americans of that period, he writes, "knew that something was wrong, something deeper than slavery. . . ." (*M*, 148).

James's refraction of history through the lens of Melville and Melville through the lens of history offers a revisionist account of Western historiography and a radically noncanonical reading of *Moby Dick*. James's status as an "outsider"—a black, West Indian who came of age in a colony on the edges of the British Empire in the New World—enables him to read the racial, class, colonial, revolutionary, and global dimensions of Melville's *Moby Dick* in ways that have eluded both the myth, symbol, and formalist critics of the cold war period and the historicist and primarily nationalist interpretations of the "new Americanists."[20] Although recent disputes over the canon have focused on *what* we read when we read American literature, James's reading of *Moby Dick*, which is rarely cited or acknowledged in either the old or the new Melville scholarship,[21] suggests that questions of canon involve changing not only *what* we read but *how* we read when we read American literature. Just as James was expelled from the United States in 1953, so his 1953 book became and still remains one of the *undesirable aliens* of American literary criticism. What exactly does James write—or read—that makes him so uncitable, so undesirable?

The Worlding of American Literature

Unlike Michael Rogin's pathbreaking rehistoricization of Melville's writings in *Subversive Genealogy: The Politics and Art of Herman Melville* (1979), which focuses on the primarily racial, familial, and national contexts of Melville's works,[22] James emphasizes the simultaneously racial, class, colonial, and global significance of Melville's writing. In his view, *Moby Dick* represents "the grandest conception that has ever been made to see the modern world, our world, as it was, and the future that lay before it" (*M*, 18). From the outset of *Mariners*, James emphasizes the worldly as opposed to the merely national or exceptionally American dimensions of Melville's work. *Mariners* is dedicated to James's son Nob, "who will be 21 years old in 1970," James writes, "by which time I hope he and his generation will have left behind them forever all the problems of nationality." The epigraph from Melville's *Redburn*—"We are not a nation, so much as a world"—further underscores James's worldly perspective: he focuses throughout on the ways global events in the twentieth century—such as the massive colonial uprisings against imperial rule after 1945 and his own experience as one of the colonized in the West Indies and on Ellis Island in 1952—have enabled him to understand the significance of Melville's "story" to the modern world.

Drawing attention to the social and politically prophetic dimensions of *Moby Dick*, James locates the struggle between renegade crew and authoritarian captain aboard the *Pequod* as part of the world historical struggle of the masses against capitalist and totalitarian dominance in the present. In James's reading, the *Pequod* is a factory, Ahab is a captain of industry, and "Melville is not only the representative writer of industrial civilization. He is the only one there is" (*M*, 105). Ahab, whom James singles out as Melville's most daring and prophetic creation, is a totalitarian social type: his drive to manage people, nature, and things anticipates not only Hitler and Stalin but also the totalitarianism of the American government as evidenced by McCarthyism, the McCarran Acts of 1950 and 1952, and the "barbarous" treatment of aliens in the United States as non-beings with "no human rights" (*M*, 169). Although James has been criticized for seeking to prove his American credentials by setting himself against the Communists and bringing the best possible news about American democracy,[23] his problem within the Manichean Communist/anti-Communist symbolics of the red scare years was that he—like other people and countries throughout the world—did not fit into this binarized remapping of the globe during the cold war years. Reading against a U.S. containment policy that envisioned both homeland and world as the scene of an apocalyptic struggle between Democracy and Communism, Freedom and Totalitarianism, Capitalism and Marxism, James argues that Totalitarianism is the spectral presence of both Capitalism and Marxism, American Individualism and Russian Communism. Melville's main theme, James writes, is "how the society of free individualism would give birth to totalitarianism and be unable to defend itself against it" (*M*, 60).[24]

Against a tradition of cold war literary criticism that has, in Donald Pease's terms, read *Moby Dick* as the story of "the opposition between Ishmael's freedom and Ahab's totalitarian will,"[25] James reads Ishmael not as the bearer of American consensus and the ideals of democracy but as "an intellectual Ahab": "As Ahab is enclosed in the masoned walled-town of the exclusiveness of authority, so Ishmael is enclosed in the solitude of his social and intellectual speculation" (*M*, 44, 45). Like Ahab and Pierre, Ishmael is in fact representative of the new forms of subjectivity spawned by the social crisis of industrial capitalism and later analyzed as personal "neurosis" in the psychoanalytic theories of Freud and others.

James counters these negative specters of totalitarianism and intellectual isolation by focusing on the passage from *Moby Dick* that appears on the front cover of his book: "If, then, to meanest mariners, and renegades and castaways, I shall hereafter ascribe high qualities though dark; weave round them tragic graces . . . if I shall touch that workman's arm with some ethereal light; if I shall spread a rainbow over his disastrous set of sun; then against all mortal critics bear me out in it, thou just Spirit of Equality, which hast spread one royal mantle of humanity over all my kind!" (*M*, 16–17). Among the "meanest mariners, and renegades and castaways" aboard the *Pequod*, James finds the forms of unalienated labor, association, and community that he, like Marx, envisioned as the teleology of capitalist history and the revolutionary future of the masses worldwide. "They are a world-federation of modern industrial laborers," James writes. "They owe allegiance to no nationality. . . . They owe no allegiance to anybody or anything except the work they have to do and the relations with one another on which that work depends" (*M*, 20).

Although James tends to idealize the workers, what is remarkable about his reading is the ways he makes visible and tangible not only the class and racial hierarchies aboard the *Pequod* but the *presence of labor*, of ordinary human work, at the center of *Moby Dick*: its sensuousness, dignity, dailiness, commonness, comradeship, and communality. Whereas others have focused on the symbolic meaning of Ahab, or Ishmael, or the Whale, James focuses on passage after passage in which Melville describes workers working. "Their heroism consists in their everyday doing of their work," James writes. "The only tragic graces with which Melville endows them are the graces of men associated for common labor" (*M*, 30). Even in his reading of the final chase, James's eye drifts away from the main event—the contest between Ahab and Moby Dick—to note the scene of workers ("They were one man, not thirty," Melville writes) bound together "for common purpose" (*M*, 68).[26] Where others have emphasized the national, or racial, or universal apocalypse signified by the sinking of the *Pequod*, which was itself named after the Indian tribe decimated by New England colonists in the seventeenth century, James reads Melville's description of Tashtego—"red arm and a hammer . . . uplifted in the open air, in the act of nailing the flag faster and yet faster to the subsiding spar"—as the expression of the "undaunted" spirit of the Indian worker determined to destroy "every vestige of the world" of "Bildad, Peleg, and Starbuck" (*M*, 79). It is "this undeviating reference back of everything to a body of men working" that, in James's view, has something to say about "the conditions of survival of modern civilization" (*M*, 102, 20).

At the center of James's reading of *Moby Dick* is the problem of revolution and the desire for human community and how these are connected to the global struggle against totalitarian power in the twentieth century. Like Michael Hardt and Antonio Negri in *Empire* (2000), who see in the transnational flow of workers across national boundaries the potential for a liberation of creative energies "beyond measure," James envisions the workers both onboard the *Pequod* and in the modern world as the bearers of a desire for productive labor and collective life that exceeds the boundaries of the nation-state.[27] Although the workers aboard the *Pequod* do not revolt, James emphasizes their cooperative spirit and their ability to achieve community—even under Ahab—as a hope for the democratic future. "[A]t first sight," James writes, "in its symbolism of men turned into devils, of an industrial civilization on fire and plunging blindly into darkness, it is the world of massed bombers, of cities in flames, of Hiroshima and Nagasaki, the world in which we live, the world of Ahab, which he hates and which he will organize or destroy." "But when you look again," James adds, "you see that the crew is indestructible" (*M*, 50).

Although James might be—and, indeed, has been—accused of misreading *Moby Dick*, such an accusation misses the revolutionary act of reading—of *rearticulation* and *creolization*—in which James is engaged.[28] As a New World colonial, James rewrites the master's narrative not as the triumph of liberal individualism signified by Ishmael's survival but as the eventual triumph of the renegade masses—of Queequeg, Tashtego, Dagoo, and Pip—aboard the *Pequod*, on Ellis Island, and in the Caribbean, Africa, Asia, and elsewhere. James's "story" of Herman Melville and the world we live in is not so much a reading *of* as a reading *over* and *back to* a classic American book that gestures toward a radically experimental, more coherent, and less self-alienated form of literary criticism. The particularities of James's reading of Melville are perhaps not so important as the revolutionary model he presents of a form of criticism that yokes a multiplicity of critical modes—of disciplines—that have been driven apart by the segregationist and nationalist ethos of the American academy in the twentieth and twenty-first centuries.

Mariners is in effect a *critical hybrid* that mixes literary criticism, philosophy, history, economics, autobiography, political theory, and aesthetics with a call to action—revolutionary action—in the world. James's critical "story" interweaves readings of *Moby Dick* with reflections on the history of Western civilization, the rise of industrial capitalism, the spread of nationalism, the relation of the nation-state to racial doctrine, the rise of nazism, communism, and totalitarianism, and what James calls "the great mass labor movements and colonial revolts" that marked the modern era (*M*, introduction). There is no *disconnect* between the world James lives in and his reading of *Moby Dick*. It is, in fact, the historical events of the post-World War II period that have enhanced his appreciation of Melville's writings: "The writer of this book confesses frankly that it is only since the end of World War II, that the emergence of the people of the Far East and of Africa into the daily headlines, the spread of Russian totalitarianism, the emergence of America as a power in every quarter of the globe, it is only this that has enabled him to see the range, the power, and the boldness of Melville" (*M*, 19). In James's view, "criticism today has a popular function to perform."[29] His study of Herman Melville and the world we live in, like his larger study of American civilization, seeks to transform literature into a means for "the ordinary everyday citizen" to know the past in order to better understand the present and future.

At a time of increased policing of the boundaries between politics and culture in the post-World War II period when critics of the left and the right were retreating from "reality" and history into an aesthetics of form, symbol, romance, and myth,[30] James seeks to claim (or reclaim) a role for both literature and literary criticism as forms of social action and power in the world. "It is startling," James writes of *Moby Dick*, "but before you have read a page you get an idea of what a great imaginative writer can do, and what philosophers, economists, journalists, historians, however gifted, can never do" (*M*, 45). Ahab, James argues, represents an imaginative creation of momentous historical importance. "Such characters," he writes, "come once in many centuries and are as rare as men who found new religions, philosophers who revolutionize human thinking, and statesmen who create new political forms" (*M*, 80). Ahab's originality lies in the insight he provides into modern totalitarianism, the repressive mechanisms of capitalism and the state, the urge to mass destruction, and the global crisis of democracy.

Whereas class has tended to fall out of the mainstream of American criticism as a major category of analysis, and the study of race and postcolonialism have developed as relatively discrete fields of analysis—with race *in here* in the United States and postcolonialism *over there* and *elsewhere*—James also offers a model of literary criticism that manages to think class, race, and colonialism *together* as major and inseparable categories of social and cultural analysis.[31] In *The Black Jacobins*, James observes: "The race question is subsidiary to the class question in politics, and to think of imperialism in terms of race is disastrous. But to neglect the racial factor as merely incidental is an error only less grave than to make it fundamental."[32] In his reading of *Moby Dick* as in his reading of the slave revolt led by Toussaint L'Ouverture in San Domingo in 1792, James emphasizes the inextricable relations among black liberation, colonial struggle, and proletarian revolution. While the officers of the *Pequod* are "white Americans," James notes, each of its three harpooners—Queequeg (a "South Sea cannibal"), Tashtego ("a Gay-Head Indian from Massachusetts"), and Daggoo ("a gigantic Negro from the coast of Africa")—is "a representative of a primitive race" (*M*, 17). Along with "the ordinary people" from "all the nations of the globe" who make up the crew of the *Pequod*, these dark-skinned harpooners represent the revolutionary and collective force of the laboring classes that will, in James's view, resist the destructive power of capitalism and imperialism worldwide.[33]

Although James's aesthetic theory is not fully worked out, through his reading of Melville he seeks to formulate a social theory of art—a social aesthetics—that conjoins Aristotelian *mimesis* and Hegelian *dialectics*, the notion of art as the "imitation" of an historical event—past, present, or future—as it "might possibly occur" with the notion of art as a collective expression of both subjective consciousness and world historical movement.[34] In Jamesian aesthetics as in Hegelian dialectics, literature acts as a "reconciling medium" through which spirit makes itself articulate as *sensuous form.* "Art's peculiar feature," Hegel says in his *Introduction to the Philosophy of Art,* "consists in its ability to represent in *sensuous form* even the highest ideas, bringing them thus nearer to the character of natural phenomena, to the senses, and to feeling."[35] Whereas Lionel Trilling and other cold war literary critics represent the "liberal imagination" as an act of individual imaginative *transcendence* that opposes society with culture, history with romance, materiality with *moral realism,* James seeks to articulate a *social aesthetics*, a concept of art as a form of social creation that conjoins the terms *culture* and *society, literature* and *history, aesthetics* and *politics, art* and the *masses* that were separated by the founding figures of American literary studies in the 1940s and 1950s.[36]

In the penultimate chapter of *Mariners* titled "The Work, the Author, and the Times," James insists that "the book as a work of art" must not become "a mere expression of social and political ideas" (137). As in his chapter on cricket titled "What Is Art?" in *Beyond a Boundary,* James continues to affirm the role of "art" and "artist" through his use of such terms as *artistic genius, creativity, originality,* and *agency,* and by referring to the author as a "unique individual." However, unlike the New Critics, the Frankfurt critics, and the New York intellectuals, and unlike such founding figures of American literary studies as Matthiessen and Chase, James refuses to grant the autonomy of art. His concept of the aesthetic remains embedded in the material and the social, in what he called "the world we live in."

Like Aristotle's theory of character as an expression of "what ought to be" and like Hegel's theory of the world historical individual as a figure who expresses world spirit, James's social theory of art is grounded in a theory of character as the basis of great art. Focusing on the originality of Ahab as a character who "sum[s] up a whole epoch of human history," James defines a theory of art as the product of the dialectical relation between material conditions—what James calls the "world *outside*"—and the imaginative creation, or consciousness, of the writer. "Ahab never existed, and in fact could not exist," James asserts. "He is a composite of a realistic base from which imagination and logic build a complete whole" (*M*, 81). In James's aesthetics of human embodiment, if the "creative power" of the artist is "great enough," not only will he work in advance of theory—as Melville anticipated the theories of Darwin, Marx, and Freud; the creative artist will also work in advance of history, anticipating what James calls "the future that is in the present."[37]

In the conclusion to *Mariners, Renegades, and Castaways*, James writes, "I rest my case with the public," offering both his book and his cause to the American people. Those who share his cause are asked to write to him personally to buy copies of the book, which, he concludes, was written "to advance both the understanding of literature and the cause of freedom" (*M*, 203). In addressing his public written appeal for citizenship directly to the American people, James not only reaffirms the Revolutionary tradition of human rights, civil liberties, and popular sovereignty on which the American republic was founded. Like the Melvillean figure of America as the world's blood that opens *Mariners*— "Settled by the people of all nations, all nations may claim her for their own"—James also affirms a more cosmopolitan definition of *world citizenship* grounded in the ideals of human dignity and universal rights declared if not realized by the American and the French revolutions.

Setting the universal principles of justice and humanity against an American immigration policy "ridden with national arrogance," James observes that the Department of Justice violated the most elementary principles of justice: "I was an alien. I had no human rights. If I didn't like it, I could leave. How to characterize this otherwise than as inhuman and barbarous? And what is its origin except that overweening national arrogance which is sweeping over the world like some pestilence?" (*M*, 169). At the very moment when Trilling was celebrating the "virtual uniqueness of American security and well-being," the intellectual's association of his "native land" with "the advantages of a whole skin, a full stomach, and the right to wag his tongue as he pleases," James was ill, starving, and imprisoned on Ellis Island for laying claim to his right to wag his renegade West Indian writer's tongue on U.S. soil.[38]

And yet, here again James turns the master's language of rights to his own defense: American law, he asserts, allows an immigrant "to make as good a case for himself as possible"—to be "treated as a potential citizen" (*M*, 170). Whereas the Department of Justice pursues "a venomous anti-alien policy" that demoralizes "its own employees," who seek to keep the founding principles of the United States alive on Ellis Island through acts of "constant self-control, patience and humanity," the "despised aliens, however fiercely nationalistic, are profoundly conscious of themselves as *citizens of the world*" (*M*, 186, 176; my emphasis). Seeking to collapse the brutalizing national distinction between *citizen* and *alien* through a countervailing global politics and ethics of *world citizenship* and *international justice*, James begins to sketch more flexible non-juridical modes of *belonging* and *citizenship* that exist within and beyond the boundaries of the nation-state.[39]

As one of the many immigrants who came to the United States in the 1920s and 1930s from the colonies and former colonies of the West Indies, Latin America, Africa, and Asia, James brings the margins to the center, rereading American civilization from the outside in and the inside out. Like Jefferson's *Notes on the State of Virginia*, which locates the origins of American New World culture and politics not in the founding of Jamestown in 1607 or the Puritan mission in New England but in the first European settlement of "the Spaniards in St. Domingo in 1493" (*NV*, 281), James's "Notes on American Civilization" locates the propulsive force of American and ultimately world civilization in the popular movement toward democracy signified by the revolt led by Toussaint L'Ouverture in San Domingo in 1792 and carried on by the abolitionists and the Civil War in the nineteenth century and the popular masses in the twentieth century. Whereas the cold war consensus historians emphasized the distinctively national, New England-centered, and homogeneous origins of American culture, James sought to locate the history of the American people in what he called "One World," interpreting the American Revolution as the "first tocsin" in the transformation of Europe from the old " 'triangular trade' of mercantilism—Africa, America, and the West Indies."[40]

Writing back to the master texts of America in both *Mariners* and "Notes on American Civilization," C.L.R. James was himself a *mixed blood*—a New World *creole* of the margins and borders who set himself against notions of racial purity and who continually crossed and resisted any narrow or fixed definition of culture, race, or national boundary. "How am I to return to non-European roots?" James asked in an interview in 1984: "if it means that Caribbean writers today should be aware that there are emphases in their writing that we owe to non-European, non-Shakespearean roots, and the past in music which is not Beethoven, that I agree. But I don't like them posed there in the way they have been posed—*either-or*. I don't think so. I think *both* of them. And fundamentally we are a people whose literacy and aesthetic past is rooted in Western European civilisation."[41] Working across the geographical spaces of the Caribbean, Europe, the United States, and Africa, James formed links in his life and criticism with cultural formations and political practices beyond the fixities of nation, race, and culture—with Toussaint and Melville, Aristotle and cricket, Marx and reggae.

Affirming an international poetics and politics of *mixture* and *crossing*, James imagined a new global order of democracy that would collapse the dehumanizing distinctions between citizen and alien, labor and culture, nation and world.[42] He not only challenged earlier and persistent notions of a bounded and homogeneous American culture threatened by what Arthur Schlesinger has called the disunifying force of difference. He also anticipated a future in which the masses and the margins would play a major role in producing and shaping the democratic culture and politics that would ensure the survival of world civilization.

Notes

Preface

1. In "American Studies and Ethnic Studies at the Borderlands Crossroads," Paul Lauter astutely observes: "In a very real sense, it is the boundaries themselves rather than the contents that have most persistently defined the study of America" (*From Walden Pond to Jurassic Park: Activism, Culture, and American Studies* [Durham, N.C.: Duke University Press, 2001], 121).

2. Mikhail Bakhtin, *The Dialogic Imagination*, ed. Michael Holquist, trans. Caryl Emerson and Michael Holquist (Austin: University of Texas Press, 1981); Homi Bhabha, *The Location of Culture* (London: Routledge, 1994); Edward W. Said, *Culture and Imperialism* (New York: Alfred A. Knopf, 1993); James Clifford, *The Predicament of Culture: Twentieth-Century Ethnography, Literature, and Art* (Cambridge, Mass.: Harvard University Press, 1988); and Gloria Anzaldúa, *Borderlands/La Frontera: The New Mestiza* (San Francisco: Aunt Lute Books, 1987). Along with Anzaldúa's work on the borderlands, this study is also informed by the work of Rosaldo Renato, who focuses on "culture in the borderlands" not as a geographical space only but as an "everyday" life "crisscrossed" by the "border zones" of sex, race, class, and nationality (*Culture and Truth: The Remaking of Social Analysis* [Boston: Beacon Press, 1989], 206); and José David Saldívar, who focuses on "the U.S.-Mexico border as a paradigm of crossing, circulation, material mixing, and resistance" that challenges "dominant national centers of identity and culture" (*Border Matters: Remapping American Cultural Studies* [Berkeley: University of California Press, 1997], 13, 19).

3. Robert J. C. Young, *Colonial Desire: Hybridity in Theory, Culture and Race* (London: Routledge, 1995), 6. See also Jennifer De Vere Brody, *Impossible Purities: Blackness, Femininity, and Victorian Culture* (Durham, N.C.: Duke University Press, 1998).

4. *The Writings of Thomas Jefferson*, ed. Andrew A. Lipscomb, 20 vols. (Washington, D.C.: Thomas Jefferson Memorial Association, 1903), 14:268, 269–70. Subsequent references to this edition will be cited as *WTJ*.

5. [Edward Long], *Candid Reflections . . . On What Is Commonly Called the Negroe-Cause, By a Planter* (London: T. Lowndes, 1772), 48–49.

6. John Adams to Abigail Adams, 29 October 1775, *Adams Family Correspondence*, ed. L. H. Butterfield, 6 vols. (Cambridge, Mass.: Belknap Press of Harvard University Press, 1963–1993), 1:318–19. Subsequent references will be cited as *AFC*.

7. See, for example, Rogers Smith, who argues that "through most of U.S. history, lawmakers pervasively and unapologetically structured U.S. citizenship in terms of illiberal and undemocratic racial, ethnic, and gender hierarchies" (*Civic Ideals: Conflicting Visions of Citizenship in U.S. History* [New Haven, Conn.:

Yale Universtiy Press, 1997], 1); and Hortense Spillers, who observes: "The blood remains impervious, at the level of folk/myth, to incursions of the 'reasonable' and inscribes the unique barrier beyond which human community has not yet passed into the 'brotherhood of man' and the 'Fatherhood of God'" ("Notes on an Alternative Model—Neither/Nor," in *The Difference Within: Feminism and Critical Theory*, ed. Elizabeth Meese and Alice Parker [Philadelphia: John Benjamins Publishing Company, 1989], 183).

8. Thomas Jefferson, *Notes on the State of Virginia*, ed. William Peden (Chapel Hill: University of North Carolina Press), 281. Subsequent references will be cited as *NV*.

9. Anzaldúa, *Borderlands*, 86. In *Playing in the Dark: Whiteness and the Literary Imagination* (Cambridge, Mass.: Harvard University Press, 1992), Toni Morrison locates a similarly "dark, abiding, and signing Africanist presence" at the center of American literature and culture (5). See also Henry Louis Gates, Jr., who describes slavery as "the figure in the carpet, the shadowed essence, the silent second text of both American political economy and the American cultural imagination," in the preface to "New Perspectives on the Transatlantic Slave Trade," *William and Mary Quarterly* 58 (January 2001): 4.

Chapter 1

1. James Otis, *A Vindication of the British Colonies* (Boston: Edes and Gill, 1765), 16.

2. John Dickinson, Letter III, in *Letters from a Farmer in Pennsylvania to the Inhabitants of the British Colonies* (Boston: Mein and Fleeming, 1768), 33.

3. Tom Paine, *Common Sense*, in *The Complete Writings of Thomas Paine*, ed. Philip S. Foner, 2 vols. (New York: Citadel Press, 1945), 1:16. Subsequent references to *Common Sense* will be cited as *CS*. Jonathan Boucher, "On Civil Liberty, Passive Obedience, and Non-Resistance," sermon preached in 1775, in *A View of the Causes and Consequences of the American Revolution in Thirteen Discourses* (1797; reprint, New York: Russell and Russell, 1967), 518.

4. Benjamin Franklin, *Autobiography*, ed. J. A. Leo Lemay and P. M. Zall (New York: W. W. Norton, 1986), 110. Subsequent references will be cited as *A*.

5. See, for example, the rupture brought to the entire Jeffersonian legacy in 1998 when DNA tests provided evidence—contra a long tradition of historians—that Jefferson was the father of at least one and possibly all six of the children of his mixed-blood slave, Sally Hemings. For scientific evidence of Jefferson's paternity, see Eugene A. Foster, "Jefferson Fathered Slave's Last Child," *Nature*, 5 November 1998, 27–28; see also Annette Gordon Reed, *Thomas Jefferson and Sally Hemings: An American Controversy* (Charlottesville: University Press of Virginia, 1997); and Jan Ellen Lewis and Peter S. Onuf, eds., *Sally Hemings and Thomas Jefferson: History, Memory, and Civic Culture* (Charlottesville: University Press of Virginia, 1999).

6. Thomas Jefferson, "Autobiography," *WTJ*, 1:31, 34, 36.

7. Cornstalk, 1 June 1776, *Morgan Diary*, quoted in Richard White, *The Middle Ground: Indians, Empires, and Republics in the Great Lakes Region, 1650–1815* (New York: Cambridge University Press, 1991), 366. As White notes, despite Cornstalk's role as a mediator between whites and Indians on "the middle ground," in 1777 he was murdered by back-country Indian haters in an act of blood vio-

lence that "gradually and inexorably became the dominant American Indian policy" (384).

8. See Bernard Bailyn, ed., *The Debate on the Constitution*, 2 vols. (New York: Library of America, 1993).

9. Alexander Hamilton, James Madison, and John Jay, *The Federalist Papers*, ed. Clinton Rossiter (1961; New York: New American Library, 1999), 337; emphasis added. Subsequent references will be cited as *FP.*

10. Thomas Jefferson, *The Papers of Thomas Jefferson*, ed. Julian P. Boyd, 29 vols. (Princeton: Princeton University Press, 1950), 12:356. Subsequent references to this edition will be cited as *PTJ.*

11. *The Correspondence of Andrew Jackson*, ed. John Spencer Bassett, 7 vols. (Washington, D.C.: Carnegie Institution of Washington, 1926), 1:241.

12. Abraham Lincoln, Address delivered at the dedication of the cemetery at Gettysburg, in *The Collected Works of Abraham Lincoln*, ed. Roy P. Basler, 9 vols. (New Brunswick, N.J.: Rutgers University Press, 1953–55), 7:23; Abraham Lincoln, Second Inaugural Address, *Collected Works of Lincoln*, 8:333. However well intended, Governor George Pataki's reading of the Gettysburg Address on 11 September 2002 on the occasion of the one-year anniversary of the terrorist attacks on the World Trade Center and the Pentagon had the effect of recontaining that event within a primarily national narrative of blood sacrifice for the ideals of the founding. It *reads over* and in effect closes down any more complex historical and global understanding of the events of September 11, 2001, in relation to the United States' own imperial legacy of blood violence in the New World and elsewhere and its current position of economic and military dominance in the struggle between first world capital and third world poverty.

13. William Benjamin Smith, *The Color Line: A Brief in Behalf of the Unborn* (New York: Mc Clure, Phillips and Company, 1905), ix.

14. Étienne Balibar, "Racism and Nationalism," trans. Chris Turner, in Balibar and Immanuel Wallerstein, *Race, Nation, Class: Ambiguous Identities* (London: Verso, 1998), 61.

15. Although blood was employed as a marker of aristocratic class distinction, the distinctions of race were never far away, as in the concept of "blue blood," which derived from the Spanish term *sangre azul.* According to the OED, this term originated with the Castillean aristocracy's emphasis on the purity of its blood—with no mixture of Moor, Jewish, or other foreign body. "Blue" may have had a literal reference to the blue veins that would show in fair people as opposed to dark people.

16. [John O'Sullivan], "Annexation," *The United States and Democratic Review* 17 (July–August 1845): 5, 7.

17. The first edition of *Notes on the State of Virginia* was published in France with no author's name in 1785; the authorized edition was published by the English bookseller and publisher John Stockdale in 1787.

18. For the genetic evidence identifying Jefferson as the father of at least one of Sally Hemings's children, see Foster, "Jefferson Fathered Slave's Last Child," 27–28. Before it received the support of scientific evidence in 1998, the story of Jefferson's thirty-eight-year relationship with Hemings and their six children circulated in oral culture and in popular literature from the revolutionary period to the present. See, for example, James Callender's stories in the *Richmond Recorder,* on 1 September, 22 September, and 29 September 1802. It is one of the ironies of "Enlightenment" history that oral and written stories of Jeffer-

son's relationship with Hemings, which were denied by Jefferson, his family, and later historians, were confirmed by the very methods of scientific investigation and the test of *blood* that Jefferson championed.

19. Responding to the question of what constituted a mulatto by Virginia law in a letter to Francis Gray dated 4 March 1815, Jefferson wrote that measuring the "fractional mixtures" of white and black blood was "a mathematical problem of the same class with those of the mixtures of different liquors or different metals." Seeking to calculate the number of crosses between white and "negro blood" it would take to "clear" the blood of blackness, Jefferson presents what he calls an "algebraic notation" that only thinly disguises the "crossings" within his own mixed-blood family—crossings that would produce on the "third cross" (between himself and Sally Hemings) white progeny: "Let the third crossing be of q [one quarter negro blood] and C [white pure blood], their offspring will be $q/2 + C/2 = a/8 + A/8 = B/4 + c/2$, call this e (eighth) who having less than $1/4$ of a, or of pure negro blood, to wit $1/8$ only, is no longer a mulatto, *so that a third cross clears the blood* ("Letter to Gray," *WTJ*, 14:262; my emphasis). "It is understood in natural history that a fourth cross of one race of animals with another gives an issue equivalent for all sensible purposes to the original blood," Jefferson concludes, leaving one to wonder if his relationship with Hemings was not part of an eugenic experiment on the science of returning the nation to its "original [white] blood" through interracial sex (*WTJ*, 14:268, 269–70).

20. The reference to "this bloody war" is used in a poem by a "Daughter of Liberty" that accompanies a woodcut of a female soldier that was circulated as a broadside in 1779. See Chapter 3, p. 93 and Figure 10.

21. Letter to Anne W. Bingham, 11 May 1788 in *PTJ*, 13:151. See also the *Boston Weekly Magazine* in which one writer complained: "Warlike women, learned women, and women who are politicians, equally abandon the circle which nature and institutions have traced round their sex; they convert themselves into men" (24 March 1804, 86; quoted in Linda Kerber, *Women of the Republic: Intellect and Ideology in Revolutionary America* [Chapel Hill: University of North Carolina Press, 1980], 199). Subsequent references will be cited as *WR*.

22. Letter to Samuel Kercheval, 5 September 1816, *WTJ*, 15:72.

23. Jay Fliegelman, *Prodigals and Pilgrims: The American Revolution against Patriarchal Authority, 1750–1800* (New York: Cambridge University Press, 1982), 138–39. The lines "Her face besmear'd with blood, her raiment dyed" appeared in one of the popular ballads inspired by McCrea's violent death.

24. James Fenimore Cooper, *The Last of the Mohicans: A Narrative of 1757* (1826; New York: New American Library, 1980), 73, 83, 142, 148, 216, 217, 312. Subsequent references will be cited as *LM*.

25. Leslie Fiedler, *Love and Death in the American Novel* (1960, 1966; reprint, Normal, Ill.: Dalkey Archive Press, 1997), 205. For others who have discussed the theme of miscegenation in *The Last of the Mohicans*, see Jane Tompkins, *Sensational Designs: The Cultural Work of American Fiction, 1790–1860* (New York: Oxford University Press, 1985), 114–16; and Shirley Samuels, *Romances of the Republic: Women, the Family, and Violence in the Literature of the Early American Nation* (New York: Oxford University Press, 1996), 96–112.

26. David G. Croly, *Miscegenation: The Theory of the Blending of the Races, Applied to the American White Man and Negro* (New York: H. Dexter, Hamilton and Company, 1864).

27. In 1985 the Supreme Court decided in favor of a claim by the Oneida tribe to land taken illegally by the state of New York in violation of a treaty dating

back to George Washington's administration. Numerous other Iroquois claims to land in the same area where Cooper's historical narrative takes place are still pending. Thus, the doom and death of the Indians and the historical triumph of whiteness toward which Cooper's historical romance moves were not at all inevitable or assured. In fact, the prospect that the Iroquois will win the legal battle to return to land formerly stolen by the state of New York suggests an historical reversal of Tamenund's prophecy as "the Red Men" come again and "[t]he palefaces" are no longer "masters of the earth." As David W. Chen writes in an article titled "Battle over Iroquois Land Claims Escalates": "It is not just a matter of the Iroquois asking for land that would quadruple the area of all current Indian holdings in the state. It is the specter of the Iroquois accruing land, removing them from the tax rolls and surrounding landowners and local businesses in checkerboard fashion to where non-Indians feel compelled to sell out" (*New York Times*, 16 May 2000, A1, A22).

28. D. H. Lawrence, *Studies in Classic American Literature* (1923; New York: Viking Press, 1964), 65.

29. Edgar Allan Poe, *Essays and Reviews*, ed. G. R. Thompson (New York: Library of America, 1984), 76. Subsequent references to this edition will be cited as *ER*.

30. "[T]he 'neuroses' we see about us today are a specific historical form of psychic conflict," writes Norbert Elias in *The History of Manners*, vol. 1 of *The Civilizing Process*, trans. E. Jephcott (New York: Pantheon, 1978), 150. See also Luce Irigaray, who asks: "What is the relation between the discovery and the definition of the unconscious and those 'others' that have been (mis)recognized by philosophic discourse?" in *This Sex Which Is Not One*, trans. Catherine Porter (Ithaca, N.Y.: Cornell University Press, 1985), 124.

31. "Edgar Poe's Significance," in *Walt Whitman: Prose Works*, ed. Floyd Stovall, 2 vols. (New York: New York University Press, 1964), 1:231–32. Subsequent references to Whitman's *Prose Works* will be cited as *PW*.

32. *Franklin Evans* was originally published as an "extra" in the *New World*, a popular weekly journal aimed at creating and reaching a mass audience.

33. Edgar Allan Poe, *Poetry and Tales*, ed. Patrick F. Quinn (New York: Library of America, 1984), 827. Subsequent references to this edition will be cited as *PT*.

34. Walt Whitman, *The Early Poems and the Fiction*, ed. Thomas L. Brasher (New York: New York University Press, 1963), 179. Subsequent references to this edition will be cited as *EPF*.

35. Michael Moon, *Disseminating Whitman: Revision and Corporeality in* Leaves of Grass (Cambridge, Mass.: Harvard University Press, 1991), 53–58; Michael Warner, "Whitman Drunk," in *Breaking Bounds: Whitman and American Cultural Studies*, ed. Betsy Erkkila and Jay Grossman (New York: Oxford University Press, 1996), 30–43.

36. See Sylvester Graham, *Lecture to Young Men on Chastity* (Boston: Light and Stearns, 1834); and Oscar Fowler, *Amativeness: Or Evils and Remedies of Excessive and Perverted Sexuality Including Warning and Advice to the Married and Single* (New York: Fowler and Wells, 1844). See also *A Treatise on Diseases of the Sexual System* (1845), in which the American physician Edward Dixon warns of the dangers of masturbation to the blood, the nervous system, the reproductive organs, and male virility; and *Self Preservation. Manhood, Causes of Its Premature Decline* (1830), in which Robert James Culverwell writes of the male onanist: "All the intellectual faculties are weakened. The man becomes a coward: sighs and weeps like a hysterical woman. He loses all decision and dignity of character" (quoted in

Charles E. Rosenberg, "Sexuality, Class and Role in 19ᵗʰ-Century America," *American Quarterly* 25 [May 1973]: 146).

37. Subjection to the impulses of the body is associated with both the savage and the slave in *Franklin Evans*. The epigraph to the chapter that introduces the creole slave Margaret begins with the following lines by "Willis": "They say 'tis pleasant on the lip, / And merry on the brain—/ They say it stirs the sluggish blood / And dulls the tooth of pain" (*EPF*, 204). Within Whitman's narrative the "it" that "stirs the sluggish blood" is ambiguous: it could be wine, but it could also be cross-race sex or sex between men. The lines are taken from the poem "Look not upon the wine when it is red," which were attributed to N. P. Willis in George B. Cheever's popular anthology, *The American Common-place Book of Poetry* (Boston: Carter, Hendee, 1831).

38. Emory Holloway, introduction to *Franklin Evans; or The Inebriate, A Tale of the Times* (New York: Random House, 1929), xvi.

39. Henry Bryan Binns, *Life of Whitman* (London: Methuen, 1905), 51–53.

40. Emory Holloway, "Walt Whitman's Love Affairs," *The Dial* 69 (November 1920): 473–83.

41. As Ed Folsom observes, the poet Yusef Komunyakaa revives in his 1992 poem "Kosmos" "the discredited story of Walt's affair with an octoroon mistress in New Orleans in order to celebrate a hybrid Whitman whose passion came from crossing borders" ("Talking Back to Walt Whitman: An Introduction," in *Walt Whitman: The Measure of His Song*, ed. Jim Perlman, Ed Folsom, and Dan Campion [Duluth, Minn.: Holy Cow! Press, 1998], 45).

42. Walt Whitman, *Leaves of Grass: The First (1855) Edition*, ed. Malcolm Cowley (New York: Viking Press, 1959), 121. Subsequent references to this edition will be cited in the text as *LG* 1855.

43. "Live Oak, with Moss," in *Whitman's Manuscripts: Leaves of Grass (1860) A Parallel Text*, ed. Fredson Bowers (Chicago: University of Chicago Press, 1955), 94.

44. Walt Whitman, *Leaves of Grass: Facsimile Edition of the 1860 Text*, ed. Roy Harvey Pearce (Ithaca: Cornell University Press, 1961), 377. The poem was entitled "Confession Drops" in manuscript. Subsequent references to this edition will be cited as *LG* 1860.

45. Seyla Benhabib, "Models of Public Space: Hannah Arendt, the Liberal Tradition, and Jürgen Habermas," in *Habermas and the Public Sphere*, ed. Craig Calhoun (Cambridge, Mass.: MIT Press, 1992), 84. For a contemporary critical attack on Whitman's "public onanism," his "public performance of what most of us would only do in private," see Robert S. Frederickson, "Public Onanism: Whitman's 'Song of Himself,'" *Modern Language Quarterly* 2 (June 1985): 143–60.

46. George Kateb, "Walt Whitman and the Culture of Democracy," *Political Theory* 18 (November 1990): 545. See also Samuel H. Beer, "Liberty and Union: Walt Whitman's Idea of the Nation," *Political Theory* 12 (August 1984): 361–86.

47. See, for example, Richard Rorty, who writes, "Whitman's image of democracy was of lovers embracing," in *Achieving Our Country: Leftist Thought in Twentieth-Century America* (Cambridge, Mass.: Harvard University Press, 1998), 25; and Martha Nussbaum, who presents Whitman's democratic poet as a model of the role that the literary imagination and sympathetic identification might play in public rationality, legal judgment, and "political relations among citizens," in *Poetic Justice: The Literary Imagination and Public Life* (Boston: Beacon Press, 1995), xii. For a more extensive discussion of the affective homoerotic poetics that shapes Whitman's theory of democracy, see Betsy Erkkila, "Public

Love: Whitman and Political Theory," in *Whitman East and West*, ed. Ed Folsom (Iowa City: University of Iowa Press, 2002), 115–44.

48. Emily Dickinson, *The Letters of Emily Dickinson*, ed. Thomas H. Johnson, 3 vols. (Cambridge, Mass.: Belknap Press of Harvard University Press, 1958), 3:830. Subsequent references to this edition of Dickinson's *Letters* will be cited as *LD*.

49. Sandra M. Gilbert, "The American Sexual Poetics of Walt Whitman and Emily Dickinson," in *Reconstructing American Literary History*, ed. Sacvan Bercovitch (Cambridge, Mass.: Harvard University Press, 1986), 124, 125, 126.

50. Ibid., 128, 140.

51. According to Richard B. Sewall, "the Dickinsons were pure stock, without even a wife in seven generations from outside New England," in *The Life of Emily Dickinson* (New York: Farrar, Straus and Giroux, 1974), 26. On both the paternal and maternal sides, intermarriage among blood relatives was not uncommon. Lavinia Norcross, Dickinson's mother's sister, married her cousin Loring Norcross after they were raised together as brother and sister. "For some reason," Alfred Habegger writes, "this marriage made more talk than the truly incestuous 1838 union between Edward's younger brother Timothy and a *double* first cousin," in *My Wars Are Laid Away in Books: The Life of Emily Dickinson* (New York: Random House, 2001), 84. The word *fusion* was used negatively by conservative Whig Otis P. Lord, Speaker of the Massachusetts House of Representatives and close friend of the Dickinson family, to describe the various hybrid political formations, including the Know-Nothing and the Republican parties, that were created in the wake of the demise of the Whig Party after 1852 (Speech to the Whig State Convention, 2 October 1855; reprinted in Millicent Bingham Todd, *Emily Dickinson's Home: Letters of Edward Dickinson and His Family* [New York: Harper, 1955], 393). For a discussion of the massive mobility, immigration, and migration that characterized American society from 1815 to the end of the century, see Rowland Berthoff, "The American Social Order: A Conservative Hypothesis," *American Historical Review* 65 (April 1960): 495–514.

52. MSS in the Todd-Bingham Family Papers at Yale University, reprinted in Sewall, *Life of Dickinson*, appendix 2, p. 282.

53. For a discussion of the "incestuous" dimension of Dickinson's relationship with Sue, see Betsy Erkkila, *The Wicked Sisters: Women Poets, Literary History, and Discord* (New York: Oxford University Press, 1992), 37–38. See also Eva Saks, who observes that "state criminal codes usually listed miscegenation next to incest as two crimes of 'blood,'" in "Representing Miscegenation Law," *Raritan* 8 (fall 1988): 53. For an illuminating discussion of the relation and conflation of incest and miscegenation from the eighteenth to the twentieth century, see Werner Sollors, *Neither Black Nor White But Both: Thematic Explorations of Interracial Literature* (New York: Oxford University Press, 1997), 286–335.

54. Dickinson, *The Poems of Emily Dickinson: Variorum Edition*, ed. R. W. Franklin, 3 vols. (Cambridge, Mass.: Belknap Press of Harvard University Press, 1998), 409A. Subsequent references to this edition of Dickinson's *Poems* will be cited as *Fr* followed by the number of the poem.

55. Edward Dickinson to Salmon P. Chase, 23 July 1855; reprinted in Todd, *Emily Dickinson's Home*, 568.

56. In his letter declining nomination as the Republican candidate for lieutenant governor of Massachusetts in 1861, Edward Dickinson denounced "as subversive of all constitutional guarantees, if we expect to reconstruct the Union, the heretical dogma that immediate and universal emancipation of

slaves should be proclaimed by the government, as the means of putting an end to the war" (*Springfield Daily Republican,* "Personal and Political," 17 October 1861). For a more extensive discussion of the political contexts of Dickinson's poetry in the Civil War years and later, see Betsy Erkkila, "Dickinson and the Art of Politics," in *A Historical Guide to Emily Dickinson,* ed. Vivian Pollak (New York: Oxford University Press, 2003).

57. "'Leaves of Grass'—Smut in Them," *Springfield Daily Republican,* 16 June 1860, 1.

58. Quoted in Millicent Bingham Todd, *Ancestor's Brocades: The Literary Début of Emily Dickinson* (New York: Harper and Brothers, 1945), 169.

59. "'Leaves of Grass'—Smut in Them."

60. William Dean Howells, "Editor's Study," *Harper's New Monthly Magazine* 82 (January 1891): 320.

61. Allen Tate, "New England Culture and Emily Dickinson," *Symposium: A Quarterly Journal in Modern Foreign Literature* 3 (April 1932): 206.

62. See, for example, R. P. Blackmur, "Emily Dickinson: Notes on Prejudice and Fact," *Southern Review* 3 (autumn 1937): 332, 324, 347. John Crowe Ransom later cited Blackmur's essay on Dickinson as a model of the New Critical method in *The New Criticism* (Norfolk, Conn.: New Directions, 1941), vii–x. *Understanding Poetry: An Anthology for College Students* (New York: Henry Holt and Company, 1938), ed. Cleanth Brooks and Robert Penn Warren, includes an extended New Critical analysis of language, image, form, and tone in "After great pain, a formal feeling comes –" (468–71). See also Tate, "New England Culture"; and Yvor Winters, "Emily Dickinson and the Limits of Judgment," *Maule's Curse: Seven Studies in the History of American Obscurantism* (Norfolk, Conn.: New Directions, 1938), 149–68. More recently, Susan Howe and others have used the language of undefiled genius to emphasize Dickinson's aesthetic purity—her separation from the messiness of politics and history. For a more detailed discussion of past and recent critical and editorial contests around Dickinson's work, see Betsy Erkkila, "The Emily Dickinson Wars," in *The Cambridge Companion to Emily Dickinson,* ed. Wendy Martin (New York: Cambridge University Press, 2002), 11–29.

63. Toni Morrison, "Unspeakable Things Unspoken: The Afro-American Presence in American Literature," *Michigan Quarterly Review* 28 (1989): 6, 8.

64. In "Is There a 'Neo-Racism?'" Étienne Balibar argues that in the contemporary era culture has come to play the role of biology as a marker of racial distinction (in *Race, Nation, Class,* 17–28). See also Avery Gordon and Christopher Newfield, "White Mythologies," *Critical Inquiry* 20 (summer 1994): 737–57.

65. Betsy Erkkila, "Ethnicity, Literary Theory, and the Grounds of Resistance," *American Quarterly* 42 (December 1995): 563–94.

66. Cherríe Moraga and Gloria Anzaldúa, eds., *This Bridge Called My Back* (New York: Kitchen Table, 1981), 23. See also Hortense Spillers, who writes that the New World order, "with its human sequence written in blood, represents for its African and indigenous peoples a scene of actual mutilation, dismemberment, and exile," in "Mama's Baby, Papa's Maybe: An American Grammar Book," *Diacritics* 17 (summer 1987): 67.

67. Stuart Hall, "New Ethnicities," in *Black Film, British Cinema,* ed. Kobena Mercer (London: Institute of Contemporary Arts, 1988), 27.

68. For the history of the dispute over the authenticity of Jacobs's work, see Jean Fagin Yellin, "Written by Herself: Harriet Jacobs' Slave Narrative," *American Literature* 53 (November 1981): 479–86; and Jean Fagin Yellin, "Texts and Contexts of Harriet Jacobs' *Incidents in the Life of a Slave Girl: Written by Herself*," in

The Slave's Narrative, ed. Charles T. Davis and Henry Louis Gates, Jr. (New York: Oxford University Press, 1985), 262–82. For discussions of the black female authorship of *Incidents,* see Hazel Carby, *Reconstructing Womanhood: The Emergence of the Afro-American Woman Novelist* (New York: Oxford University Press, 1987), 45–61; Valerie Smith, *Self-Discovery and Authority in Afro-American Narrative* (Cambridge, Mass.: Harvard University Press, 1987), 28–43; Elizabeth Fox-Genovese, "My Statue, My Self: Autobiographical Writings of Afro-American Women," in *The Private Self: Theory and Practice of Women's Autobiographical Writings,* ed. Shari Benstock (Chapel Hill: University of North Carolina Press, 1988), 63–89; Claudia Tate, "Allegories of Black Female Authority," in *Changing Our Own Words: Essays on Criticism, Theory, and Writing by Black Women,* ed. Cheryl A. Wall (New Brunswick, N.J.: Rutgers University Press, 1989); and Frances Foster, *Written by Herself: Literary Production by African American Women, 1746–1892* (Bloomington: Indiana University Press, 1993), 95–116.

69. See, for example, Houston A. Baker's criticism of the historical work of black women critics who seek "to incorporate themselves comfortably into an essentialist, northern, history" (*Workings of the Spirit: The Poetics of African-American Women's Writing* [Chicago: University of Chicago Press, 1991], 19).

70. Harriet A. Jacobs, *Incidents in the Life of a Slave Girl: Written by Herself,* ed. Jean Fagan Yellin (Cambridge, Mass.: Harvard University Press, 1987), 1.

71. Hall, "New Ethnicities," 27.

72. Henry Louis Gates, Jr., *The Signifying Monkey: A Theory of African-American Literary Criticism* (New York: Oxford University Press, 1988), 130. See Michael Awkward's response to Deborah E. McDowell, "Boundaries: Or Distant Relations and Close Kin," in *Afro-American Literary Study in the 1990s,* ed. Houston A. Baker, Jr., and Patricia Redmond (Chicago: University of Chicago Press, 1989), 76.

73. Thayer and Eldridge was the same press that published the 1860 edition of Walt Whitman's *Leaves of Grass.* An English edition of Jacobs's book, *The Deeper Wrong: Or, Incidents in the Life of a Slave, Written by Herself,* ed. L. Maria Child, was published in London in 1862.

74. Jacobs, *Incidents,* 242. John Blasingame, *The Slave Community* (New York: Oxford University Press, 1972), 234; Sterling A. Brown, Arthur P. Davis, and Ulysses Lee, *The Negro Caravan: Writings by American Negroes* (New York: The Citadel Press, 1941); Arna Bontemps, "The Slave Narrative: An American Genre," *Great Slave Narratives* (Boston: Beacon Press, 1969). In "Mama's Baby, Papa's Maybe," Spillers describes the narrative of Brent/Jacobs as "dictated to Lydia Maria Child" (76).

75. Spillers, "Mama's Baby, Papa's Maybe," 76.

76. Lydia Maria Child to Harriet Jacobs, 13 August 1860, in *Incidents,* ed. Yellin, 244.

77. C.L.R. James, *Mariners, Renegades, and Castaways: The Story of Herman Melville and the World We Live In* (New York: Privately printed, 1953). Subsequent references to this edited will be cited as *M.* See also Michael Hardt and Antonio Negri, who envision the achievement of "global citizenship" by "the mobile multitude" as a means of resisting "the slavery of belonging to a nation, an identity, and a people." "Nomadism and miscegenation," they write, "appear here as figures of virtue, as the first ethical practices on the terrain of Empire" (*Empire* [Cambridge, Mass.: Harvard University Press, 2000], 361–62).

78. C.L.R. James, *American Civilization,* ed. Anna Grimshaw and Keith Hart (Cambridge, Mass.: Blackwell, 1993), 276.

Chapter 2

1. Perry Miller, *Errand into the Wilderness* (Cambridge, Mass.: Belknap Press of Harvard University Press, 1956), vii, viii; emphasis added.

2. Morrison,"Unspeakable Things Unspoken," 6, 8. See also Amy Kaplan's introduction to *Cultures of United States Imperialism*, in which she discusses Miller's "errand" in the context of "the absence of empire from the study of American culture" and the reciprocal relation between U. S. imperialism at home and abroad ("'Left Alone with America': The Absence of Empire in the Study of American Culture," in *Cultures of United States Imperialism*, ed. Amy Kaplan and Donald Pease [Durham, N.C.: Duke University Press, 1993], 11).

3. In 1780, Marbois, who was secretary to the French legation in Philadelphia, circulated twenty-two queries about the American states to members of the Continental Congress as part of a semi-official effort to gather information about each of the thirteen states for the French government. Jefferson received a handwritten copy of the queries in the fall of 1780 from Joseph Jones, a member of the Virginia delegation to Congress. The list of twenty-two queries is in *PTJ*, 4:166–67.

4. See, for example, Foucault's classic study of transformations in the prison system and the power to punish in relation to the emergence of a new "political technology of the body," in *Discipline and Punish: The Birth of the Prison*, trans. Alan Sheridan (1975; reprint, New Haven, Conn.: Yale University Press, 1979), 24. For a discussion of the vexed heritage of the Enlightenment, its contradictory legacy of freedom and control, see Max Horkheimer and Theodor W. Adorno, *Dialectic of Enlightenment*, trans. John Cumming (New York: Continuum, 1995).

5. Reserved almost exclusively for unruly blacks and occasionally Indians, castration was, according to Jordan, "a peculiarly American experiment, for there was no basis for it in English law." In 1769, Jordan writes, "Virginia almost entirely abandoned castration as a lawful punishment" (*White over Black: American Attitudes Toward the Negro, 1550–1812* [Chapel Hill: University of North Carolina Press, 1968], 155). Subsequent references will be cited as *WOB*.

6. The grotesque body is, in Bakhtin's terms, associated with bodily functions and the lower body parts, with "[e]ating, drinking, defecation, and other elimination (sweating, blowing the nose, sneezing), as well as copulation, pregnancy, dismemberment, swallowing up by another body." In contrast to the modern individualist body, which "presents an entirely finished, completed, strictly limited body," the grotesque body is associated with the transgression of bodily bounds, between body and body, animal and human, body and world (*Rabelais and His World*, trans. Helen Iswolsky [Bloomington: Indiana University Press, 1984], 317, 320).

7. The Jamaican writer Edward Long makes a similar case for "amorous intercourse" between apes and Negroes in *History of Jamaica* (1774), portions of which were reprinted in the *Columbian Magazine* during the constitutional debates. "Ludicrous as it may seem, I do not think that an oran-outang husband would be any dishonour to an Hottentot female" (quoted in *WOB*, 492–93). "[B]efore the Revolution," Jordan observes, "the English colonists generally felt no need to expound or even mention the Negro-ape connection" because "[e]veryone knew—then—that man possessed a soul and rationality" (*WOB*, 239, 231).

8. Jefferson's proposal is at the center of past and recent debates about his

attitudes toward the black race. Peden has argued that if Jefferson's views on "the natural inferiority of the Negro seem less than liberal today, his attitude toward that race and toward the institution of slavery was startlingly advanced for eighteenth-century Virginia." "Jefferson took every opportunity he could to strike at the 'infamous practice' of slavery," Peden writes (*NV,* 286–87, n. 6). John Chester Miller also observes: "The significance of the *Notes on Virginia* is not that Jefferson presented a brief for black inferiority, but that he demanded the extinction of slavery" ("Slavery," in *Thomas Jefferson: A Reference Biography,* ed. Merrill D. Peterson [New York: Scribner, 1986], 426). See also William Freehling, "The Founding Fathers and Slavery," *American Historical Review* 77 (1972): 81–93; and Dumas Malone, *Jefferson the Virginian,* vol. 1 of *Jefferson and His Time* (Boston: Little Brown, 1948), 264–68. Jefferson himself insisted on circulating the first printed edition of *Notes,* which was privately published in France in 1785, among only a few select individuals for fear that if it were "to go to the public at large," its proposal regarding slavery would damage the cause of emancipation in Virginia and his desire to revise the Virginia code of laws (*NV,* xvii). However, during the Revolution, as John Chester Miller points out, "Jefferson and his colleagues actually tightened the slave code in their revision and codification of the laws" (*The Wolf by the Ears: Thomas Jefferson and Slavery* [New York: Free Press, 1977], 20). Some have argued that Jefferson's views on race were, in the words of Robert McColley, "not ahead, but rather far behind" his time (*Slavery and Jeffersonian Virginia* [1964; 2nd ed., Urbana: University of Illinois Press, 1973], 131). George M. Fredrickson also notes that the notion of innate black inferiority was a minority view in the eighteenth century: "despite the fact that Jefferson speculated in the 1780s about the possibility that blacks were inherently inferior in some respects to whites, no one in the United States actually defended institutionalized inequality on the basis of racial theory until well into the nineteenth century" (*The Arrogance of Race: Historical Perspectives on Slavery, Racism, and Social Inequality* [Middletown, Conn.: Wesleyan University Press, 1988], 202). See also Thomas F. Gossett, *Race: The History of an Idea in America* (Dallas: Southern Methodist University Press, 1963). Although Jefferson later claimed in his "Autobiography" that nothing came of his proposal to emancipate slaves because "the public mind would not yet bear the proposition" (*The Writings of Thomas Jefferson,* ed. Paul L. Ford, 10 vols. [New York: G. P. Putnam's Sons, 1892–99], 1:68), Paul Finkelman notes that the Virginia legislature's adoption of a liberal manumission law after Jefferson left the governorship "suggests that on the question of manumission the 'public mind'—and certainly the collective mind of the Virginia legislature—was far in advance of Jefferson's" (*Slavery and the Founders: Race and Liberty in the Age of Jefferson* [Armonk, N.Y.: M. E. Sharpe, 1996], 121). Countering Malone's claim that Jefferson "proposed a plan of gradual emancipation for his own commonwealth" (Dumas Malone, *Ordeal of Liberty,* vol. 3 of *Jefferson and His Time* [Boston: Little Brown, 1962], 207), Finkelman observes: "If Jefferson or anyone else ever prepared such an amendment, no copy of it has survived. The first appearance of the text of this amendment was in the *Notes"* (*Slavery and the Founders,* 120). Jefferson's proposed emancipation of slaves may have been a purely imaginative act for the eyes of the French and a select group of his friends only.

9. In *Les époques de la nature,* which is part of his influential *Histoire naturelle, générale et particulière* (Paris: l'Imprimerie Royale, 1778), the famous French naturalist, Georges Louis Leclerc, Comte de Buffon, argued that in the New World physical nature, including the indigenous population of North and South

America, is smaller and degenerate in comparison with Europe. In *Histoire philosophique et politique des établissemens et du commerce des européens dans les deux Indes* (Amsterdam: s.n., 1770), Guillaume Thomas François Raynal extended this charge of New World inferiority to include what Jefferson called "the race of whites, transplanted from Europe" (*NV,* 64).

10. See, for example, Kant's observation of "A few curiosities about the blacks" in *Physical Geography,* excerpted in *Race and the Enlightenment: A Reader,* ed. Emmanuel Chukwudi Eze (Cambridge, Mass.: Blackwell, 1997), 58–64. "The Negroes, if they do not mix with white people, remain over many generations Negroes, even in Virginia" (61), he writes, in a comment that suggests that Virginia existed in the European imagination as the very scene of excess, mixture, and unstable boundaries between black and white.

11. Benedict Anderson, *Imagined Communities: Reflections on the Origin and Spread of Nationalism* (1983; rev. ed. New York: Verso, 1991), 46. For a discussion of what Anderson calls "creole" nationalism, see especially "Creole Pioneers," 47–65.

12. Anderson defines "creole" (*criollo*) as a "person of (at least theoretically) pure European descent but born in the Americas (and, by later extension, anywhere outside Europe)" (*Imagined Communities,* 47).

13. Monogenism, the belief in the unity of the human species, dominated eighteenth-century racial theory. It was not until the nineteenth century that polygenism, the belief in the separate origins of different races, came to dominate American scientific thought. See Gossett, *Race,* 32–53, 54–83. For a contemporary attack on Jefferson for the religious infidelity of his notion of separate racial origins, see *Observations upon certain passages in Mr. Jefferson's* Notes on Virginia *which appear to have a tendency to subvert religion, and establish a false philosophy,* published anonymously by Clement Clark Moore in 1804.

14. Benjamin Franklin advances a similar argument in *Observations Concerning the Increase of Mankind* (1751): "why increase the Sons of Africa, by Planting them in America, where we have so fair an Opportunity, by excluding all Blacks and Tawneys of increasing the lovely White and Red?" (*The Papers of Benjamin Franklin,* ed. Leonard W. Labaree, 34 vols. [New Haven, Conn.: Yale University Press, 1959], 4:234). Against the racially hierarchized arguments of Jefferson and Franklin, Benjamin Rush argued that the mulatto was superior to the pure blood: "The mulatto has been remarked, in all countries, to exceed, in sagacity, his white and black parent. The same remark has been made of the offspring of the European, and North American Indian" ("On the Influence of Physical Causes," in *Sixteen Introductory Lectures* [Philadelphia: Bradford and Innskeep, 1811], 117).

15. Thomas Jefferson to Colonel Benjamin Hawkins, 18 February 1803, in *The Writings of Thomas Jefferson,* ed. Andrew A. Lipscomb and Albert Bergh, 20 vols. (Washington, D.C.: Thomas Jefferson Memorial Association, 1903), 10:363.

16. William Byrd makes a similar connection among sexual intermixture, peaceful land acquisition, and "blanching" the native American population in *Histories of the Dividing Line betwixt Virginia and North Carolina* (written in 1728; published posthumously). "[T]here is but one way of Converting these poor Infidels, and reclaiming them from Barbarity, and that is, Charitably to intermarry with them," Byrd observes. "Besides," he argues, "the poorest Indians would have had less reason to Complain that the English took away their Land, if they had received it by way of Portion with their Daughters. Had such Affinities been contracted in the Beginning, how much Bloodshed had been pre-

vented. . . . Nor wou'd the Shade of the Skin have been any reproach at this day; for if a Moor may be washt white in 3 Generations, Surely an Indian might have been blancht in two" (*Histories of the Dividing Line betwixt Virginia and North Carolina*, ed. William K. Boyd [Raleigh, N.C.: North Carolina Historical Commission, 1929], 120, 4).

17. The relations among bodily incorporation, sexual mixture, and the continental aspirations of the United States are particularly evident in a speech Jefferson gave to the Delawares, Mohicans, and Munries on 21 December 1808: "you will unite yourselves with us, join in our Great Councils and form one people with us, and we shall all be Americans," Jefferson says; "you will mix with us by marriage, your blood will run in our veins, and will spread with us over this great island" (Jefferson, *Writings*, ed. Lipscomb and Bergh, 16:452). Historically, incorporation turned out to be an ambiguous ground for American Indian policy since there was considerable uncertainty about what it meant and how it was to take place. Did it mean sexual mixture or a mixture of cultural and social forms? Did it mean absorption of the red by the white race, a blending of the two races into something different, or an incorporation of Indian tribes as sovereign bodies—or states—within the United States? Ironically, Jefferson's policy of incorporation turned out to be most controversial when it appeared to be most successful. The passage and implementation of Jackson's removal policy in 1830 was prompted by the fact that the Cherokee nation assimilated American economic and political structures to specifically tribal forms and then sued for legal status as a sovereign nation within the United States. These complicated questions of Indian citizenship, sovereignty, and incorporation are still being debated and fought in the courts. See Chapter 1, n. 27. See also Robert F. Berkhofer, *The White Man's Indian: Images of the American Indian from Columbus to the Present* (New York: Knopf, 1978); Bernard Sheehan, *Seeds of Extinction: Jeffersonian Philanthropy and the American Indian* (Chapel Hill: University of North Carolina Press, 1973); William G. McLaughlin, "Thomas Jefferson and the Beginning of Cherokee Nationalism, 1806 to 1808," *William and Mary Quarterly* 32 (1975): 547–80; and Anthony F. C. Wallace, *Jefferson and the Indians: The Tragic Fate of the First Americans* (Cambridge, Mass.: Belknap Press of Harvard University Press, 1999).

18. Peter Stallybrass and Allon White, *The Politics and Poetics of Trangression* (Ithaca: Cornell University Press, 1986), 192.

19. Quoted in James Hugo Johnston, *Race Relations in Virginia & Miscegenation in the South, 1776–1860* (Amherst: University of Massachusetts Press, 1970), 170.

20. See, for example, Johnston, *Race Relations*; Joel Williamson, *New People: Miscegenation and Mulattoes in the United States* (New York: Free Press, 1980); Lerone Bennett, "Thomas Jefferson's Negro Grandchildren," *Ebony* 10 (November 1954): 78–80; and Mechal Sobel, *The World They Made Together: Black and White Values in Eighteenth-Century Virginia* (Princeton, N.J.: Princeton University Press, 1987). In *An Essay on the Causes of the Variety of Complexion and Figure in the Human Species* (Philadephia: Robert Aitken, 1787), Samuel Stanhope Smith, a Virginian, advocated racial mixture as a solution to Virginia's racial problems. See also Jordan, who observes that "in all the English colonies," there was more "intermixture . . . during the eighteenth century than at any time since" (*WOB*, 137).

21. Williamson, *New People*, 35.

22. "Mais je fus étonné de voir appeler noirs et traiter comme tels des enfants aussi blancs que moi," Volney wrote in his journal (quoted in Jean Gaulmier, *Un grand témoin de la Révolution et de L'empire, Volney* [Paris: Hachette, 1959], 211).

23. Rumors of a relationship between Jefferson and Hemings began circulating among the Virginia gentry in the 1790s. The story was originally reported by James Callender in the Federalist *Richmond Recorder* on 1 September 1802. Despite heated controversy in the press, Jefferson never publicly denied either the relationship or the story. In 1873, Hemings's son Madison Hemings gave an account of the relationship between Jefferson and Hemings to the the the *Pike County (Ohio) Republican* that corroborates many of the details of Callender's story ("Life among the Lowly, No. 1," 13 March 1873). While historians such as Merrill D. Peterson and Dumas have dismissed the story as inconsistent with Jefferson's character, others have argued that, in the words Robert H. Cooley III, a Hemings family descendant, it's "not a story. It's true" (*Richmond Times Dispatch,* 1992; quoted in Scot A. French and Edward L. Ayers, "The Strange Career of Thomas Jefferson: Race and Slavery in American Memory," in *Jeffersonian Legacies,* ed. Peter S. Onuf [Charlottesville: University Press of Virginia, 1993], 450). See also Lerone Bennett; Fawn M. Brodie, "The Great Jefferson Taboo," *American Heritage* 22 (June 1972): 48ff.; and Brodie, *Thomas Jefferson,* 293–318. For the best account of the evidence, see Gordon Reed, *Thomas Jefferson and Sally Hemings.* In their excellent review of public debates on the Jefferson-Hemings relationship over the last fifty years, French and Ayers note that "new archaeological evidence" from three of Jefferson's houses "tends to confirm . . . the often-discounted stories that the United States third president had children with Sally Hemings, one of his slaves" ("The Strange Career of Thomas Jefferson," 451). The story was supported by scientific evidence in 1998, when Dr. Eugene A. Foster published the results of DNA tests conducted on the male descendants of Hemings and Jefferson. According to Foster and his associates, "The simplest and most probable explanations for our molecular findings are that Thomas Jefferson, rather than one of the Carr brothers [Jefferson's nephews], was the father of Eston Hemings Jefferson, and that Thomas Woodson was not Thomas Jefferson's son" ("Jefferson Fathered Slave's Last Child," 27). Hemings's heirs claim that Jefferson had six other children with Hemings: Thomas, Edy, Harriet, Beverly, Harriet (no. 2), and Madison. See also Lewis and Onuf, ed., *Sally Hemings & Thomas Jefferson.*

24. *Richmond Recorder,* 1 and 22 September 1802; see also 29 September, 5 November, and 1 December 1802. Significantly, given his controversial reference in *Notes* to the "preference of the Oran-ootan for the black women over those of his own species," Jefferson described himself as "an animal of a warm climate, a mere Oran-ootan" in a letter to Maria Cosway written at the same time he may have been forming a relationship with Hemings (14 January 1789, *PTJ,* 14:446).

25. Randolph claimed that Jefferson's nephews, Peter and Samuel Carr, had sexual liaisons with Sally and her sister, which accounted for "the progeny which resembled Mr. Jefferson." Jefferson himself was "chaste and pure"—as "immaculate a man as God ever created" (Henry S. Randall to James Parton, 1 June 1868; reprinted in Gordon Reed, *Thomas Jefferson and Sally Hemings,* 254–55).

26. "[U]nless Jefferson was capable of *slipping badly out of character in hidden moments at Monticello,*" writes Merrill D. Peterson, "it is difficult to imagine him caught up in a miscegenous relationship. Such a mixture of the races, such a ruthless exploitation of the master-slave relationship, revolted his whole being" (*Thomas Jefferson and the New Nation* [New York: Oxford University Press, 1970], 707; emphasis added). In his 1997 biography, Joseph J. Ellis also asserts that "a long-term sexual relationship with one of his slaves was *not in character* for Jeffer-

son" (*American Sphinx: The Character of Thomas Jefferson* [New York: Knopf, 1997], 219; emphasis added). See also Virginius Dabney, *The Jefferson Scandals: A Rebuttal* (New York: Dodd, Mead, 1981); and Douglass Adair, "The Jefferson Scandals," in *Fame and the Founding Fathers: Essays by Douglass Adair*, ed. Trevor Colbourn (New York: W. W. Norton, 1974).

27. The conflict between historians and popular culture over the public representation of Jefferson is itself an interesting instance of cultural contest over purity and contamination. In dismissing the Hemings relation as "out of character" for Jefferson, his defenders insist on the unity and self-coherence of a liberal subject and the purity of a republican father that will brook no contradiction—or mixture. Their fierce assertions of racial purity register the horror of racial mixture they attribute to Jefferson at the same time that they reinstate the implicit hierarchy of white over black, written over oral, and literate over popular forms. See, for example, Douglass Adair's reference to the tale of Jefferson and Hemings living together as a "subliterary oral tradition" ("The Jefferson Scandals," 166). See also Merrill D. Peterson, *The Jefferson Image in the American Mind* (New York: Oxford University Press, 1960).

28. As Gossett observes, "before the eighteenth century physical differences among peoples were so rarely referred to as a matter of great importance that something of a case can be made for the proposition that race consciousness is largely a modern phenomenon" (*Race*, 3). See also Benedict Anderson, who notes that "in the older imagining, where states were defined by centres, borders were porous and indistinct, and sovereignties faded imperceptibly into one another" (*Imagined Communities*, 19).

29. For an eloquent consideration of the "irrelevance of boundary to topography" in Jefferson's *Notes*, see Mitchell Robert Breitwieser, "Jefferson's Prospect," *Prospects* 10 (1985): 326–30.

30. It was not until 1 March 1784 that Virginia ceded its claims to western lands to Congress. As Frank Shuffelton notes: "In Query I Jefferson mentions Virginia's 1784 cession of claims to western territories as a condition of its own boundaries, but Query II, on rivers, is shaped by his state's earlier claims to a western empire" (Introduction to *Notes on the State of Virginia*, ed. Frank Shuffelton [New York: Penguin, 1999], xv).

31. In a letter dated 24 November 1801, Jefferson wrote to James Monroe of the white destiny of America: "nor can we contemplate with satisfaction either blot or mixture on that surface" (*WTJ*, 10: 296).

32. On the "agrarian myth" as myth, see Richard Hofstadter, *The Age of Reform: From Bryan to F. D. R.* (New York: Knopf, 1955), 23–36.

33. James Boswell, *Boswell's Life of Dr. Johnson*, ed. George Birkbeck Hill, 6 vols. (1791; reprint, Oxford: Clarendon Press, 1934), 2:476.

34. Edmund S. Morgan, *American Slavery, American Freedom: The Ordeal of Colonial Virginia* (New York: W. W. Norton, 1975), 380.

35. *The Papers of George Washington*, ed. W. W. Abbot and Dorothy Twohig, 10 vols. (Charlottesville: University Press of Virginia, 1983–95), 10:155.

36. As Brodie observes, it was in 1770 that the words "all men are born free" "first came to [Jefferson's] lips publicly in the legal defense of a black man" who claimed he was free because his grandmother was the daughter of a white woman and a black man (*Thomas Jefferson*, 104). See *Howell v. Netherland*, April 1770, in Jefferson, *Writings*, ed. Ford, 2:376. See also Jefferson's *Summary View of the Rights of British America*, in which he accuses the king of "a deliberate, systematical plan of reducing us to slavery" (*PTJ*, 1:125). Northerners also invoked the

slave as a defining figure of American freedom. We are "the most abject sort of slaves," wrote John Adams. "We are taxed without our consent expressed by ourselves and our representatives. We are therefore—Slaves," John Dickinson asserted (quoted in Bernard Bailyn, *The Ideological Origins of the American Revolution* [1967; enlarged ed., Cambridge, Mass.: Belknap Press of Harvard University Press, 1992], 232–33).

37. Jefferson's "Act for establishing Religious Freedom," which was printed as a pamphlet in Paris in 1786, was included as appendix 3 in the 1787 edition of *Notes*. The act was passed by the Virginia General Assembly in January 1786. Along with his authorship of the Declaration of Independence and his founding of the University of Virginia, Jefferson's "Act for Religious Freedom" is one of the three achievements listed on his grave site.

38. David Brion Davis suggests that Jefferson's record of inaction on race is explained by his membership in and loyalty to the Southern planter class (*The Problem of Slavery in the Age of Revolution, 1770–1823* [Ithaca, N.Y.: Cornell University Press, 1975], 169–84). For a discussion of Jefferson's failure to act against slavery, see also J. Miller, "Slavery" and *The Wolf by the Ears*; and Finkelman, *Slavery and the Founders*, 105–37.

39. Hegel, "Independence and Dependence of Self-Consciousness: Lordship and Bondage," *Phenomenology of Spirit*, trans. A. V. Miller (Oxford: Clarendon Press, 1977), 111–19. My reading of Hegel is informed by Alexandre Kojève's translation and commentary, titled "Autonomy and Dependence of Self-Consciousness: Mastery and Slavery," in *Introduction to the Reading of Hegel: Lectures on the Phenomenology of Spirit*, ed. Allan Bloom, trans. James H. Nichols, Jr. (New York: Basic Books, 1969), 3–30. For a fascinating contemporary account of Jefferson's relationship to his slaves, see Volney, who described Jefferson's efforts to frighten (*effrayer*) his slaves out of their indolence as "une scène comique," in which Jefferson gesticulated, scolded, and threatened with his whip, but each time he turned around, the blacks changed their attitude: those who faced him worked harder and those he couldn't see, stopped working at all (Gaulmier, *Un grand témoin*, 210–11). Volney's description of Monticello as a kind of theater of the absurd in which the white master and his black slaves appear to "play" the roles of master and slave suggests the instability—the literally performed nature—of racial identity. His account also exemplifies recent theories of the potentially subversive effects of shadowing, doubling, mimesis, and performance. See, for example, Spillers, "Notes on an Alternative Model," 165–87; Bhabha, *The Location of Culture*; and Judith Butler, *Gender Trouble: Feminism and the Subversion of Identity* (New York: Routledge, 1990).

40. See also Query XIV ("Laws"), in which Jefferson defends the black person's moral sense and his "right" to steal from—or "slay"—a master who has violated his right to "property" in himself (*NV*, 142).

41. As Peden observes, "This is one of the very rare examples of Jefferson's speaking of miracles with anything less than extreme skepticism" (*NV*, 292).

42. A year before his death, Jefferson told Frances Wright that the problem of slavery in the American republic was the subject "through life" of his "greatest anxieties" (Jefferson to Wright, 7 August 1825, in Jefferson, *Writings*, ed. Ford, 10:344). Jefferson's persistent fear of racial apocalypse was heightened historically by the slave insurrection in San Domingo in 1791. Emancipation would come, he wrote Edward Coles in 1814, whether "by the generous energy of our own minds; or by the bloody process of St. Domingo" (24 August 1814, in Jefferson, *Writings*, ed. Ford, 9:478).

43. Madison to Thomas L. McKenney, 10 February 1826, in *Letters and Other Writings of James Madison*, 4 vols. (New York: R. Worthington, 1884), 3:516.

44. For a study of Jeffersonian Indian policy see Sheehan, *Seeds of Extinction* and "American Indians," in Peterson, *Jefferson: A Reference Biography*, 399–415; and Wallace, *Jefferson and the Indians*. See also McLaughlin, "Thomas Jefferson and the Beginning of Cherokee Nationalism."

45. Roy Harvey Pearce, *Savagism and Civilization: A Study of the Indian and the American Mind* (1953; rev. ed., Berkeley: University of California Press, 1988), 94, 73, 5.

46. For Jefferson, Ronald Takaki argues, "everything . . . threatening to republican society had to be purged": "British corruption, luxury, monarchical ideas, 'licentious' immigrants, the instinctual life, the passions, the body, blacks, and Indians" (*Iron Cages: Race and Culture in Nineteenth-Century America* [New York: Knopf, 1979], 65). "Nestled under Jefferson's philanthropy was an ominous will to exterminate," writes Richard Drinnon. "Jefferson's hostility to mysticism, impulse, and the pleasures of the body was scarcely less than John Adams's and John Winthrop's" (*Facing West: The Metaphysics of Indian-Hating and Empire Building* [Minneapolis: University of Minnesota Press, 1980], 96, 102).

47. "As an amateur archaeologist, among the very earliest on the North American continent," writes Peden, "Jefferson anticipated by a century the aims and methods of modern archaeological science" (*NV*, 281).

48. Horkheimer and Adorno, *Dialectic of Enlightenment*, 25.

49. The image of America as a graveyard emerged during the Revolutionary period as a recurrent trope, one to which later American writers would return with obsessive frequency. See, for example, Cooper's *Last of the Mohicans* (1826), "The Bean-Field" in Thoreau's *Walden* (1854), and Whitman's *Leaves of Grass*, especially "This Compost" (1856).

50. "The controlling principle of Jefferson's politics is not to be found in any fixed image of society," writes Leo Marx. "Rather it is dialectical" (*The Machine in the Garden: Technology and the Pastoral Ideal in America* [New York: Oxford University Press, 1964], 139). See also Breitwieser's analysis of the tension between empiricism and speculation in Jefferson's *Notes* in "Jefferson's Prospect"; and Robert A. Ferguson's discussion of the conflict between the demands of law and the disorder of the real in Jefferson's *Notes* in "'Mysterious Obligation': Jefferson's *Notes on the State of Virginia*," *American Literature* 52 (November 1980): 381–406.

51. Jefferson's version of the mammoth legend was reprinted in 1959 along with a Shawnee version of the legend recorded in 1829 by N. Guilford in *The Mammoth Legend, as Related by Thomas Jefferson in His Notes on the State of Virginia, 1781, and Being One of the First Folk Tales or Legends of the Indians of the Ohio Valley Ever Recorded or Preserved in Printed Form, and an Account of the Shawnee Version of the Mammoth Legend as Related by N. Guilford, 1829* (Chillocothe, Ohio: Ross County Historical Society, 1959).

52. "There is a wonder somewhere," Jefferson says earlier in the same query when he is unable to account for the existence of seashells in the Andes by scientific means (*NV*, 33).

53. While he was in France in the 1780s, Jefferson was in the habit of asserting his savagism as a means of affirming his Americanism against what he perceived to be the artifice, pretense, and corruption of European society. See also Jefferson's later comment to John Adams: "As for France and England, with all their pre-eminence in science, the one is a den of robbers, and the other of pirates.

As if science produces no better fruits than tyranny, murder, rapine, and destitution of national morality, I would rather wish our country to be ignorant, honest and estimable as our neighboring savages are" (Jefferson to Adams, 21 January 1812, in *The Adams-Jefferson Letters*, ed. Lester J. Cappon, 2 vols. [Chapel Hill: University of North Carolina Press, 1959], 2:291).

54. Jefferson solicited Thomson's response to the manuscript version of *Notes* in 1781; he appended Thomson's comments to the privately printed first edition of *Notes* in 1785, and they were included as appendix 1 in the 1787 Stockdale edition.

55. "To Jefferson, as well as Franklin," writes Bruce E. Johansen, "the Indians had what the colonists wanted: societies free of oppression and class stratification" (*Forgotten Founders: How the American Indian Helped Shape Democracy* [Boston: Harvard Common Press, 1982], xvi). According to Johansen, Canassetego had urged the colonists to unite themselves on the model of the Five Nations tribes as early as 1744. A few years before the Albany Congress met in 1754 to vote on a plan of federal union for the colonies, Franklin wrote to James Parker: "It would be a very strange Thing, if Six Nations of ignorant Savages should be capable of forming a Scheme for such an Union, and be able to execute it in such a Manner, as that it has subsisted Ages, and appears indissoluble, and yet that a like Union should be impracticable for ten or a Dozen English colonies" (Franklin to Parker, 20 March 1751, in Franklin, *Papers*, 4:118–19). See also Donald A. Grinde and Bruce Johansen, *Exemplar of Liberty: Native America and the Evolution of Democracy* (Los Angeles: American Indian Studies Center, 1991); and "The Iroquois Influence Thesis—Con and Pro," special issue of *William and Mary Quarterly* 53 (July 1996): 587–636.

56. In *Rites of Assent,* Sacvan Bercovitch calls for "a model of cross-cultural criticism," but the cultural tradition he traces begins with "the symbolic construction of America" among the Puritans in New England and ends by absorbing all forms of opposition from Jefferson and Douglass to Gloria Steinem and Martin Luther King into what Bercovitch calls "the ritual of American consensus" (*Rites of Assent: Transformations in the Symbolic Construction of America* [New York: Routledge, 1993], 5, 29).

57. James Adair, *The History of the American Indians* (1775; New York: Johnson Reprint Corporation, 1968), 378.

58. Brathwaite distinguishes between two forms of creolization: "*ac/culturation,* which is the yoking (by force and example, deriving from power/prestige) of one culture to another"; "and *inter/culturation,* which is an unplanned, unstructured but osmotic relationship proceeding from this yoke" (*Contradictory Omens: Cultural Diversity and Integration in the Caribbean* [Mona, Jamaica: Savacou Publications, 1974], 6). See also James Clifford, who writes: "Stories of cultural contact and change have been structured by a pervasive dichotomy: absorption by the other or resistance to the other. . . . Yet what if identity is conceived not as the boundary to be maintained but as a nexus of relations and transactions actively engaging a subject? The story or stories of interaction must then be more complex, less linear and teleological" (*The Predicament of Culture*, 344). For an influential theoretical consideration of the fluid and unstable processes of cultural struggle and exchange, see Bhabha's attempt to conceptualize what he calls "an *inter*national culture" based on "the inscription and articulation of culture's *hybridity*" (*The Location of Culture*, 38).

59. White, *The Middle Ground*, x.

60. As Arnold Krupat observes: "Indian texts are always the consequence of a

collaboration" (*For Those Who Came After: A Study of Native American Autobiography* [Berkeley: University Of California Press, 1985], 7). The speech was translated by Gibson and delivered to Lord Dunmore, the governor of Virginia, at the end of Lord Dunmore's War in 1774. Jefferson recalls that he heard it in Williamsburg, at Lord Dunmore's: "I find in my pocket-book of that year (1774) an entry of the narrative, as taken from the mouth of some person, whose name, however, is not noted" (*NV*, 227).

61. "The speech was published in the Virginia Gazette of that time," Jefferson recalls. "[I]t was so admired, that it flew through all the public papers of the continent, and through the magazines and other periodical publications of Great Britain" (*NV*, 227). Washington Irving cites the first lines of Logan's speech as an epigraph to "Traits of Indian Character" in *The Sketch Book of Geoffrey Crayon, Gent.* (New York: C. S. Van Winkle, 1819–20). In 1840, the Logan Society was organized, which published a monthly periodical, the *American Pioneer*, for two years at Chillicothe, Ohio. Logan's speech appeared in editions of the McGuffey *Reader* during the 1850s and 1860s. In 1913, the state of Ohio established Logan Elm State Park at the site where Logan is said to have delivered his speech near Chillicothe. See E. D. Seeber, "Critical Views of Logan's Speech," *Journal of American Folklore* 60 (April 1947): 130–46.

62. According to White, "He was not a chief. Kayashuta and White Mingo were the Mingo chiefs. Logan was merely a war leader, the Indian equivalent of Cresap." He was "a deeply disturbed man who believed himself pursued by evil manitous" (*The Middle Ground*, 358, 361). Others, however, including Theodore Roosevelt in *The Winning of the West*, have argued that Logan "was a man of splendid appearance" and manly character (*The Winning of the West*, 4 vols. [New York: G. P. Putnam's Sons, 1889], 1:203–4). In point of fact, almost everything about Logan is open to contest: his birthplace, his parentage, his physical demeanor and character, his status, whether or not he delivered his famous "speech," and, if so, to whom. Beginning with Jefferson's *Notes*, the figure of "Logan" and his "speech" have themselves become bound up with broader contests in American literature, culture, and history about Indian nature, problems of translation and representation, and the "truth" of Native and Euro-American history in the New World. See for example, Wallace, *Jefferson and the Indians*, 1–20, and Laura Rigal, "Framing the Fabric: A Luddite Reading of Penn's Treaty with the Indians," *American Literary History* 12 (fall 2000): 557–84). Both read Logan's words as a proleptic sign of the conquest of the Native by Euro-American imperialism.

63. "Nothing Jefferson ever wrote has evoked more controversy than the passage and its revision on the murder of Logan's family," writes Peden (*NV*, 298). For a discussion of the historical contests surrounding this passage, see *NV*, 298–301, n. 1.

64. Here, as elsewhere in *Notes*, Jefferson's identification with alternative and resistant points of view often manifests itself textually in the deletions, revisions, additions, and marginalia of his manuscript. At one point in his narrative he appears to identify with the Indian against his own republican argument that "the lands of this country were taken from them" by purchase rather than "by conquest." "I find in our historians and records, repeated proofs of purchase" (*NV*, 96), he writes. But in the original manuscript, he admits and later crosses out: "it is true that these purchases were sometimes made with the price in one hand and the sword in the other" (*NV*, 281).

65. See also Shuffelton, who argues that Jefferson's appendix moves toward a more public and democratic form of writing: "The private communications

and contributions of his invisible philosophical society, a select group of gentle-men, were increasingly displaced by a public conversation about truth and jus-tice carried on by ordinary citizens of the republic, represented here as the men of the West who testified about the 1774 murder of Logan's family" (Shuffelton, introduction, *Notes*, xviii).

66. See also Benjamin Franklin, "A Narrative of the Late Massacres" (1764); Robert Montgomery Bird, *Nick of the Woods, or the Jibbernainosay; a tale of Kentucky* (1837); and Melville's criticism of "the metaphysics of Indian-hating" in *The Confidence Man: His Masquerade* (1857), vol. 10 of *The Writings of Herman Melville*, ed. Harrison Hayford, Hershel Parker, and G. Thomas Tanselle (Evanston: Northwestern University Press, 1984), 144–51.

67. Gilbert Chinard, *Thomas Jefferson: The Apostle of Americanism* (Boston: Little Brown, 1929), 118.

68. An exception to this is Shuffelton's 1999 Penguin edition of *Notes on the State of Virginia,* which preserves Jefferson's many non-English quotations as they originally appeared in the 1787 Stockdale edition.

69. "The hemisphere . . . was not manifestly Anglo-Saxon in the eyes of Europe," writes Eric Wertheimer. "It was a place whose land and history were contested primarily by colonizers who, after the Peace of Paris of 1763 and then the Treaty of 1783, spoke either English or Spanish" ("Imagined Empires: Incas, Aztecs, and the Columbian Trope in American Literature, 1771–1876" [Ph.D. diss., University of Pennsylvania, 1994], 67).

Chapter 3

1. In this and other quotations from the letters, Abigail Adams's unorthodox spelling and punctuation have been preserved.

2. Joan Hoff Wilson, "The Illusion of Change: Women and the American Revolution," in *The American Revolution: Explorations in the History of American Radicalism,* ed. Alfred F. Young (Dekalb, Ill.: Northern Illinois University Press, 1976), 423.

3. Bernard Bailyn, "The Transforming Radicalism of the American Revolu-tion," in *Pamphlets of the American Revolution,* ed. Bernard Bailyn (Cambridge, Mass.: Harvard University Press, 1965), 191–92.

4. Boucher, "On Civil Liberty," 510, 525, 530, 511, 553. Boucher's arguments are grounded in Sir Robert Filmer's defense of monarchy in *Patriarcha; Or the Natural Power of Kings* (1680), which traces the origins of patriarchy and the divine, absolute, and unlimited authority of kings to the "natural" authority of the father within the family.

5. For a discussion of the potentially subversive power of imitation, repeti-tion, reiteration, and citation as forms of resistance to phallocentric and hetero-normative language and power, see Irigaray's discussion of "mimesis" in *This Sex Which Is Not One,* 76; Butler's discussion of repetition as a means of making "gen-der trouble" in *Gender Trouble,* especially 142–49; and her argument for a "cita-tional politics" in *Bodies That Matter: On the Discursive Limits of "Sex"* (New York: Routledge, 1993), 1–23.

6. *The Political Writings of John Adams,* ed. George A. Peek (New York: Liberal Arts Press, 1954), 13. John's awareness of the Revolutionary logic and danger of Adams's attack on the tyranny of men is evident in a letter he wrote only a month later to James Sullivan about proposed revisions to Massachusetts law:

"Whence arises the Right of the Men to govern Women, without their Consent? . . . Depend upon it, sir, it is dangerous to open So fruitfull a Source of Controversy and Altercation. . . . There will be no End of it. New Claims will arise. Women will demand a Vote . . . and every Man, who has not a Farthing, will demand an equal Voice with any other in all Acts of State. It tends to confound and destroy all Distinctions, and prostrate all Ranks, to one common Levell" (*Papers of John Adams*, ed. Robert J. Taylor, 10 vols. [Cambridge, Mass.: Belknap Press of Harvard University Press, 1979], 4:208, 211–12).

7. Lynne Withey, *Dearest Friend: A Life of Abigail Adams* (New York: Free Press, 1981), 73.

8. Much of the political debate about the Revolution was carried out in the form of letters, both published and unpublished, fictive and private. In addition to the committees of correspondence, which were formed to facilitate communication among the colonists during the Revolutionary years, the subject of Revolution was addressed in such public epistolary forms as John Dickinson's *Letters from a Farmer in Pennsylvania* (1768); Crèvecoeur's *Letters from an American Farmer* (1782); Franklin's letters to his son that later became known as *The Autobiography*; and Washington's "Circular Letter" to the governors of the several states at the end of the war in 1783.

9. Warren published several other poems and political satires in dramatic form in support of the American cause. Although she expressed anxiety about crossing the "line" and unwomanly behavior in the political satire of *The Group* (1775), she went on to publish *Poems Dramatic and Miscellaneous* (1790) and *Observations on the New Constitution, and on the Federal Conventions* (1788), which criticized the Constitution for its lack of a Bill of Rights. Her three-volume *History*, which she began writing in the 1770s, was the only contemporary history of the American Revolution written from a Republican point of view.

10. Catharine Macaulay was the author of the multivolume *History of England, from the Accession of James I to That of the Brunswick Line* (London: J. Nourse, 1763–83). In 1771, Adams wrote to her cousin Isaac Smith in England asking him to procure a copy of Macaulay's history: "I have a curiosity to know her Education, and what first prompted her to engage in a Study never before Exhibited to the publick by one of her own sex and Country" (*AFC*, 1:77).

11. For another account of a woman who managed farm and family while her husband served in the Continental Congress, see the letters of Mary Bartlett, Josiah Bartlett Papers, New Hampshire Historical Society, Concord, N.H. Sharon M. Harris includes a selection of Bartlett's letters in *American Women Writers to 1800*, ed. Sharon M. Harris (New York: Oxford University Press, 1996), 275–78.

12. Jefferson expresses a similarly gloomy view of the future of the American republic in *Notes on the State of Virginia*: "From the conclusion of this war we shall be going downhill. . . . [The people] will forget themselves, but in the sole faculty of making money, and will never think of uniting to effect a due respect for their rights" (*NV*, 161).

13. Like the debate about republican as opposed to liberal interpretations of the American Revolution, over the last decade the term *republican womanhood* has also become a subject of contest among scholars. In 1980, in her important study, *Women of the Republic*, Kerber used the term *republican motherhood* to describe "the intersection of the woman's private domain and the polis" that defined notions of republican womanhood in the post-Revolutionary period (283). Jan Lewis later revised Kerber's formulation to argue that it was woman's

role as wife rather than mother that was emphasized in the post-Revolutionary years; it was not until the nineteenth century that woman's maternal role in the family and society became dominant ("The Republican Wife: Virtue and Seduction in the Early Republic," *William and Mary Quarterly* 44 [October 1987]: 689–721; and "Motherhood and the Construction of the Male Citizen in the United States, 1750–1850," in *Constructions of the Self,* ed. George Levine [New Brunswick, N.J.: Rutgers University Press, 1992]: 143–63). See also Ruth H. Bloch, "American Feminine Ideals in Transition: The Rise of the Moral Mother, 1785–1815," *Feminist Studies* 4 (1978): 101–26.

14. *The Poems of Phillis Wheatley,* ed. Julian D. Mason, Jr. (Chapel Hill: University of North Carolina Press, 1989), 204. Subsequent references to this edition will be cited as *PPW.* Wheatley's letter to Occom, which was published a few months after her own manumission in the fall of 1773, was one of the strongest public statements in support of antislavery in circulation in the New England colonies at that time. The letter was reprinted in the *Massachusetts Gazette,* the *Massachusetts Spy,* the *Boston Post-Boy,* and several other New England papers.

15. Along with Hutchinson and Hancock, others who signed the "Attestation" certifying that the poems were, indeed, "written by PHILLIS, a young Negro Girl, who was but a few years since, brought an uncultivated barbarian from Africa," included the lieutenant governor of Massachusetts, Andrew Oliver, the Reverends Mather Byles and Charles Chauncy, and several other ministers and councilmen (*PPW,* 48). The "Attestation" did not appear in the first London edition of *Poems,* but it was circulated in the press before the volume was published, and it appeared in subsequent London editions and American reprintings. See William H. Robinson, ed., *Phillis Wheatley and Her Writings* (New York : Garland Publishing, 1984), 28–29.

16. LeRoi Jones [Amiri Baraka], "The Myth of a Negro Literature," in *Home: Social Essays* (New York: William B. Morrow, 1966), 106.

17. Benjamin Rush, *An Address to the Inhabitants of the British Settlements in America, Upon Slave-Keeping* (Philadelphia: John Dunlap, 1773), 24. For a review of the debate on the nature of the Negro that surrounded the publication of Wheatley's *Poems,* see Henry Louis Gates, Jr., "Phillis Wheatley and the Nature of the Negro," in *Critical Essays on Phillis Wheatley,* ed. William H. Robinson (Boston: G. K. Hall, 1982), 215–33.

18. For critics who have emphasized Wheatley's absorption by white culture, see Vernon Loggins, *The Negro Author* (New York: Columbia University Press, 1931); James Weldon Johnson, ed., *The Book of American Negro Poetry* (New York: Harcourt, Brace and Company, 1922); Terence Collins, "Phillis Wheatley: The Dark Side of Poetry," in *Critical Essays,* ed. Robinson, 208–14; and Jones, "The Myth of a Negro Literature," 105–15. For those who have emphasized her black voice, see Houston A. Baker, Jr., *The Journey Back: Issues in Black Literature and Criticism* (Chicago: University of Chicago Press, 1980), 1–26; Henry Louis Gates, "In Her Own Write," in *The Collected Works of Phillis Wheatley,* ed. John Shields (New York: Oxford University Press, 1988), vii–xxii; and Frances Smith Foster, *Written by Herself,* 23–43. See also Henry Louis Gates's review of the historical contests over Wheatley's place in the black literary tradition in *The Trials of Phillis Wheatley: America's First Black Poet and Her Encounters with the Founding Fathers* (New York: Basic Books, 2003).

19. I borrow the phrase "puts on the white world" from Franz Fanon, who writes of the Negro's self-divided relationship to the language of the colonizer: "Nothing is more astonishing than to hear a black man express himself prop-

erly, for then in truth he is putting on the white world" (*Black Skins, White Masks* [1952], trans. Charles Lam Markmann [New York: Grove Weidenfeld, 1967], 36). In his major study, *The Signifying Monkey*, Gates uses the term *double-voiced* to describe the "difference" of the black writer's signifying relationship with black vernacular literary traditions that exist "outside the Western tradition" (xxii). My own use of the term *double-voicing* in this study is closer to Bakhtin's notion of the heteroglot possibilities of language: "The word in language is half someone else's," he writes. "It becomes 'one's own' only when the speaker populates it with his own intention, his own accent, when he appropriates the word, adapting it to his own semantic and expressive intention." Bakhtin also refers to this process as linguistic "hybridization," "a mixture of two social languages within the limits of a single utterance" (*The Dialogic Imagination*, 293, 358). See also Bhabha's discussion of the "hybridity of language" and the resistant uses to which it might be put in the relation of colonized to colonizer ("Interrogating identity," in *The Location of Culture*, 40–65); and Paul Gilroy's use of W.E.B. Du Bois's concept of "double-consciousness" to suggest "the inescapable hybridity and intermixture of ideas" in what he calls "the Black Atlantic" (*The Black Atlantic: Modernity and Double Consciousness*, [Cambridge, Mass.: Harvard University Press, 1993], xi).

20. Margaret G. Burroughs, "Do Birds of a Feather Flock Together?" in *Critical Essays*, ed. Robinson, 145.

21. Quoted in Charles W. Akers, "'Our Modern Egyptians': Phillis Wheatley and the Whig Campaign against Slavery in Revolutionary Boston," *Journal of Negro History* 60 (July 1975): 404.

22. Belinda, "Petition of an African Slave" (1782), *The American Museum* 1 (June 1787): 464.

23. Maya Angelou, *I Know Why the Caged Bird Sings* (New York: Random House, 1969), 215.

24. In *Bid the Vassal Soar* (Cambridge, Mass.: Harvard University Press, 1974), Merle A. Richard comments on the "warping influence" of slavery on Wheatley. "It mutilated her," he says (66). For others who have commented on Wheatley's internalization of racist attitudes, see Loggins, *The Negro Author*, 24; and Collins, "Phillis Wheatley," 208–14.

25. Wheatley met or corresponded with several figures who were actively involved in the transatlantic evangelical movement. She met Dartmouth when she went to England in 1773, and she corresponded with the Countess of Huntington, Samson Occom, John Thornton, and Samuel Hopkins. She wrote an elegy on the death of the famous English evangelical preacher George Whitefield, which was published as a broadside in 1770 and reprinted in several American and British newspapers. She may have met Whitefield through the Wheatley family. Her involvement in evangelicalism on both sides of the Atlantic also links her with the antislavery movement in England and America. She met Granville Sharpe, the founder of the English Society for the Abolition of Slavery, when she visited England. The combined evangelical and antislavery sentiment of her work also connects her with the abolitionist work and writing of African writers in England, including Ignatius Sancho (*Letters*, 1782), Olaudah Equiano (*The Interesting Narrative of the Life of Olaudah Equiano*, 1787), and Ottohbah Cugoano (*Thoughts and Sentiments on the Evil and Wicked Traffic of the Slavery and Commerce of the Human Species*, 1787). Through her African friend Obour Tanner, who was also a slave, Wheatley may have come to know Sarah Osborn, the evangelical and antislavery activist who held religious meetings for blacks, women, and many

others in her Newport, Rhode Island, home in the 1760s. For a detailed discussion of the contexts of Wheatley's work in Anglo-American evangelicalism and antislavery sentiment, see David Grimsted, "Anglo-American Racism and Phillis Wheatley's 'Sable Veil,' 'Length'ned Chain,' and 'Knitted Heart,'" in *Women in the Age of the American Revolution*, ed. Ronald Hoffman and Peter J. Albert (Charlottesville: University Press of Virginia, 1989), 338–444.

26. "[H]ow my bosom burns! / And pleasing Gambia on my soul returns," Wheatley wrote of Africa a few years later in a poem that evokes "Afric's blissful plain" as a place where "Eden blooms again" ("The Answer," *PPW*, 163). Unlike Jefferson, and later Stowe and Lincoln, however, who could not imagine the emancipation of blacks in the United States apart from their (re)colonization in Africa or elsewhere, Wheatley made it clear that her place was in America rather than as a missionary to Africa. In a 1774 letter to the English merchant and supporter of African missionaries, John Thornton, she gently mocks and reverses the discourse of colonialism as a way of turning down his proposal that she return to Africa: "Upon my arrival, how like a Barbarian Should I look to the Natives; I can promise that my tongue shall be quiet for a strong reason indeed being an utter stranger to the Language of Anamaboe" (30 October 1774, *PPW*, 211).

27. Margaretta Matilda Odell, *Memoir and Poems of Phillis Wheatley* (Boston: George W. Light, 1834), 10–11.

28. In the racial calculus of the Constitution of the United States, which was ratified in 1788, blacks would be constituted as property but counted as three-fifths of the population in apportioning the representation and taxation of each state.

29. Jefferson's judgment notwithstanding, Wheatley's work was generally well received in both England and America among blacks as well as whites. In a letter to Wheatley thanking her for her verse epistle in his honor, Washington wrote: "the style and manner exhibit a striking proof of your great poetical Talents" (28 February 1776, *PPW*, 165). The African slave poet Jupiter Hammon wrote a poem in praise of Wheatley titled "An Address to Miss Phillis Wheatly [sic], Ethiopian Poetess," which was published as a broadside in 1778. The reprinting of Wheatley's *Poems* in the United States in 1786, 1787, 1789, 1793, 1801, 1804, and 1816 indicates that her popularity as a poet continued in the post-Revolutionary period. In *An Essay on the Slavery and Commerce of the Human Species, Particularly the African*, the English writer Thomas Clarkson observed: "if the authoress *was designed for slavery* . . . the greater part of Britain must lose their claim to freedom" (Philadelphia: Joseph Crukshank, 1786), 112. See also Muktar Ali Isani, "The British Reception of Wheatley's *Poems on Various Subjects*," *Journal of Negro History* 66 (summer 1981): 144–49.

30. *Boston Evening Post*, 12 February 1770; quoted in Mary Beth Norton, *Liberty's Daughters* (Boston: Little Brown, 1980), 160–61.

31. Milcah Moore, *Miscellanies, Moral and Instructive* (Philadelphia: Joseph James, 1787).

32. Quoted in Inez Parker Cumming, "The Edenton Ladies' Tea-Party," *Georgia Review* 8 (winter 1954): 392.

33. Mercy Otis Warren, *Poems, Dramatic and Miscellaneous* (Boston: I. Thomas and E. T. Andrews, 1790), 182.

34. The Hannah Griffitts Papers at the Historical Society of Pennsylvania include some two hundred unpublished poems. For an excellent selection of women's private and published writings during the Revolutionary years, see Harris, *American Women Writers to 1800*.

35. During the American Revolution, the army had not yet been defined as a specifically male space. For a discussion of women camp followers, see Elizabeth Ellet, *Women of the American Revolution* (New York: Baker, 1850); Walter Hart Blumenthal, *Women Camp Followers of the American Revolution* (Philadelphia: George St. Manus, 1952); and Linda Grant DePauw, "Women in Combat: The Revolutionary War Experience," *Armed Forces and Society* 7 (1981): 209–26.

36. Quoted in Julia Ward Stickley, "The Records of Deborah Samppson Gannett, Woman Soldier of the Revolution," *Prologue* 5 (1972): 235. Deborah Sampson Gannett's life is fictionalized in Herman Mann's female picaresque novel *The Female Review* (Dedham, Mass.: Nathaniel and Benjamin Heaton, 1797). See also Martinette de Beauvais, who cross-dresses and goes to war, in Charles Brockden Brown's *Ormond, or, The Secret Witness* (New York: H. Caritat, 1799).

37. "The Sentiments of an American Woman (Broadside 1780)," *Pennsylvania Magazine of History and Biography* 18 (1894): 361, 364.

38. For a detailed discussion of Reed's organization, see Norton, *Liberty's Daughters*, 178–88.

39. For studies of the changes in American women's lives in the Revolutionary and post-Revolutionary period, see Kerber, *Women of the Republic;* Norton, *Liberty's Daughters;* and Nancy Cott, *The Bonds of Womanhood: "Woman's Sphere" in New England, 1780–1835* (New Haven, Conn.: Yale University Press, 1977). For changes in the family, see Fliegelman, *Prodigals and Pilgrims;* Bloch, "American Feminine Ideals in Transition"; and Lewis, "The Republican Wife" and "Motherhood."

40. In his letter offering the painting *Liberty Displaying the Arts and Sciences* to the Philadelphia Library Company, whose directors wanted him to stress the antislavery symbolism of the painting, Samuel Jennings wrote: "Liberty is in the Act of placing the Catalogue of the Philadelphia Library on a Pedestal, with some other Books, & as an Emblem of her aversion to Slavery, a broken Chain is placed under her Feet—The Groups of Negroes in the Fore Ground are paying homage to Liberty, for the boundless blessings they secure through her, those in the Back Ground are in attitudes expressive of Ease & Joy, & the Shipping denotes Commerce" (13 March 1792; Philadelphia Library Company).

41. Murray's argument in support of female education in "On the Equality of the Sexes," which was composed in 1779 and published in the *Massachusetts Magazine* (April/May 1790) under the pseudonym "Constantia," begins by asserting sexual equality: "nature with *equality* imparts" (132). But she grounds her defense of women's education in the fact that "they would thus be rendered fit companions" for men (134). Acknowledging that women's "more peculiar department" is home, marriage, and family, she concludes: "Shield us then, we beseech you, from external evils, and in return *we* will transact *your* domestick affairs" (224).

42. Benjamin Rush, *Medical Inquiries and Observations* (Philadelphia: Thomas Dobson, 1794), 277.

43. John Adams, *Correspondence between the Hon. John Adams . . . and the late Wm. Cunningham, Esq.* (Boston: E. M. Cunningham, 1823), 19. For a fascinating analysis of the political significance of Samuel Richardson's *Clarissa* in the early national period, see Fliegelman, *Prodigals and Pilgrims*, 83–89.

44. *Virginia Gazette and Alexandria Advertiser,* 22 April 1790, quoted in Kerber, *Women of the Republic*, 281. See also Benjamin Rush, who insists on the need for "degrees of inferiority and contrast between the two sexes." "Many of the disor-

ders, not only of domestic but of political society," he writes, "originate in the inversion of this order" (*Lectures on the Mind,* ed. Eric T. Carlson, Jeffrey L. Wollock, and Patricia S. Noel [Philadelphia: American Philosophical Society, 1981], 698).

45. Ironically, as a playwright and writer Royall Tyler was himself rejected as a suitable partner for Abigail (Nabby) Adams, the daughter of Abigail and John Adams.

46. Annette Kolodny studies "The Panther Captivity" as a female wilderness myth in "Turning the Lens on 'The Panther Captivity,' A Feminist Exercise in Practical Criticism," *Critical Inquiry* 8 (winter 1981): 329–45.

47. See also "The Vision, an Ode to Washington" (1789) by the New Jersey poet Annis Boudinot Stockton, in which the Federalist speaker envisions "free born" minds giving up "Their native rights" to "*Men,* who can those rights define" and to Washington as enthroned "Sov'reign" (*Gazette of the United States,* 16 May 1789; reprinted in vol. 2 of *The Heath Anthology of American Literature,* ed. Paul Lauter [Lexington: D. C. Heath and Company, 1994], 678).

48. *The Lady's Magazine and Repository of Entertaining Knowledge,* 1 December 1792.

49. Hannah Foster, *The Coquette; or The History of Eliza Wharton* (1797), ed. Cathy N. Davidson (New York: Oxford University Press, 1986), 5.

50. "The sentimental plot simply would not serve the objectives which the conservative writers had drafted it to advance," writes Cathy Davidson (*Revolution and the Word: The Rise of the Novel in America* [New York: Oxford University Press, 1986], 128). Elaborating on Davidson's reading of *The Coquette* as a criticism of the plight of women in the new republic, Carroll Smith-Rosenberg writes of Eliza: "It is the relinquishing of her social and intellectual independence, not of her sexual virginity, that constitutes her true fall" ("Domesticating 'Virtue': Coquettes and Revolutionaries in Young America," in *Literature of the Body: Essays on Populations and Persons,* ed. Elaine Scarry [Baltimore: Johns Hopkins University Press, 1988], 176). For a reading that emphasizes "the auditory apparition of Eliza's voice" as it "resonates beyond the bleakness of *The Coquette*'s ending" (151), see Julia A. Stern, *The Plight of Feeling* (Chicago: University of Chicago Press, 1997), 71–151.

51. *Virginia Gazette,* 11 February 1773, p. 4.

52. [Judith Sargent Murray], *The Gleaner, A Miscellaneous Production by Constantia* (1798; reprint Schenectady, N.Y.: Union College Press, 1992), 703; Priscilla Mason, "The Salutatory Oration," delivered 15 May 1793 (in *The Rise and Progress of the Young Ladies Academy of Philadelphia* [Philadelphia: Stewart and Cochran, 1794], 93); *Massachusetts Magazine* 4 (September 1794): 566.

53. *Adams-Jefferson Letters,* 2:455.

54. *FP,* No. 54, 305.

55. *Correspondence Between John Adams and Mercy Warren,* ed. Charles Francis Adams (New York: Arno, 1972), 493–94. See also Benjamin Rush's comment on the ongoing revolution in *Address to the People of the United States* (1787): "There is nothing more common, than to confound the terms of *American revolution* with those of *the late American war.* The American war is over: but this is far from being the case with the American revolution. On the contrary, nothing but the first act of the great drama is closed. It remains yet to establish and perfect our new forms of government" (in *Principles and Acts of the Revolution in America,* comp. Hezekiah Niles [Baltimore: W. O. Niles, 1822], 402).

Chapter 4

1. Walter Benjamin, *Charles Baudelaire: A Lyric Poet in the Era of High Capitalism*, trans. Harry Zohn (London: New Left Books, 1973), 105.

2. *Letters of Edgar Allan Poe*, ed. John Ward Ostrom, 2 vols. (1948; New York: Gordian Press, 1966), 1:8. Subsequent references will be cited as *LP*.

3. The bill of sale, dated 10 December 1829, indicates that Poe acted as an agent in the sale of a slave named Edwin to Henry Ridgway, who may also have been a person of color (cited in John C. Miller, "Did Edgar Poe Really Sell a Slave?" *Poe Studies* 9 [1976]: 52).

4. Vernon Parrington, *Main Currents in American Thought*, 3 vols. (New York: Harcourt, Brace, 1927–30), 2:57, 56.

5. Toni Morrison, *Playing in the Dark*, 6, 33. For recent discussions of Poe and race, see Kenneth Alan Hovey, "Critical Provincialism: Poe's Poetic Principle in Antebellum Context," *American Quarterly* 4 (1987): 341–54; Joan Dayan, "Romance and Race," in *The Columbia History of the American Novel*, ed. Emory Elliott (New York: Columbia University Press, 1991), 89–109; Joan Dayan, "Amorous Bondage: Poe, Ladies, and Slaves," *American Literature* 66 (June 1994): 239–73; John Carlos Rowe, "Poe, Antebellum Slavery, and Modern Criticism," in *Poe's Pym: Critical Explorations*, ed. Richard Kopley (Durham, N.C.: Duke University Press, 1992), 117–38; Dana Nelson, *The Word in Black and White: Reading "Race" in American Literature, 1638–1867* (New York: Oxford University Press, 1993), 90–108; Terence Whalen, "Subtle Barbarians: Poe, Racism, and the Political Economy of Adventure," in *Styles of Cultural Activism: From Theory and Pedagogy to Women, Indians, and Communism*, ed. Philip Goldstein (Newark: University of Delaware Press, 1994), 169–83; and Teresa Goddu, "The Ghost of Race: Edgar Allan Poe and the Southern Gothic," in *Criticism and the Color Line: Desegregating American Literary Studies*, ed. Henry B. Wonham (New Brunswick, N.J.: Rutgers University Press, 1996), 230–50. See also J. Gerald Kennedy and Liliane Weissberg, eds., *Romancing the Shadow: Poe and Race* (New York: Oxford University Press, 2001).

6. Morrison, *Playing in the Dark*, 44.

7. Terence Whalen, "Edgar Allan Poe and the Horrid Laws of Political Economy," *American Quarterly* 44 (September 1992): 398.

8. *The Collected Works of Edgar Allan Poe*, ed. Thomas Ollive Mabbott, 3 vols. (Cambridge, Mass.: Belknap Press of Harvard University Press, 1969–78), 1:22. Subsequent references to this edition will be cited as *CW*.

9. According to Mabbott, Poe read Chateaubriand's *Itinéraire* (1810–11) in F. Shoberl's translation, *Travels in Greece, Palestine, Egypt, and Barbary* (1813). For a discussion of Orientalism, see Edward Said, *Orientalism* (New York: Random House, 1979).

10. As Melville notes in *Typee*, the first American arrived in the South Pacific in 1791, when Captain Ingraham of Boston "discovered" three islands of the Marquesas and named them "the Washington Group." During the War of 1812, Melville observes, another American, Captain David Porter, sought to annex the Marquesas for the United States (Herman Melville, *Typee: A Peep at Polynesian Life* [1846], vol. 1, *The Writings of Herman Melville*, ed. Hayford, Parker, and Tanselle [Evanston, Ill.: Northwestern University Press, 1968], 11). Poe favorably reviewed and drew from Jeremiah N. Reynolds's *Address on the Subject of a Surveying and Exploring Expedition to the Pacific Ocean and South Seas* (1836).

11. See, for example, John Rowe's discussion of the ways "the racial hierar-

chies recognizable in nineteenth-century British imperialism" are shifted to African Americans and Native Americans in Poe's "Tale of the Ragged Mountains" and "The Journal of Julius Rodman" (*Literary Culture and U. S. Imperialism: From the Revolution to World War II* [New York: Oxford University Press, 2000], 54).

12. George Sale, "A Preliminary Discourse," *The Koran*, trans. George Sale (London: J. Wilcox, 1734), 94.

13. Quoted in John M. Blum, Edmund S. Morgan, Willie Lee Rose, Arthur M. Schlesinger, Jr., Kenneth M. Stampp, and C. Vann Woodward, eds., *The National Experience: A History of the United States to 1877* (New York: Harcourt Brace Jovanovich, 1981), 232; emphasis added.

14. In 1832, the proslavery advocate Thomas R. Dew observed with some alarm that blacks were everywhere "intertwined" with whites in Southern society: "a race of people differing from us in colour and in habits, and vastly inferior in the scale of civilization, have been increasing and spreading—'growing with our growth and strengthening with our strength'—until they have become intertwined with every fibre of society" ("Abolition of Negro Slavery" [1832], in *The Ideology of Slavery: Proslavery Thought in the Antebellum South, 1830–1860*, ed. Drew Gilpin Faust [Baton Rouge: Louisiana State University Press, 1981], 23).

15. For a discussion of the relationship among the "needs of an alienated Southern intellectual class," the defense of Southern culture, and the proslavery argument, see Drew Gilpin Faust, "A Southern Stewardship: The Intellectual and Proslavery Argument," *American Quarterly* 31 (spring 1979): 63–80. See also David Herbert Donald, who argues that the defenders of slavery sought to escape the national and regional crisis by fleeing to some "bygone pastoral Arcadia" that had been lost ("The Proslavery Argument Reconsidered," *Journal of Southern History* 37 [February 1971]: 3–18).

16. Drew Gilpin Faust, "The Proslavery Argument," in *The Ideology of Slavery*, 4. In *The Black Image in the White Mind: The Debate on Afro-American Culture and Destiny, 1817–1914* (New York: Harper and Row, 1971), George M. Frederickson also notes that after 1830, in response to growing attacks by Northern abolitionists, Southerners began to articulate an increasingly coherent proslavery ideology grounded in notions of African savagery and inferiority and the socially beneficent effects of Southern enslavement (45).

17. W. J. Cash, *The Mind of the South* (New York: Knopf, 1941), 86. Although Stallybrass and White do not explicitly address the question of the racial body in *The Politics and Poetics of Transgression*, their comments on the social ideal of the pure classical body are relevant to the entangled dependencies of whiteness and blackness in Poe's work: the "closure and purity [of the classical body] are quite illusory and it will perpetually rediscover in itself, often with a sense of shock or inner revulsion, the grotesque, the protean and the motley, the neither/nor, the double negation of high and low which is the very precondition of its social identity" (113). See also Dayan's splendid analysis of the ways "Poe's unlinked Great Chain completely mixes men, nature, women, reason, and dreams" ("Amorous Bondage," 246).

18. Fiedler notes that Poe was one of the first "to express a peculiarly American dilemma of identifying the symbolic blackness of terror with the blackness of the Negro and the white guilt he embodies" (*Love and Death in the American Novel*, 378). Although the black and white symbolism in Poe's work cannot be reduced to race, it cannot be entirely separated from race either. As critics from Harry Levin and Fiedler in the 1950s and 1960s to Toni Morrison in the 1990s

have noted, given the racial struggles of the nineteenth century and the Judeo-Christian and Enlightenment symbology of darkness and lightness, it would be difficult to separate Poe's pervasive use of black and white symbolism from any racial reference. In a comment on the "esthetic effect" of blackness in Poe's work, Levin observes: "[s]uch effects do not pre-exist in a vacuum, although the artist may obtain them subconsciously; he chooses one shade, rather than an alternative, because it bears some connotation for him and for others" (*The Power of Blackness: Hawthorne, Poe, Melville* [New York: Knopf, 1970], 28–29). Whether slavery caused the cultural denigration of blackness or the cultural denigration of blackness caused African enslavement, as Jordan observes: "Blackness had become so thoroughly entangled with the basest status in American society that at least by the beginning of the eighteenth century it was almost indecipherably coded into American language and literature" (*WOB,* 258). Moreover, in the history of Western aestheticism, blackness had a longstanding association with dark skin. Thus, for example, by the mid-eighteenth century, the association of the horror of darkness with horror of dark skin had become so pervasive that in his *Philosophical Enquiry into the Origin of our Ideas of the Sublime and the Beautiful* (1757; New York: Oxford University Press, 1990), Edmund Burke equates sublime terror with terror at the first sight of a Negro. Citing William Cheselden's account of a boy who had been born blind and regained his eyesight at age thirteen or fourteen, Burke notes that "the first time the boy saw a black object, it gave him great uneasiness; and that some time after, upon accidentally seeing a negro woman, he was struck with great horror at the sight" (131).

19. *The Complete Works of Edgar Allan Poe,* ed. James A. Harrison, 17 vols. (New York: Kelmscott Society, 1902), 8:119.

20. See, for example, "The Masque of the Red Death," in which Prince Prospero seeks to build a pleasure palace of Beauty in order to wall himself off from the contagion of the "Red Death" that "had long devastated the country." "Blood was its Avatar," we are told, "and its seal—the redness and the horror of blood" (*CW,* 1:670).

21. *The Confession, Trial, and Execution of Nat Turner, the Negro Insurrectionist,* dictated to Thomas R. Gray (1831; reprint, New York: AMS Press, 1975), 4.

22. Dew, "Abolition of Negro Slavery," 57.

23. As editor of the *Southern Literary Messenger,* Poe wrote a laudatory review of one of Dew's speeches that concludes with the following excerpt on the "awful conflict" of the times: "Never were the opinions of the world more unsettled and more clashing than at this moment. Monarchists and democrats, conservatives and radicals, whigs and tories, agrarians and aristocrats, slave-holders and non-slave-holders, are all now in the great field of contention. What will be the result of this awful conflict, none can say" (quoted in Bernard Rosenthal, "Poe, Slavery, and the *Southern Literary Messenger:* A Reexamination," *Poe Studies* 7 [December 1974]: 30).

24. The review was included in volume 8 of *The Complete Works of Edgar Allan Poe,* ed. Harrison, 265–75. Subsequent references to the review will be cited as *SLM.* In a 1941 doctoral dissertation, William Doyle Hull II argued that it was written not by Poe but by Poe's proslavery friend, Judge Beverly Tucker ("A Canon of the Critical Works of Edgar Allan Poe with a Study of Poe as Editor and Reviewer" [Ph.D. diss., University of Virginia, 1941]). Hull's conclusions were later challenged by Rosenthal in "Poe, Slavery, and the *Southern Literary Messenger."* Although some critics continue to argue that the review was written

by Poe (see, for example, Dayan, "Amorous Bondage"), the current critical consensus seems to be that it was written by Tucker; see, for example, Joseph V. Ridgely, "The Authorship of the 'Paulding-Drayton Review,'" *Poe Studies Association Newsletter* 20 (fall 1992): 1–6; and Terence Whalen, "Average Racism," *Edgar Allan Poe and the Masses* (Princeton, N.J.: Princeton University Press, 1999): 111–46. In making the case against Poe's authorship, Ridgely notes that "the issue here is not the fact of Poe's racist attitudes": "Poe shared in the racism and pro-slavery sentiment of his time and place; he also expressed contempt for abolitionists" (2).

25. *The Narrative of Arthur Gordon Pym,* in *The Imaginary Voyages,* vol. 1 of *Collected Writings of Edgar Allan Poe,* ed, Burton R. Pollin and Joseph V. Ridgely (New York: Gordian Press, 1994), 201. Subsequent references will be cited as *IV.*

26. In *The Confession,* Gray also refers to Nat Turner's insurrection as a "massacre" committed by "a band of savages" (4).

27. Walter E. Bezanson reads the final scene as Pym's return home: "Home to mother through a warm cosmic milk bath. . . . Or, if one prefers older conventions, welcomed into his dream of oblivion by the White Goddess" ("The Troubled Sleep of Arthur Gordon Pym," in *Essays in Literary History,* ed. Rudolf Kirk and C. F. Main [New Brunswick, N.J.: Rutgers University Press, 1960], 173). Teresa Goddu, on the other hand, observes: "Given the timing of Nu-Nu's death, it is possible to see the shrouded figure at the end as the spiritual revivification of Nu-Nu. Pym might be embracing precisely what he hopes to evade" ("The Ghost of Race," 246).

28. *CW,* 1:317; and George Woodberry, *The Life of Edgar Allan Poe,* 2 vols. (Boston: Houghton Mifflin, 1909), 2:420. A version of Henry B. Hirst's parody published in *Sartain's Magazine* 10 (May 1852), substitutes the following lines: "Never negro took a nip in / Fabric half so black and bare" (434). In "Abolition of Negro Slavery" (1832), Dew uses the term *fairy palace* to describe the luxurious world of whiteness to which black people are denied access. See also "The Murders in the Rue Morgue" (1841), in which the *"excessively outré"* murder and mutilation of an old woman and her daughter is committed by a "large fulvous Ourang-Outang," which, as in Jefferson, is associated in the popular imagination with the "imitative propensities" and ape-like inferiority of blacks (*CW,* 1:559). For a discussion of the racial sources of Poe's orangutan in a contemporary newspaper account of the violent and "atrocious murder" of a black woman by a black man, see Richard Kopley, *Edgar Allan Poe and "The Philadelphia Saturday News"* (Baltimore: Enoch Pratt Library, 1991).

29. For a consideration of the relation between Poe's theory of taste and his "philosophical" attack on Enlightenment rationalism, see Allen Tate, "The Angelic Imagination: Poe as God," in *The Forlorn Demon: Didactic and Critical Essays* (Chicago: Regnery, 1953). See also Robert D. Jacobs, "Poe and the Agrarian Critics," *Hopkins Review* 5 (1952): 43–54.

30. Hovey, "Critical Provincialism," 350, 349.

31. In his proslavery essay "Abolition of Negro Slavery," Dew similarly notes that "schemes of emancipation . . . are admirably calculated to excite plots, murders, and insurrections" (57).

32. Hervey Allen, *Israfel: The Life and Times of Edgar Poe,* 2 vols. (London: Brentano's, 1927), ix.

33. Arthur Hobson Quinn, *Edgar Allan Poe: A Critical Biography* (New York: D. Appleton-Century, 1941), 439.

34. If slaves were emancipated, wrote Dew in 1832, "The whites would either

gradually withdraw, and leave whole districts or settlements in their possession, in which case they would sink rapidly in the scale of civilization; *or the blacks, by closer intercourse, would bring the whites down to their level*" ("Abolition of Negro Slavery," 57; emphasis added).

35. John O'Sullivan, "Annexation," *United States and Democratic Review* 17 (July–August 1845): 5, 7; emphasis added.

36. Stallybrass and White's discussion of "the contradictory and unstable representation of low-Others" is relevant here. They observe:

A recurrent pattern emerges: the "top" attempts to reject and eliminate the "bottom" for reasons of prestige and status, only to discover, not only that it is in some way frequently dependent upon that low-Other (in the classic way that Hegel describes in the master-slave section of the *Phenomenology*), but also that the top *includes* that low symbolically, as a primary eroticized constituent of its own fantasy life. The result is a mobile, conflictual fusion of power, fear and desire in the construction of subjectivity: a psychological dependence upon precisely those Others which are being rigorously opposed and excluded at the social level. It is for this reason that what is *socially* peripheral is so frequently *symbolically* central. (*Politics and Poetics of Transgression*, 5)

37. Poe uses black animals recurrently in racially inflected contexts in his writings: the orangutan that is provoked to acts of "frightful mutilation" by his master's "use of a whip" in "The Murders in the Rue Morgue" (*CW*, 1:547, 565); the "perverse" relation between black cat and master in "The Black Cat"; the ape that is worshipped and the "wild beasts" that periodically rise up against their masters in "Four Beasts in One—The Homo-Cameleopard"; the black cat capable of reason in "Instinct vs Reason—A Black Cat"; and the figure of the condor as ominous black bird of prey in the poems "Sonnet—To Science" and "The Conqueror Worm." In these and other poems and tales, such as "The Haunted Palace," *Pym*, "Ligeia," "The Fall of the House of Usher," "The System of Doctor Tarr and Professor Fether," and "Hop-Frog," Poe returns over and over to fantasies of revenge and reversal of the master-slave (or male-female) relation. See also Poe's 1836 review of Robert Bird's *Sheppard Lee*, in which he praises a sequence in which the ghost of the white man, Sheppard Lee, assumes the body of a black man, Nigger Tom: "In his character of Nigger Tom, Mr. Lee gives us some very excellent chapters upon abolition and the exciting effects of incendiary pamphlets and pictures, among our slaves in the South. This part of the narrative closes with a spirited picture of a negro insurrection, and with the hanging of Nigger Tom" (*ER*, 399).

38. See also John F. Adams, who observes: "Classical mythology has Pallas, the embodiment of wisdom, as the raven's original master, a tradition Poe evidently drew upon in perching his raven on her white bust" ("Classical Raven Lore and Poe's Raven," *Poe Studies* 5 [1972]: 53).

39. David Hume, "Of National Characters" (1748), in *David Hume: Political Essays*, ed. Knud Haakonssen (New York: Cambridge University Press, 1994), 86; emphasis added.

40. Later, for example, in the preface to *The Clansman: An Historical Romance of the Ku Klux Klan* (1905; Lexington: University Press of Kentucky, 1970), Thomas Dixon makes explicit what was only implicit in Poe's "Raven" by representing the darkness that hangs over the post-Civil War South as a "Vulture" that grips the "wounded people" of the South in its "beak and talon."

41. Poe delivered his lecture titled "The Poetic Principle" in Providence, Rhode Island, on 20 December 1848; in Richmond, Virginia, on 17 and 24 Sep-

tember 1849; and in Norfolk, Virginia on 14 and 17 September 1849 (Dwight Thomas and David K. Jackson, *The Poe Log: A Documentary Life of Edgar Allan Poe, 1809–1849* [New York: G. K. Hall, 1987]). The lecture was published posthumously in 1850.

42. In response to Poe's lecture in Richmond on 17 August 1849, John M. Daniels in the *Semi-Weekly Examiner* (Richmond) praises Poe for exploding "the poetic 'heresy of modern times'" by insisting that poetry should have no "end to accomplish beyond that of ministering to our sense of the beautiful.—We have in these days poets of humanity and poets of universal suffrage, poets whose mission is to break down the corn laws and poets to build up workhouses" (Thomas and Jackson, *Poe Log*, 827).

43. Ralph Waldo Emerson, *Essays and Lectures*, ed. Joel Porte (New York: Library of America, 1993), 307.

44. Whereas earlier critics, including Woodberry, Killis Campbell, *The Mind of Poe, and Other Studies* (1933; New York: Russell and Russell, 1962), Floyd Stovall, *Edgar Poe the Poet: Essays New and Old on the Man and His Work* (Charlottesville: University Press of Virginia, 1969), and Marvin Laser, "The Growth and Structure of Poe's Concept of Beauty," *ELH* 15 (1948): 9–84, have emphasized the determining influence of Coleridge on Poe's aesthetic ideas, Glen A. Omans argues convincingly that Poe's tripartite division of the mind derives not from Coleridge but from Kant's *Critique of Judgment*: "Not only are Poe's three faculties, pure intellect, taste, and the moral sense, translations of Kant's German terms, *Verstand, das Geschmacksurteil*, and *Vernunft*, but also Poe, like Kant, places the faculty of taste between those of the intellect and moral sense and emphasizes its function as a 'connecting link in the triple chain'" ("Intellect, Taste, and the Moral Sense: Poe's Debt to Kant," *Studies in the American Renaissance* 4 [1980]: 128). For a discussion of Poe in relation to eighteenth-century moral sense philosophers, see Robert D. Jacobs, *Poe: Journalist and Critic* (Baton Rouge: Louisiana State University Press, 1969), especially 3–34.

45. Burke, *Philosophical Enquiry*, 11.

46. Baumgarten's two-volume *Aesthetica* was published in Germany in 1750–58. For a discussion of the historical emergence of the term *aesthetic* in Germany and England in the eighteenth and nineteenth centuries, see Raymond Williams, *Keywords: A Vocabulary of Culture and Society* (rev. ed.; New York: Oxford University Press, 1983), 31–32. In *The Ideology of the Aesthetic* (Oxford: Blackwell, 1990), Terry Eagleton argues: "Aesthetics is born as a discourse of the body" (13).

47. Immanuel Kant, *Observations on the Feeling of the Beautiful and the Sublime*, trans. John T. Goldthwait (1764; Berkeley: University of California Press, 1960), 110–11.

48. Jay B. Hubbell, "Edgar Allan Poe," in *Eight American Authors: A Review of Research and Criticism*, ed. James Woodress (rev. ed., New York: Norton, 1972), 8.

49. Rufus Wilmot Griswold, "The 'Ludwig' Article," *New York Daily Tribune*, 9 October 1949 (reprinted in Eric W. Carlson, ed., *The Recognition of Edgar Allan Poe: Selected Criticism since 1829* [Ann Arbor: University of Michigan, 1966], 33–34); *PW*, 1: 232, 231; Henry James, *French Poets and Novelists* (New York: Macmillan, 1878), 76.

50. In a footnote to his discussion of "Method and Scope" in *American Renaissance: Art and Expression in the Age of Emerson and Whitman* (New York: Oxford University Press, 1941), Matthiessen says that he excluded Poe from his study because he "was bitterly hostile to democracy" and lacked "the moral depth of Hawthorne and Melville" (xii).

51. Edmund Wilson, "Poe at Home and Abroad," *New Republic* 8 (December 1926), reprinted in Carlson, *The Recognition of Edgar Allan Poe*, 145, 143.

52. See also Patrick F. Quinn, *The French Face of Edgar Allan Poe* (Carbondale: Southern Illinois University Press, 1957).

53. T. S. Eliot, *From Poe to Valéry* (New York: Harcourt Brace, 1948), 26.

54. Eliot, *From Poe to Valéry*, 32, 9, 29; Tate, "The Angelic Imagination," 60.

55. Charles Baudelaire, "New Notes on Edgar Poe," in *Baudelaire on Poe: Critical Papers*, ed. Lois and Francis E. Hyslop (State College, Pa.: Bald Eagle Press, 1952), 124. Subsequent references will be cited as *NN*. Baudelaire's essays on Poe appeared in *Edgar Allan Poe: Sa vie et ses ouvrages* (1852), *Edgar Poe: Sa vie et ses oeuvres* (1856), and *Notes nouvelles sur Edgar Poe* (1857).

56. "Edgar Allan Poe" (1852), in *Baudelaire on Poe*, 67. In this first published essay on Poe, Baudelaire wrote: "He went through life as if through a Sahara desert, and changed his residence like an Arab" (63). Given the racially marked nature of Baudelaire's response to Poe, it is significant that his interest in Poe was aroused by a reading of "The Black Cat," a story that he discusses at length as a fable of human perversity in his 1852 essay on Poe.

57. Stéphane Mallarmé, *Oeuvres complètes*, ed. Henri Mondor and G. Jean-Aubry (Paris: Gallimard, 1945), 70. In his own pursuit of technical perfection and a poetic language purified of all social reference, Mallarmé regarded Poe as "my great master" (quoted in Henri Mondor, *Vie de Mallarmé* [Paris: Gallimard, 1941], 104). Claiming that he learned English in order to translate Poe, he published translations of several of Poe's poems. See Stéphane Mallarmé, *Les poèmes de Edgar Poe, traduits par Stéphane Mallarmé* (Paris: Gallimard, 1928).

Chapter 5

1. *Selected Correspondence of Kenneth Burke and Malcolm Cowley: 1915–1981*, ed. Paul Jay (New York: Viking, 1988), 273.

2. Malcolm Cowley, "Introduction," *LG* 1855, xii.

3. In letters to his lover, Russell Cheyney, F. O. Matthiessen had also drawn sympathetic attention to Whitman's erotic attachments to men. But in his influential book *American Renaissance*, he dismissed the "vaguely pathological and homosexual" quality of Whitman's work and sought to reclaim him for serious national and international attention through a formalist approach to *Leaves of Grass* as a "language experiment" with analogues in oratory, opera, the ocean, and the visual arts (517–625). For a review of Whitman criticism and homosexuality, see Robert K. Martin, *The Homosexual Tradition in American Poetry* (Austin: University of Texas Press, 1979), 3–8; and Scott Giantvalley, "Recent Whitman Studies and Homosexuality," *Cabirion and Gay Books Bulletin* 12 (spring/summer 1985): 14–16. Justin Kaplan, in "The Biographer's Problem," *Mickle Street Review* 11 (1989): 80–88, begins by observing that "the history of over a century of Whitman biography is to a large extent the history of a pussyfooting accommodation to the issue of sexuality, more specifically, homosexuality. One sees biography being skewed in the interests of literary public relations" (83–84). But he concludes by reconsigning the "issue" of Whitman's homosexuality to the margins when he notes that "perhaps it's time to move on to a broader focus" (88).

4. Robert K. Martin pioneered in the field of gay studies and in the study of Whitman and homosexuality in his groundbreaking article, "Whitman's *Song of Myself*: Homosexual Dream and Vision," *Partisan Review* 42 (1975): 80–96. See

also Martin's chapter on Whitman in *The Homosexual Tradition*, 3–89; Joseph Cady, "Not Happy in the Capitol: Homosexuality and the Calamus Poems," *American Studies* 19 (fall 1978): 5–22; Cady, "*Drum-Taps* and Nineteenth-Century Male Homosexual Literature," in *Walt Whitman: Here and Now*, ed. Joann P. Krieg (Westport, Conn.: Greenwood Press, 1985), 49–60; Charley Shively, *Calamus Lovers: Walt Whitman's Working Class Camerados* (San Francisco: Gay Sunshine Press, 1987); Charley Shively, ed., *Drum Beats: Walt Whitman's Civil War Boy Lovers* (San Francisco: Gay Sunshine Press, 1989); and Alan Helms, "Whitman's 'Live Oak with Moss,'" in *The Continuing Presence of Walt Whitman*, ed. Robert K. Martin (1992), 185–205. Michael Moon focuses on Whitman's "sexual politics" in *Disseminating Whitman*, but in emphasizing the split between the corporeal and the social self in Whitman's work, he maintains the bounds between the private and the public, homosexuality and democracy, as separate and relatively distinct realms. Gary Schmidgall maintains a similar distinction between homosexual love and the public rhetoric of democracy in his biography, *Walt Whitman: A Gay Life* (New York: Plume, 1998). For an approach that challenges the public/private binary in critical interpretations of Whitman's work, see Jay Grossman, "'The Evangel-Poem of Comrades and Love': Revising Whitman's Republicanism," *American Transcendental Quarterly* 4 (September 1990): 201–18. See also Erkkila, "Democracy and (Homo)Sexual Desire," in *Whitman the Political Poet* (New York: Oxford University Press, 1989), 155–89.

5. David Warner, "The Good G(r)ay Poet," *Philadelphia City Paper*, 12–19 January 1990.

6. Given the controversial decision of the National Endowment for the Arts to deny funding to several homosexual artists in the early 1990s, it cannot be entirely coincidental that the Library of Congress, which holds the largest and most substantial collection of Whitman materials in the world, sponsored no exhibit or other series of events in commemoration of the centennial of Walt Whitman's death in 1992. More recently, in January 2003 First Lady Laura Bush cancelled a series of *purely literary* discussions of great American writers at the White House when she realized that a symposium on the poetry of Walt Whitman, Emily Dickinson, and Langston Hughes might be "politicized" in the context of the U.S. invasion of Iraq.

7. The exhibit was designed by Ralph Applebaum, who designed the Holocaust Museum in Washington, D.C.; Joann Krieg, a Whitman scholar and President of the Board of the Whitman Birthplace Association, served as the exhibit's script consultant. The exhibit has been opposed by the Calamus Preservation Society, a group of scholars and activists who threw erasers at the official opening of the exhibit in protest against the decision to erase any specific reference to Whitman's homosexuality.

8. For a study of the relation between capitalist transformation and the male purity movement, see Carroll Smith-Rosenberg, "Sex as Symbol in Victorian Purity: An Ethnohistorical Analysis of Jacksonian America," *American Journal of Sociology* 84 (Supplement 1978): S212–S247.

9. Jeffrey Weeks, *Sexuality and Its Discontents: Meanings, Myths, and Modern Sexualities* (London: Routledge and Kegan Paul, 1985), 6. See also Michel Foucault's comment on the emergence of the homosexual as a distinct personage in the nineteenth century: "The sodomite had been a temporary aberration; the homosexual was now a species" (*The History of Sexuality: An Introduction* [1976], trans. Robert Hurley [New York: Vintage, 1990], 43).

10. *An American Primer by Walt Whitman*, ed. Horace Traubel (1904; reprint, San Francisco: City Lights Press, 1970), 21.

11. Ibid.

12. See Shively, *Calamus Lovers*, 11–12; and Moon, *Disseminating Whitman*, 26–36. See also Michael Warner's "Whitman Drunk" for a discussion of the dialectics of self-abandonment and self-mastery in Whitman's temperance writings and his poetry (in *Breaking Bounds*, ed. Erkkila and Grossman, 30–43).

13. This association of temperance with the future of the American republic is further supported by the iconography of the *New World*, which bears as its logo a triumphant image of Columbus arriving in the New World over the inscription: "No pent-up Utica contracts our powers; For the whole boundless continent is ours" (*New World*, extra series, 2 [November 1842]: 1).

14. *The Uncollected Poetry and Prose of Walt Whitman*, ed. Emory Holloway, 2 vols. (Garden City, N.Y.: Doubleday, Page, 1921), 2:72. Subsequent references will be cited as *UPP*.

15. Shively, *Calamus Lovers*, 21.

16. James E. Miller, Jr., " 'Song of Myself' as Inverted Mystical Experience," *PMLA* 70 (September 1955): 636.

17. Cady, "Not Happy," 15. M. Jimmie Killingsworth makes a similar distinction between sentimental rhetoric and homosexual love in Whitman's "Calamus" poems (*Whitman's Poetry of the Body: Sexuality, Politics, and the Text* (Chapel Hill: University of North Carolina Press, 1989), 99. See also Helms, "Whitman's 'Live Oak with Moss' "; Hershel Parker, "The Real 'Live Oak, with Moss': Straight Talk about Whitman's 'Gay Manifesto,' " *Nineteenth-Century Literature* 51 (September 1996): 145–60; and Herschel Parker and Steven Olsen-Smith, " 'Live Oak, with Moss' and 'Calamus': Textual Inhibitions in Whitman Criticism," *Walt Whitman Quarterly* 14 (spring 1997): 153–65.

18. For studies of Whitman and phrenology, see Edward Hungerford, "Walt Whitman and His Chart of Bumps," *American Literature* 2 (1931): 350–84; Harold Aspiz, *Walt Whitman and the Body Beautiful* (Urbana: University of Illinois Press, 1980); and Michael Lynch, " 'Here Is Adhesiveness': From Friendship to Homosexuality," *Victorian Studies* 29 (autumn 1985): 67–96.

19. *Whitman's Manuscripts*, ed. Fredson Bowers, 114.

20. See, for example, Gay Wilson Allen, who writes that Whitman "left convincing evidence in his notebooks that ["Enfans d'Adam"] was an after-thought, growing not from an inner compulsion but used for the strategic purpose of balancing 'Calamus'—or more accurately the cluster of twelve poems first called 'Live-Oak Leaves,' before Whitman had thought of his calamus plant symbol" (*The Solitary Singer: A Critical Biography of Walt Whitman* [1955; New York: New York University Press, 1967], 250).

21. Walt Whitman, *Notes and Fragments*, ed. Richard Maurice Bucke (Ontario, Canada: A. Talbot, 1899), 169.

22. See also Whitman's deletion of the reference to "the perfect girl" in "Enfans" 2 ("From Pent-Up Aching Rivers") and the explicit references to the female in "Enfans" 6 ("One Hour to Madness and Joy").

23. Lynch, " 'Here is Adhesiveness,' " 91, 67.

24. See, for example, Helms, who argues that Whitman's decision to disperse the "Live Oak, with Moss" poems in the 1860 "Calamus" sequence represented not only a "retreat from his sexuality" but also a "degeneration" in the style of his later work ("Whitman's Live Oak with Moss," 192). Moon also distinguishes between the "visionary and utopian project" of the pre–Civil War Whitman and the Whitman of the post–Civil War years (*Disseminating Whitman*, 221). See also Schmidgall, *Walt Whitman*, 147.

25. Cady makes a similar point in *"Drum-Taps* and Nineteenth-Century Male Homosexual Literature," but he continues to distinguish between the private poet of homosexual love and the more public figure of the soldier-comrade through whom Whitman self-protectively masks his homosexual desire. What I want to stress is the inseparability of the private discourses of male homosexual desire from the more public discourses of combat and democratic union in Whitman's poems of the Civil War.

26. *Drum-Taps (1865) and Sequel to Drum-Taps (1865–66): A Facsimile Reproduction*, ed. F. DeWolfe Miller (Gainesville, Fla.: Scholars' Facsimiles and Reprints, 1959), 6, 37. Subsequent references will be cited as *DT.*

27. On 30 June 1865, Whitman was fired from his job as a clerk in the Department of Interior when Secretary James Harlan "found" a marked copy of the 1860 *Leaves of Grass* in Whitman's desk. Although Whitman was reemployed the next day in the attorney general's office, his friend William D. O'Connor undertook an impassioned defense of the poet against charges of moral turpitude in a pamphlet titled *The Good Gray Poet,* which was published in 1866. For a study of the erotic bonds Whitman formed with soldiers during the Civil War, see Shively's *Drum-Beats,* which includes a selection of "Soldiers' Letters" written to Whitman during and after the war.

28. Horace Traubel, *With Walt Whitman in Camden,* 5 vols. (New York: Mitchell Kennerly, c. 1906–1914), 3:582.

29. *Walt Whitman: The Correspondence,* ed. Edwin Haviland Miller, 6 vols. (New York: New York University Press, 1961–77), 2:47, 84, 104. Subsequent references will be cited as *CORR.*

30. Shively discusses Whitman's love relationship with Fred Vaughan and reprints the letters Vaughan wrote to Whitman in 1860–62 and 1874 in *Calamus Lovers,* 36–50. Shively argues that it was Vaughan who "inspired Whitman to write the Calamus poems—perhaps the most intense and successful celebration of gay love in our language" (38).

31. Ed Folsom, "Whitman's Calamus Photographs," in *Breaking Bounds,* ed. Erkkila and Grossman, 193–219.

32. In a series titled "Suggestions for Posing," which was published in *Anthony's Photographic Bulletin* between 1870 and 1871, for example, seventy-one different examples of posing are suggested, but none is men together; and in a section titled "On Groups" in the popular 1883 book *About Photography and Photography,* Henry Baden Pritchard argues that nonfamily groups are "usually a failure as an artistic work" (quoted in John Ibson, *Picturing Men: A Century of Male Relationships in Everyday American Photography* [Washington, D.C.: Smithsonian Institution Press, 2002], 16). As Ibson observes, the portraits that men took together before the primarily male gaze of the studio camera in the nineteenth century reveal a world of male intimacy that "would largely disappear from view" in the late nineteenth and early twentieth centuries as taboos about male homosexuality and communality took hold in the culture.

33. Schmidgall describes the changes Whitman made in his poems after 1860 as "a lengthy and meticulous sexual suicide" (*Walt Whitman,* 145). See also Killingsworth, who writes: "Propriety had become a central tenet for the postwar Whitman" (*Whitman's Poetry of the Body,* 148).

34. *Leaves of Grass,* ed. Sculley Bradley and Harold W. Blodgett (New York: Norton, 1973), 121. Subsequent references will be cited as *LG.*

35. See also *Specimen Days* (1882), in which Whitman finds among the workers and crowded city streets of "Human and Heroic New York" "a palpable out-

cropping of that personal comradeship I look forward to as the subtlest, strongest future hold of this many-item'd Union" (*PW*, 1:172).

36. See Havelock Ellis and John Addington Symonds, *Sexual Inversion* (London: Wilson and Macmillan, 1897). See also Robert K. Martin, who emphasizes the class difference between Whitman and Symonds, and thus the ways Whitman's response to Symonds might be read as an attempt to "put on" and "put down" Symonds as an effete member of the British aristocracy who knows nothing about American working-class comradeship and sexuality ("Whitman and the Politics of Identity," in *Walt Whitman: The Centennial Essays*, ed. Ed Folsom [Iowa City: University of Iowa Press, 1994], 172–81).

37. Lynch, " 'Here Is Adhesiveness,' " 67.

Chapter 6

1. See Erkkila, *Whitman the Political Poet;* Erkkila, "Emily Dickinson and Adrienne Rich: Toward a Theory of Female Influence," *American Literature* 56 (December 1984): 541–59; "Emily Dickinson on Her Own Terms," *Wilson Quarterly* 9 (spring 1985): 98–109; Erkkila, *The Wicked Sisters.*

2. For the debate between Marxists and feminists about sex and class as categories of analysis, see, for example, Lillian Robinson, "Dwelling in Decencies: Radical Criticism and the Feminist Perspective," *Sex, Class, Culture* (New York: Methuen, 1986), 3–21; Catharine MacKinnon, "Feminism, Marxism, Method, and the State: An Agenda for Theory," *Signs* 7 (1982): 515–44; Toril Moi, *Sexual/Textual Politics: Feminist Literary Theory* (New York: Methuen, 1985); Frank Lentricchia, "Patriarchy against Itself—The Young Manhood of Wallace Stevens," *Critical Inquiry* 13 (1987): 743–86; Frank Lentricchia, "Andiamo!" *Critical Inquiry* 14 (1988): 407–13; and Sandra Gilbert and Susan Gubar, "The Man on the Dump versus the United Dames of America; or, What Does Frank Lentricchia Want?" *Critical Inquiry* 14 (1988): 386–406. For more recent arguments that race is the shaping presence in American society, culture, and politics, see Morrison, *Playing in the Dark;* and Henry Louis Gates, Jr., who emphasizes "the central shaping role that slavery has played in the creation of all America's social, political, and economic institutions" (preface to "New Perspectives on the Transatlantic Slave Trade," 5).

3. Rebecca Patterson, *The Riddle of Emily Dickinson* (Boston: Houghton Mifflin, 1951); Adrienne Rich, "Vesuvius at Home: The Power of Emily Dickinson" (1975), in *On Lies, Secrets, and Silence: Selected Prose, 1966–1978* (New York: Norton, 1979), 157–83; Sandra Gilbert, "The American Sexual Poetics of Walt Whitman and Emily Dickinson," 123–54; Joanne Feit Diehl, *Dickinson and the Romantic Imagination* (Princeton, N.J.: Princeton University Press, 1981); Barbara Mossberg, *Emily Dickinson: When a Writer Is a Daughter* (Bloomington: Indiana University Press, 1982); Vivian Pollak, *Dickinson: The Anxiety of Gender* (Ithaca, N.Y.: Cornell University Press, 1984); Wendy Martin, *An American Triptych: Anne Bradstreet, Emily Dickinson, Adrienne Rich* (Chapel Hill: University of North Carolina Press, 1984).

4. This ahistoricism in Dickinson studies is by no means limited to feminist critics. Commenting on the underlying vision of Dickinson's work in *Emily Dickinson* (New York: Sloane, 1951), Richard Chase observes: "Emily Dickinson's eschatological cast of mind, on the whole a departure from New England Puritanism, was entirely a personal vision of life and has no direct historical or social

implications" (186). In *Beneath the American Renaissance: The Subversive Imagination in the Age of Emerson and Melville* (New York: Knopf, 1988), David Reynolds argues that it is precisely in transcending politics that Dickinson becomes a major woman artist (387–437).

5. William S. Tyler, *History of Amherst College during Its First Half Century* (Springfield, Mass.: Clark W. Bryan, 1873), 539.

6. Ideology, writes Terry Eagleton, is "that complex structure of social perception which ensures that the situation in which one social class has power over the others is either seen by most members of the society as 'natural' or not seen at all" (*Marxism and Literary Criticism* [Berkeley: University of California Press, 1976], 5).

7. Friedrich Engels, *The Origin of the Family, Private Property, and the State* (New York: International, 1942), 89. Feminists are less certain about the relation and relevance of class in the history of women. In *The Second Sex* (trans. H. M. Parshley [New York: Knopf, 1953]), Simone de Beauvoir argues that women are dispersed among men and divided from other women along class lines: "If they belong to the bourgeoisie, they feel solidarity with men of that class, not with proletarian women; it they are white, their allegiance is to white men, not to Negro women" (xix). In *Sexual Politics* (Garden City, N.Y.: Doubleday, 1970), on the other hand, Kate Millett rejects class altogether as a significant category of analysis, arguing that patriarchy is the fundamental system of domination, independent of capitalism or any other mode of production. Whereas American feminist historians, most notably Gerda Lerner (*The Majority Finds Its Past: Placing Women in History* [New York: Oxford University Press, 1979]) and Elizabeth Fox-Genovese ("Placing Women's History in History," *New Left Review* 133 [1982]: 5–29), have tended to follow de Beauvoir in emphasizing the class and race divisions among women in the US, American feminist literary critics have tended to follow Millett in emphasizing the communality of interests among women across race, class, and cultural bounds.

8. Bingham, *Emily Dickinson's Home*, 413–14; emphasis added.

9. For a speculative account of the interactive relationship Emily Dickinson may have had with her Irish servant, Margaret Maher, who came to work at the Dickinson Homestead in 1869 and remained in the household for some thirty years, see Aife Murray, "Miss Margaret's Emily Dickinson," *Signs* 24 (spring 1999): 697–732.

10. For a study of New England squirearchy, see Robert A. Gross, "Squire Dickinson and Squire Hoar," *Massachusetts Historical Society Proceedings* 101 (1989): 1–23.

11. "My Personal Acquaintance with Emily Dickinson," quoted in Sewall, *Life of Emily Dickinson*, 60. Clara Newman and her sister Anna came to live with their uncle, Edward Dickinson, in 1852. The two sisters lived with Austin and Sue beginning in 1858.

12. See Polly Longsworth, *Austin and Mabel: The Amherst Affair and Love Letters of Austin Dickinson and Mabel Loomis Todd* (New York: Farrar, Straus and Giroux, 1984).

13. Todd-Bingham Family Papers, reprinted in Sewall, *Life of Emily Dickinson*, 282. For an opposing view of class, see Edward Pessen, *Jacksonian America: Society, Personality, and Politics* (Chicago: Dorsey, 1969) and *Riches, Class, and Power before the Civil War* (Lexington: Mass.: Heath, 1973). He argues that far from being an age of equality and "the democratic mixing of upper and lower classes," the antebellum decades featured an inequality among classes that surpassed anything that came afterward.

14. See George R. Taylor, "The Rise and Decline of Manufactures and Other Matters," in *Essays on Amherst's History,* ed. Theodore P. Greene (Amherst, Mass.: Vista Trust, 1978); Christopher Clark, "The Household Economy, Market Exchange and the Rise of Capitalism in the Connecticut Valley, 1800–1860," *Journal of Social History* 13 (1979): 169–90; Richard D. Brown, "The Emergence of Urban Society in Rural Massachusetts," *Journal of American History* 61 (1974): 29–51.

15. In *History of Amherst College,* William S. Tyler says of Samuel Fowler Dickinson: "His business which was so large as to require all his time and care, suffered from his devotion to the public. He became embarrassed and at length actually poor. And in his poverty he had the additional grief of feeling that his services were forgotten" (121). For a discussion of the complicated financial negotiations that led to the bankruptcy of Samuel Fowler Dickinson in 1828 and the sale of his half of the Dickinson mansion at public auction in 1833, see Habegger, *My Wars Are Laid Away in Books,* especially 55–60, 82–90.

16. Jay Leyda, *The Years and Hours of Emily Dickinson,* 2 vols. (New Haven, Conn.: Yale University Press, 1960), 1:30. Subsequent references will be cited as *YH.* Edward Dickinson's marriage in 1828 to Emily Norcross, who came from a family of wealthy entrepreneurs who had made much money in land speculation, may itself have been linked to his attempt to secure his social position against the impending losses of his father. For a discussion of the socioeconomic background of the Norcross family, see Mary Elizabeth Bernhard, "Portrait of a Family: Emily Dickinson's Norcross Connection," *New England Quarterly* 40 (1987). She notes: "At a time when the Dickinson family fortunes were in jeopardy, the Norcross family resources were secure as a result of Joel [Norcross]'s business acumen" (376).

17. On 20 April 1855, the *Franklin and Hampshire Express* noted under "SALE OF REAL ESTATE": "The elegant place where the late venerable Dea. Mack resided for upwards of twenty years, has been recently sold by his son, Samuel E. Mack, of Cincinnati, to the Hon. Edward Dickinson, whose father, Samuel F. Dickinson, formerly owned the place. Thus has the worthy son of an honored sire the pleasure of possessing the 'Old Homestead'" (*YH,* 1:331). How Edward Dickinson obtained the money to repurchase the "Old Homestead" is open to question. His wife, Emily Norcross Dickinson, may have received an inheritance from her father's estate. However, Barton Levi St. Armand (*Emily Dickinson and Her Culture: The Soul's Society* [New York: Cambridge University Press, 1984]) and Cynthia Griffin Wolff (*Emily Dickinson* [New York: Knopf, 1986]) both argue that Edward Dickinson embezzled from his nieces, Clara and Anna Newman, who came to live with the Dickinson family in the early 1850s.

18. Sketch of Emily Dickinson by Emily Fowler Ford published in *Letters of Emily Dickinson,* ed. Mabel Loomis Todd (New York: Harper, 1931), 132.

19. Emily Fowler Ford, "Eheu! Emily Dickinson," *Springfield Daily Republican,* 11 January 1891, p. 2.

20. As Rogers M. Smith observes: "The Irish were 'savages,' like 'negroes, Indians, Mexicans' and indeed were sometimes called 'Irish niggers'" (*Civic Ideals,* 210).

21. Speech delivered on the occasion of the completion of the Bunker Hill Monument, 17 June 1843 (*The Great Speeches of Daniel Webster,* ed. Edwin P. Whipple [Boston: Little, Brown, and Co., 1879], 143, 144; my emphasis).

22. Todd-Bingham Papers, reprinted in Sewall, *Life of Emily Dickinson,* 297, 299.

23. Pollak, *Anxiety of Gender*, 156.

24. For a discussion of the relation between Dickinson and other more socially engaged women writers of her time, see Joanne Dobson, *Dickinson and the Strategies of Reticence: The Woman Writer in Nineteenth-Century America* (Bloomington: Indiana University Press, 1989), 78–98.

25. Beecher defended the home as the site of national renewal in such books as *The Duty of American Women to Their Country* (1844). Hale was the editor of *Godey's Lady's Book* (1837–77) and the author of several humanitarian works, including the antislavery novel *Northwood: A Tale of New England* (Boston: Bowles and Dearborn, 1827).

26. Gerda Lerner, "The Lady and the Mill Girl: Changes in the Status of Women in the Age of Jackson," in *The Majority Finds Its Past*, 25–26.

27. In "Ideology and Ideological State Apparatuses," Louis Althusser comments on the relation between the state and what he calls "Ideological State Apparatuses" such as the church, the family, the educational system, and the arts. These institutions are, he argues, "not only the *stake,* but also the *site* of class struggle, and often of bitter class struggle" because "the former ruling classes are able to retain strong positions there for a long time" and because "the resistance of the exploited classes is able to find means and occasions to express itself there" (*Lenin and Philosophy and Other Essays* [New York: Monthly Review, 1971], 147).

28. For a discussion of the "country party" tradition as it was embodied by such figures as John Quincy Adams, see Daniel Walker Howe, *The Political Culture of the American Whigs* (Chicago: University of Chicago Press, 1979) and Tamara Plakins Thornton, *Cultivating Gentlemen: The Meaning of Country Life among the Boston Elite, 1785–1860* (New Haven, Conn.: Yale University Press, 1989).

29. See Taylor, "The Rise and Decline of Manufacturers."

30. Matthiessen, *American Renaissance*, ix.

31. Stow Persons, *The Decline of American Gentility* (New York: Columbia University Press, 1973), 4.

32. "The Works of Alexander Dumas," *North American Review* 56 (1843): 110.

33. The two editors to whom Dickinson refers may be Samuel Bowles and Josiah Holland, the editors of the *Springfield Republican*.

34. Sandra Gilbert and Susan Gubar, *The Madwoman in the Attic: The Woman Writer and the Nineteenth-Century Literary Imagination* (New Haven, Conn.: Yale University Press, 1979), 71.

35. Julia Kristeva, "Oscillation between Power and Denial," in *New French Feminisms*, ed. Elaine Marks and Isabelle de Courtivon (Amherst: University of Massachusetts Press, 1980), 166.

36. Hélène Cixous and Catherine Clément, *The Newly Born Woman*, trans. Betsy Wing (Minneapolis: University of Minnesota Press, 1986), 159.

Chapter 7

1. Perhaps not coincidentally, in *Empire*, Michael Hardt and Antonio Negri also cite Melville's words on America as the world's blood as an epigraph to their chapter on the possibilities of "Generation and Corruption" within the new global order presided over by America (371–92). Through generation in postmodernity, they write, the "already hybrid" bodies of intellectual and cooperative power become bodies "beyond measure." Corruption appears in the form

of "disease, frustration, and mutilation" as well as "psychosis, opiates, anguish, and boredom" (392).

2. Paul Buhle, *The Artist as Revolutionary: C.L.R. James* (London: Verso, 1988); Martin Glaberman, "The Marxism of C.L.R. James," in *C.L.R. James: His Intellectual Legacies*, ed. Selwyn R. Cudjoe and William E. Cain (Amherst: University of Massachusetts Press, 1995), 304–16; Anna Grimshaw, ed., *The C.L.R. James Reader* (Cambridge, Mass.: Blackwell, 1992); Anthony Bogues, *C.L.R. James and Marxism* (London: Pluto Press, 1992) and *Caliban's Freedom: The Early Political Thought of C.L.R. James* (London: Pluto Press, 1997); Aldon Nielsen, *C.L.R. James: A Critical Introduction* (Jackson: University Press of Mississippi, 1997); and Nicole King, *C.L.R. James and Creolization: Circles of Influence* (Jackson, University Press of Mississippi, 2001). See also Kent Worcester, *C.L.R. James: A Political Biography* (New York: State University Press of New York, 1996).

3. Matthiessen, *American Renaissance*; Miller, *Errand into the Wilderness*.

4. For attempts to read beyond the nationalist frames of American studies, see especially Donald E. Pease, *Nationalist Identities and Post-Americanist Narratives* (Durham, N.C.: Duke University Press, 1994); Benjamin Lee, "Critical Internationalism," *Public Culture* 7 (1995): 559–92; and John Carlos Rowe, ed., *Post-Nationalist American Studies* (Berkeley: University of California Press, 2000). In "Resituating American Studies in a Critical Internationalism," Jane C. Desmond and Virginia R. Dominguez note how seldom international scholars are cited in the new American scholarship (*American Quarterly* 48 [September 1996]: 475–90). See also Günter H. Lenz, who observes that "the various attempts at 'internationalizing' American Studies tend to be built on a unidirectional perspective." He proposes "a new 'dialogics' of International American Culture Studies, of the encounter of American and foreign scholars in a bi- or multidirectional joint venture" ("Toward a Dialogics of International Culture Studies: Transnationality, Border Discourses, and Public Culture(s)," *Amerikastudien/American Studies* 44 [1999]: 5).

5. "Cricket had plunged me into politics long before I was aware of it. When I did turn to politics I did not have too much to learn," James wrote in *Beyond a Boundary*, 71.

6. *Congressional Record*, 81st Cong., 2nd sess., 23 September 1950, 987.

7. Here as elsewhere in this chapter, my use of the term *creolization* is informed by Nicole King's superb study of James's mixed heritage as a West Indian who was raised on Western European cultural traditions in *C.L.R. James and Creolization*. See especially, "Mapping Creolization," in which King uses the term *creolization* to describe the layers of history, literature, philosophy, and political theory that coalesce in many of James's works (3–29). See also Brathwaite, *Contradictory Omens*; and Edouard Glissant's post-negritude theorization of a cross-cultural poetics of creolization, movement, and relation in *Caribbean Discourse: Selected Essays*, trans. Michael Dash (Charlottesville: University Press of Virginia, 1989) and *Poetics of Relation*, trans. Betsy Wing (Ann Arbor: University of Michigan, 1997).

8. Buhle, *The Writer as Revolutionary*, 82. For a discussion of James's work and writing for the Socialist Workers Party and the Workers Party, see also Worcester, *C.L.R. James*, 55–81.

9. Glaberman, "The Marxism of C.L.R. James," 304.

10. C.L.R. James, "The Revolutionary Answer to the Negro Problem in the USA" (1948), in *The C.L.R. James Reader*, ed. Grimshaw, 188. Worcester describes this document, which was presented to the Socialist Worker's Party Convention

in 1948, as "one of the most stimulating and exciting documents to come out of the American far left" (*C.L.R. James*, 80).

11. C.L.R. James, *Notes on Dialectics: Hegel, Marx, Lenin* (London: Allison and Busby, 1980), 117.

12. Gregory Jay, "White Out: Race and Nationalism in American Studies," *American Quarterly* 55 (December 2003): 787.

13. James, *American Civilization*, 119.

14. For a perceptive analysis of James's cultural criticism as "a singular extension of *dialectical* reasoning into customary notions of the 'popular'" and his ability "to think beyond the standpoint of cultural studies to a genuinely popular aesthetic," see Neil Larsen, "Negativities of the Popular: C.L.R. James and the Limits of 'Cultural Studies,'" in *Rethinking C.L.R. James*, ed. Grant Farred (Cambridge, Mass.: Blackwell, 1996), 86.

15. Internal Security Act of 1950, *Congressional Record*, 23 September 1950, p. 989.

16. For a discussion of the controversy surrounding the final chapter and its repression in subsequent editions of *Mariners*, see Donald E. Pease's introduction to his new edition of James's *Mariners, Renegades and Castaways* (Hanover, N.H.: University Press of New England, 2000), xviii–xxviii. This is the first edition since 1953 to include James's final chapter.

17. Internal Security Act of 1950, *Congressional Record*, p. 1007.

18. Although Lionel Trilling's *Liberal Imagination: Essays on Literature and Society* (New York : Harcourt Brace Jovanovich, 1950) calls for a liberal criticism that assumes "the connection between literature and politics," he uses the term *politics* in its "wide sense" to mean "the politics of culture," which he defines as "the quality of human life" (preface, n.p.). In Trilling's literary criticism, the literary imagination—the art of fantasy, romance, symbol, and myth—becomes a primary means of defending liberal freedom against both Stalinist totalitarianism and home-grown modes of writing associated with social realism, the left, the masses, and the 1930s. See, for example, the opening essay, "Reality in America," 3–20. By equating liberalism with the imagination and the qualities of "complexity and difficulty" valued by high modernism (preface, n.p.), Trilling empties politics of its association with a particular order of power and the *historical reality* of oppression that many—including James himself on Ellis Island—suffered at the hands of an increasingly powerful and paranoid liberal capitalist state during the cold war years and after. For other critics who emphasized the primarily mythic, symbolic, and romance qualities of American literature during the cold war years, see Henry Nash Smith, *Virgin Land: The American West as Symbol and Myth* (Cambridge, Mass.: Harvard University Press, 1950); Charles Feidelson, *Symbolism and American Literature* (Chicago: University of Chicago Press, 1953); R. W. B. Lewis, *The American Adam: Innocence, Tragedy, and Tradition in the Nineteenth Century* (Chicago: University of Chicago Press, 1955); Richard Chase, *The American Novel and Its Tradition* (Baltimore: Johns Hopkins University Press, 1957); Levin, *The Power of Blackness*; and Fiedler, *Love and Death in the American Novel*.

19. Matthiessen, *American Renaissance*, ix. See also Trilling's seminal reading of *Huckleberry Finn* in which he argues that the antebellum years represented a magical time of innocence before the fall into an era of machines, money, and city dwellers brought "a deterioration of American moral values" ("Huckleberry Finn," in *The Liberal Imagination*, 109).

20. In "Notes toward a Politics of 'American' Criticism," Paul Bové suggests

that "the best critical emblem for our time" might be "the postcolonial subject," a subject who is cognizant of the relation of global issues to regional and national concerns (*In the Wake of Theory* [Hanover, N.H.: Wesleyan University Press, 1992], 63).

21. See, for example, William V. Spanos, *The Errant Art of Moby-Dick: The Canon, the Cold War, and the Struggle for American Studies* (Durham, N.C.: Duke University Press, 1995), in which he draws attention to the need for "the perspectives of the outside of this inside" as a means of challenging "the totalizing American imaginary," but he never discusses James's reading of *Moby Dick* from the "outside" as part of the cold war struggle for American studies. Nor is James's study of Melville cited by Donald Pease in his influential essay, "*Moby Dick* and the Cold War" (in *The American Renaissance Reconsidered,* ed. Walter Benn Michaels and Donald E. Pease [Baltimore: Johns Hopkins University Press, 1985], 113–55), even though Pease's effort to read against *Moby Dick* as a cold war text bears a striking resemblance to James's interpretation of Ahab and Ishmael in *Mariners, Renegades and Castaways.* Even Toni Morrison, whose *Playing in the Dark,* has inspired a major rethinking of what she calls the "Africanist presence" (6) in classic American literature, makes her argument without ever taking note of the fact that as early as *The Black Jacobins* (1938), James had begun the process of historical, political, and cultural reconstruction that would locate blacks not only at the center of New World history but at the center of modernity and political struggles against capitalism and colonialism worldwide. For a discussion of James's relevance to recent work in American studies, see Darryl E. Levi, who observes: "Many of his insights have scarcely been explored, particularly by mainstream scholars" ("C.L.R. James: A Radical West Indian Vision of American Studies," *American Quarterly* 43 [September 1991]: 500). See also Pease's introduction to his new edition of *Mariners,* which focuses on the primarily national political contexts of James's struggle with the American cold war state at the same time that it links the "republication" of *Mariners* with the transition to what Pease calls "Transnational Americas Studies" ("C.L.R. James's *Mariners* and the World We Live In," xxxi). Oddly, given James's commitment to revolutionary Marxism from the mid-1930s onward and his emphasis throughout his writing on the emancipatory possibilities of labor, race, and colonial struggle under the conditions of global capitalism, Pease observes: "Marxism will only incompletely illuminate the significance of James's network of interests" ("C.L.R. James's *Mariners,*" xii).

22. Michael Rogin argues that "there was a crisis of bourgeois society at midcentury on both continents, but that in America it entered politics by way of slavery and race rather than class" (*Subversive Genealogy: The Politics and Art of Herman Melville* [Berkeley: University of California Press, 1979], ix).

23. See Paul Buhle, who observes that James's "defense of American society" against the Communist detainees on Ellis Island "more nearly approached an apologia for social life under capitalism than at any other time before or since" (*The Artist as Revolutionary,* 110).

24. For a suggestive discussion of Derrida's *Specters of Marx: The State of the Debt, the Work of Mourning, and the New International,* trans. Peggy Kamuf (London: Routledge, 1994) in relation to James's increasing emphasis on totalitarianism and state capitalism as the shadow presence at the "secret origins" of Marxism, see Nielsen, *C.L.R. James,* 103.

25. Pease, "*Moby Dick* and the Cold War," 141.

26. As Robert A. Hill points out in his "Literary Executor's Afterword" to

American Civilization, the popular desire for what James called "free association, for common social ends" was at the center of his reading of American civilization and his theory of popular culture as the realm through which the collective fears, fantasies, and desires of the American masses are expressed (*American Civilization*, 316). At a time when social and literary critics were turning toward *aestheticism* and *culture* as a means of escaping the political turmoil and disillusionment of the cold war years, James sought to theorize the radical force of culture, especially the mass culture of comic strips and gangster films, jazz and soap opera, Sid Caesar and the television comedies, in expressing and giving shape to the ongoing popular struggle for democracy in America and worldwide.

27. Hardt and Negri, *Empire*, 392.

28. James is not an objective reader of either Shakespeare or Melville, William E. Cain has argued: "by over-honoring the crewmen and dissociating them from Ahab, James misreads Melville's novel" ("The Triumph of the Will and the Failure of Resistance," in *C.L.R. James: His Intellectual Legacies*, ed. Cudjoe and Cain, 270, 260). For a theorization of the ways the colonized have written back to and resisted the master narratives of the West through acts of revolutionary rearticulation, see especially Gates on signifying in *The Signifying Monkey*; Bhabha on hybridity in *The Location of Culture*; and Said's discussion of resistance and opposition in *Culture and Imperialism*, 191–281.

29. James, "Popular Art and Cultural Tradition" (1954), in *C.L.R. James Reader*, ed. Grimshaw, 252.

30. See, for example, Richard Chase, *Herman Melville: A Critical Study* (New York: Macmillan, 1949), in which he seeks "to ransom liberalism from the ruinous sellouts, failures, and defeats of the thirties." The "new liberalism," Chase writes, "must present a vision of life capable, by a continuous act of imaginative criticism, of avoiding the old mistakes: the facile ideas of progress and 'social realism' . . . the belief that historical reality is merely a question of economic or ethical values, the idea that literature should participate directly in the economic liberation of the masses, the equivocal relationship to communist totalitarianism and power politics" (preface, vii). See also Trilling's *Liberal Imagination*, in which he sets the values of individual creative imagination, complexity, and *moral realism* represented by Henry James and Mark Twain against the nonaesthetic and merely reflective values of *social realism* represented by the intellectual historian Vernon L. Parrington and writers such as Theodore Dreiser, Sherwood Anderson, and John Steinbeck.

31. James's recognition of the global relations among race, class, nation, and capital in *Mariners* and elsewhere anticipates the work of recent cultural critics, including Balibar and Wallerstein, *Race, Nation, Class*; Said, *Culture and Imperialism*; Paul Gilroy, *Against Race: Imagining Political Culture beyond the Color Line* (Cambridge, Mass.: Belknap Press of Harvard University Press, 2000); and Hardt and Negri, *Empire*.

32. James, *The Black Jacobins: Toussaint L'Ouverture and the San Domingo Revolution* (1938; New York: Vintage Books, 1989), 283.

33. In a report on the "Negro Question" delivered to the Socialist Workers Convention in July 1948, James argued that "the independent Negro struggle . . . is able to exercise a powerful influence upon the revolutionary proletariat . . . and that it is in itself a constituent part of the struggle for socialism." Countering the notion that the independent struggles of Negro people were danger-

ous to the labor movement and the Marxist party, James concluded "that the Negro movement logically and historically and concretely is headed for the proletariat" and might indeed "be the means whereby the proletariat is brought on to the scene" ("The Revolutionary Answer to the Negro Problem in the USA," in *C.L.R. James Reader,* ed. Grimshaw, 183, 187, 185).

34. "The difference between the historian and the poet," Aristotle writes in *Poetics,* "lies in the fact that the historian narrates events that have actually happened, whereas the poet writes about things as they might possibly occur." The poet, Aristotle says, carries out his "imitations" in three possible ways: "he must imitate the things that were in the past, or are now, or that people say and think to be or those things that ought to be"; in *Poetics,* reprinted in *The Critical Tradition: Classic Texts and Contemporary Trends,* ed. David H. Richter (New York: St. Martin's Press, 1989), 48, 62.

35. Hegel, *Introduction to the Philosophy of Art,* in *The Critical Tradition,* ed. Richter, 346.

36. In *The Liberal Imagination,* Trilling criticizes liberal critics who praise Dreiser for his representation of reality: "the question for criticism is how he *transcended* the imposed limitations of his time and class," Trilling asserts (16; my emphasis). See also Matthiessen's critical distinction between historical "background" and aesthetic "foreground" in *American Renaissance* ("Method and Scope," ix); Chase's call for a "new" liberal criticism that will seek to come to terms with Melville not primarily as "a political thinker" but as "an enormous cultural fact" (*Melville,* ix); and the 1952 symposium conducted by *Partisan Review* titled "Our Country and Our Culture," in which intellectuals were asked to respond to the possibility that "a democratic society necessarily leads to a leveling of culture, to a mass culture which will overrun intellectual and aesthetic values traditional to Western civilization" (quoted in Lionel Trilling, *The Moral Obligation to Be Intelligent: Selected Essays,* ed. Leon Wieseltier [Farrar, Straus and Giroux, 2000], 278). In a review of Raymond Williams's *Culture and Society* (1958) and *The Long Revolution* (1961), James criticized Williams for failing to grasp the "materialist, internationalist, historic basis" of socialism or Marxism (Buhle, *The Artist as Revolutionary,* 135); in other words, James is critical of the very modes of cultural as opposed to materialist criticism that have made Williams fashionable among left intellectuals.

37. "Dialectical Materialism and the Fate of Humanity" (1947), in *C.L.R. James Reader,* ed. Grimshaw, 161.

38. Trilling, "The Situation of the American Intellectual at the Present Time" (1952), reprinted in *The Moral Obligation to Be Intelligent,* 279.

39. James's attempt to formulate alternative modes of *world citizenship* might be compared with recent efforts to rethink both democracy and citizenship outside the nation form. See for example, Bonnie Honig's call for a "democratic politics that is more cosmopolitan than nationalist in its aspirations." She proposes a resistant myth of "democratic cosmpolitanism" grounded in "a narrative of democratic activism whose heroes are not nationals of the regime but insist, nonetheless, on exercising national citizen rights while they are here" (*Democracy and the Foreigner* [Princeton, N.J.: Princeton University Press, 2001], 72, 101); Hardt and Negri, who describe *global citizenship* as "the first political demand" of the mobile multitude in its resistance to empire: "all should have the full rights of citizenship in the country where they live and work" (*Empire,* 400); and Sylvia Wynter, who asks if we can "now be empowered to postulate laws of culture and therefore regulations of behaviors that should hold in *all*

human orders?" ("Columbus, the Ocean Blue, and Fables That Stir the Mind: To Reinvent the Study of Letters," *Poetics of the Americas: Race, Founding, and Textuality,* ed. Bainard Cowan and Jefferson Humphries [Baton Rouge: Louisiana State University Press, 1997], 146; emphasis added).

40. C.L.R. James, "The American People in 'One World': An Essay in Dialectical Materialism," in *C.L.R. James and Revolutionary Marxism: Selected Writings of C.L.R. James, 1939–1949,* ed. Scott McLemee and Paul Le Blanc (Atlantic Highlands, N.J.: Humanities Press, 1994), 169. See also James, *American Civilization.* For cold war consensus historians who emphasized the distinctiveness of American national experience and character see especially Daniel J. Boorstin, *The Genius of American Politics* (Chicago: University of Chicago Press, 1953); David M. Potter, *People of Plenty: Economic Abundance and the American Character* (Chicago: University of Chicago Press, 1954); and Louis Hartz, *The Liberal Tradition: An Interpretation of American Political Thought since the Revolution* (New York: Harcourt Brace, 1955).

41. "An Audience with C.L.R. James," *Third World Book Review* 1 (1984): 7.

42. James anticipates recent calls for a global and cosmopolitan perspective beyond the nation-state. See, for example, James Clifford, who uses the term *discrepant cosmopolitanisms* to describe the "hybrid, cosmopolitan experiences" in which the local and the particular are always enmeshed ("Traveling Cultures," in *Cultural Studies,* ed. Lawerence Grossberg, Cary Nelson, and Paula A. Treichler [New York: Routledge, 1992], 108, 100). Bruce Robbins seeks to reconceive an older cosmopolitanism associated with both capitalist imperialism and universalist detachment as a move toward "some new, de-nationalized internationalism," "an international competence or mode of citizenship that is the monopoly of no one class or civilization" ("Comparative Cosmopolitanism," *Social Text* 31–32 [1992]: 183–84). Paul Gilroy calls for a "pragmatic, planetary humanism" to replace "race-thinking" (*Against Race,* 17). Hardt and Negri envision the possibility of "*cosmopolitical liberation*" in "the absolute constitution of labor and cooperation, the earthly city of the multitude" (*Empire,* 65, 396). Honig seeks to rethink "democracy as also a cosmopolitan and not just a nation-centered set of solidarities, practices, and institutions" (*Democracy and the Foreigner,* 8). For an exploration of the limits and possibilities of cosmopolitanism as an alternative to nationalism in contemporary politics and culture, see Pheng Cheah and Bruce Robbins, eds., *Cosmopolitics: Thinking and Feeling beyond the Nation* (Minneapolis: University of Minnesota Press, 1998). Although the term *postnationalism* has been used by Arjun Appadurai and others to describe contemporary efforts to think beyond that nation-state, the terms *cosmopolitanism, transnationalism,* and *internationalism* might better describe the current moment of tension and negotiation among residual and emergent forms of nationalisms and cosmopolitanisms. For Appadurai's notion of "postnational identities" see his "Patriotism and Its Futures," *Public Culture* 5, no. 3 (1993): 418. As Pheng Cheah observes in "Given Culture: Rethinking Cosmopolitan Freedom in Transnationalism," nationalism and the nation-state are far from dead; in fact, under conditions of global capitalism, they may have a positive role to play as forms of popular empowerment, political transformation, and resistance (*Cosmopolitics,* ed. Cheah and Robbins, 290–328). See also Paul Lauter, who expresses a reservation about the ways "a strong international emphasis" on "the interaction between American and overseas cultures" might "marginalize the intense struggles of minority and queer communities *within* the United States" ("American Studies and Ethnic Studies at the Borderlands Crossroads," 133).

Index

Acknowledgments

I want to thank the many colleagues and friends whose scholarly work, inspiration, friendship, and support have contributed to my completion of this book. I especially want to thank Northwestern University and my former dean, Eric Sundquist, for giving me research leave during my term as chair of the English Department. I also want to thank my dedicated and hard-working department assistant, Kathy Daniels, whose deep knowledge and strong support helped me find time to write even while I was chair.

At Northwestern, I have been blessed with wonderful colleagues— Brian Edwards, Larry Lipking, Carl Smith, and Julia Stern—whose feedback on different parts of this book at different stages of writing has been invaluable to me. My current and former graduate students, Matt Frankel, Hunt Howell, Coleman Hutchison, and Sarah Blackwood, have provided expert research assistance; and I am particularly grateful to Katy Chiles for her excellent work on the illustrations. I also want to thank Russell Maylone, the curator of Special Collections at Northwestern University Library, for his knowledge and love of books and his help in locating (and sometimes even buying) difficult-to-find editions and illustrations.

I owe a particular debt of gratitude to Paul Lauter, whose 1982 summer institute at Yale on "Reconstructing American Literature" changed my life. His support and friendship over the past two decades have meant the world to me. My Whitman and Dickinson "chums," Ed Folsom, Jerry Loving, Robert K. Martin, Vivian Pollak, and Ken Price, have been especially dear in attending to and responding to my work even when they disagree. I am grateful to Donald Pease for his genius, generosity, and friendship; Jerry Kennedy and Liliane Weissberg for inspiring me to write on Poe and race; Nicole King and Aldon Nielsen for many memorable conversations about C.L.R. James; and Katherine Kinney, Teresa Goddu, and Judith Jackson Fossett for brilliant work and treasured moments of friendship and exchange. I also want to thank my editors, Jerry Singerman and Erica Ginsburg, whose support, good humor, and expertise at every stage of the editorial process have made it a particular pleasure to publish this book with the University of Pennsylvania Press.

I gratefully acknowledge permission to reprint material from the following sources: passages from *The Poems of Emily Dickinson*. Reprinted by permission of the publishers and the Trustees of Amherst College from *The Poems of Emily Dickinson*, Ralph W. Franklin, ed., Cambridge, Mass.: The Belknap Press of Harvard University Press, Copyright © 1998 by the President and Fellows of Harvard College. Copyright © 1951, 1955, 1979 by the President and Fellows of Harvard College; a passage from *The Letters of Emily Dickinson*. Reprinted by permission of the publishers from *The Letters of EmilyDickinson*, edited by Thomas H. Johnson, ed., Cambridge, Mass.: The Belknap Press of Harvard University Press, Copyright © 1958, 1986 by the President and Fellows of Harvard College.

I am also grateful to the following presses for permission to publish revised versions of earlier essays: Tulsa University Press for an early version of Chapter 3 in *Tulsa Studies in Women's Literature* (1987); Oxford University Press for Chapter 4 in *Romancing the Shadow: Poe and Race* (2001), ed. J. Gerald Kennedy and Liliane Weissberg, and a version of Chapter 6 in *American Literary History* (1992); and the University of Iowa Press for an earlier version of Chapter 5 in *Walt Whitman Centennial Essays*, ed. Ed Folsom (1994).

My family, especially Jan and Tim, who helped with the index, has been invaluable to me. I also want to thank my second mom, Lillie, for her loving support and her sense of humor. As always, Larry and Suli fill my life with love and joy and help me keep everything else in perspective. I dedicate this book to my students who have been—along with Larry, Suli, Marah, and Luc—my inspiration and my heartbeat.